Blue
Fairways

Blue Fairways

A Route 1 Golf Odyssey

CHARLES SLACK

AN OWL BOOK

HENRY HOLT AND COMPANY

NEW YORK

Henry Holt and Company, LLC
Publishers since 1866
115 West 18th Street
New York, New York 10011

Henry Holt ® is a registered trademark
of Henry Holt and Company, LLC.

Published in Canada by Fitzhenry & Whiteside Ltd.,
195 Allstate Parkway, Markham, Ontario L3R 4T8

Library of Congress Cataloging-in-Publication Data
Slack, Charles.
Blue fairways: a Route 1 golf odyssey /
Charles Slack.
p.   cm.
ISBN 0-8050-5994-6
1. Slack, Charles—Journeys—Atlantic States. 2. Golfers—Travel—
Atlantic States. 3. Golf Courses—Atlantic States. I. Title.
GV964.S54A3   1999   99-13639
796.352'06'874—DC21   CIP

Henry Holt Books are available for special promotions and
premiums. For details contact: Director, Special Markets.

First published in hardcover in 1999 by Henry Holt and Company

First Owl Books Edition 2000

Designed by Paula Russell Szafranski

Printed in the United States of America

1   3   5   7   9   10   8   6   4   2

For Barbara, Natalie, and Caroline,
who make my foursome complete

Contents

Acknowledgments and Author's Note

Perhaps the most hazardous sentence a man can utter to his pregnant wife is this: "Honey, I'm going golfing." The fact that I said to my pregnant wife, "Honey, I'm going golfing for nearly three months," and am still married is testament to the debt of support, encouragement, and trust that I will always owe to my wife, Barbara Slack. A skilled editor, she overcame her lack of interest in golf to provide helpful readings of each draft. I would like to thank my parents, Carolyn and Warner Slack, for their constant support. I would like to thank Dean King, without whose generous counsel and guidance at every step this project would not have happened. Thanks also to my agent, Andrew Blauner, for believing from the start, and to my editor, David Sobel, for his careful reading and thoughtful suggestions. I would like to thank the friends along the way whose hospitality provided welcome relief from another night in a hotel room or another road meal, among them my sisters, Alison Slack and Jennifer Slack-Gans, and their husbands, Chris Peters and Erik Gans, Tony and Jo-Ann DiPanni, Ed and Lisa Goldfinger, Bruce and Carol Leonard, Claudio and Betsy Phillips, Lamar and

Laura Flatt, Logan and Heather Ward, Bret Schundler, and Tony Hatch. For advice and other help at crucial times I would like to thank Bruce Schoenfeld, Chip Jones, Ed Crews, Munford Ashworth and Jann Malone. Several golf guides and regional histories provided useful information. These include *Golf Digest*'s indispensable *4,200 Best Places to Play*; *The Maine Golf Guide*, by Bob Labbance and David Cornwell; *Down Rae's Creek*, by Michael C. White; *A Place Called Pinehurst*, by Mary Elle Hunter; *The Allagash*, by Lew Dietz, and *The Place We Call Home*, by the staff of the *Augusta Chronicle* in Georgia. Finally, I would like to thank William Least Heat Moon, whose classic travel book, *Blue Highways*, inspired the title of this book, for his belief in the random goodness of Americans.

Author's Note: From the early days of my journey it became clear to me that my original plan to play each course in strict geographical and chronological order would prove unworkable. I quickly realized that such an approach, while satisfying to the purist in me, would have reduced my travel pace to an intolerable crawl, and robbed me of flexibility, when needed, to dart ahead and fill in gaps later. Also, the call of my family meant completing the trip in stages. Although the trip moved inexorably southward from Maine to Florida, I played one small section of courses near my home in Virginia several months after the trip was completed. To present each course in the book in the exact order in which I played would have been unduly confusing. They are presented in uninterrupted geographical order here in the interest of narrative flow and clarity.

Blue
Fairways

Part One

New England

1

Speed Skating Through Jell-O

My tires crunched to a stop in the gravel parking lot of the Fort Kent Golf Club, a nine-hole course on a hillside three miles west of Fort Kent, Maine.

"On parle français ici," a sign in the neat, white clubhouse read.

"American or Canadian money?" asked the young woman behind the lunch/green fees counter.

"American," I said. "Will you take a credit card?"

"Oh *oui*," she said.

The greens fee was $10.

There were a few groups already on the course but nobody waiting to tee off, and nobody in the clubhouse. I now could understand the manager's casual "yes" when I had phoned the day before asking if they might squeeze in a single the next morning.

Fort Kent, population 2,100, marks the northern terminus of Route 1, near the northernmost tip of the continental United States. This section of Maine lies a couple of hundred miles inland from the rocky coast and is rounded by a sort of camel's hump defined by the St. John River. The river runs north from Fort Kent for a few miles before turning south on its long run to the Atlantic Ocean. Route 1 pushes north with the river, peaks at a town called Madawaska, then plunges south for 2,200 miles to Key West, Florida.

I arrived in Fort Kent on a cool, bright Sunday morning in June, just as the local Catholic churches—not quaint, cozy New England churches of lore, but tall, austere, European-looking structures with pointed arches—were letting out. I inched my car through throngs of parishioners exchanging hugs and playing with their children on roadside fields strewn with wildflowers. The golf course lies along Route 161, which is actually an extension of Route 1. Follow 161 for about thirty more miles and you would pass the tiny outpost towns of Allagash and Dickey, and then come quite literally to the end of the road, the last paved frontier before the start of the Allagash Wilderness Waterway and the interminable forests of northern Maine.

I headed to the first tee box alone. An urban golfer in such a setting is like a starving man who continues to hoard food after the famine is over. I hurried out to the tee box without even lacing up my golf shoes, as if at any moment some assistant manager might appear with the news that there had been a mistake, I must actually wait for a couple of slow foursomes to tee off in front of me. When it was clear this would not happen, I slowed down.

I stood for a moment on the tee box, staring up the fairway, not wanting to smudge the crisp, virgin canvas of my adventure. So far, my scorecard read even par. You can't avoid getting old, but if you play golf you know what it feels like to have life begin all over again with each new round. You have a shot at redemption, a chance to correct past mistakes, erase regrets; all is forgiven. Today will be different. There is the smell of wet grass, the crisp cardboard of an unbent scorecard, a sharp pencil, a new ball still cool and slightly sticky to the touch. It's the moment of infinite possibility, when all drives will land in the fairway, wedge shots will float like angels to welcoming greens, and putts will roll true. And here I was on the cusp of not just one round but an entire summer's worth of golf, the road trip of a lifetime.

The idea had first come to me one summer evening about a year earlier as I drove home after a round of golf near my home in Richmond, Virginia. Some great old rock song, "Mony Mony," "Louie Louie," something like that, blared from the radio. A fresh breeze rushed through my opened windows. I had played well; well enough, that is, to be thinking about the next time I could golf instead of thinking about throwing my clubs into the nearest body of water. A thought popped into my head. What if I just kept driving? What if I extended this sublime moment, and, instead of going home to prepare for another workweek, I just *kept driving,* with my only destination being the next golf course down the line?

I stowed the idea with the thousand other harmless fantasies of the sort that get you through your chicken salad on wheat toast at the lunch place around the corner from the office. But over the next several months this particular fantasy returned at odd times, such as the middle of the night or the middle of some phone call at work. Unlike, say, the fantasy involving the copra schooner and forgotten coral atolls in the South Seas, this one seemed just doable enough to unsettle me. Finally, I broached the subject with Barbara, my wife, assuming (hoping?) that her incredulous reaction would jolt me into forgetting about the idea. Surprisingly, she seemed positive, after raising a few basic questions, such as how we would pay our mortgage and feed ourselves and our daughter. Women are so practical.

Perhaps Barbara sensed, as I did, that I had reached a point in my career and my life that demanded some sort of action, or at least an elaborate gesture. At thirty-five, I had been reporting for the same newspaper in Richmond for a decade, first as a general assignment feature writer, then as a business reporter on the transportation beat. I had arrived at the paper in 1986 as an eager twenty-five-year-old cub. Richmond was going to be a two-year stop. Then we'd move to Boston, Washington, New York. But somehow the years slipped by. We bought a house, had a daughter, started worrying about taxes and school districts. Roots sprouted despite our stubborn protestations that we'd be moving on at any moment. I was no longer the youth of twenty-five. I had morphed into a veteran, a reliable pro, a solid member of the team—all those double-edged plaudits guaranteed to fuel the quiet desperation Thoreau wrote about.

Lately, I'd found it harder and harder to jump-start my professional engines over airline strikes, trucking regulations, highway construction contracts. I'd been around long enough by now to see the same stories, the same conflicts and characters, disappear and come around again like carousel ponies. The crush of daily deadlines, amid the barely controlled chaos of the newsroom, no longer gave me that terrifying thrill. More and more it felt like speed skating through Jell-O—a furious expense of energy in order to wind up more or less where I had started.

"So, what is this, some kind of midlife crisis?" a fellow reporter demanded, after I'd wangled a six-month leave of absence from my job.

I hadn't thought of it that way. I didn't know I was old enough to qualify for a midlife crisis. But what the hell. These days you qualified for senior citizen discounts in your fifties. Perhaps they were offering midlife crises to thirty-five-year-olds. Crisis, burnout, call it what you will. Staring at that ever-shrinking buffer zone between Someday and Today, I could tell it was time to do . . . something.

"I didn't know you were a big-time golfer," another reporter said, as if I were a source who'd been withholding key information all these years.

"I'm not," I said. And that was true. Not if "big-time" meant highly skilled.

But I loved the game. I'd hacked around the local course near my home in Boston as a teenager, but I didn't start golfing in earnest until thirty. With predictable results. Regardless of how badly the adult mind wishes to master the game, the adult body hates to learn golf. Golf demands all sorts of strange grips, postures and motions that are utterly useless in the rest of life.

Learning to golf means ignoring those marquee muscles (biceps, pecs and so forth) that one has spent a lifetime training, preening, fretting over in the bathroom mirror. Instead, you demand precise movements from an odd assortment of B-list muscles that have lain around forgotten for years, like an old casserole in the back of the freezer.

I started with a weekly trip to a driving range, mainly to let off steam after work. Then my father-in-law offered to lend me an old set of clubs. I joined a group from work for the occasional round. I took a lesson here and there, studied some tapes and books. Progress came slowly, fitfully. For months I straddled a fence, unsure why I kept playing, whether I was enjoying myself or just wasting time.

Then one afternoon at a tough, pond-filled course near my home in Richmond, I played the par-four sixth hole, the hardest hole, to perfection. I waggled my driver, brought my arms back in a slow, steady motion, rotated my hips, shifted my weight and swung. The ball sailed straight, missed an outcropping branch on the left side by a foot, crossed the dogleg and rolled to a stop on the right side of the fairway, about 260 yards away. For my approach, I hit a graceful, arcing eight-iron that landed three feet from the cup. I calmly sank my putt for a birdie. On the next hole, of course, I brought my arms back slowly, rotated my hips and all the rest. The ball whizzed through the grass in front of the tee for a few ugly yards and stopped. The spell was broken, I was average again. But that sixth hole! Any professional golfer in the world would love to play that hole just the way I had played it. The memory sustained me for weeks. Without consciously knowing it, I had been initiated into the mysterious brotherhood of golf fanatics. So much of life encourages the prosaic, the mundane, the cynical. Golf appeals to a better, more youthful side of our nature, eternally hopeful and expectant, as if something fine and noble is certain to happen soon, if only we give it a chance. Here's the thing: In that moment I had come close to achieving perfection. I wanted to do it again. Lord help me, I was hooked.

My goals for the journey were relatively simple. I wanted to shave at least ten strokes off my game. Although I had never bothered to establish a formal handicap, my scores had wallowed far too long in the dreary mid- to high-nineties (with plenty of forays into triple digits). I just didn't get to play enough to build any consistency. I felt certain that if I could lower my scores to the mid- to high-80s I could be satisfied, and just have fun. Also, I established a goal of breaking 80 on at least one round. Nobody breaks 80 by a fluke; do so even once and you may justly say that you know how to play the game.

Beyond improving my own ability, the trip would allow me to meet other American golfers on public courses in large cities and small towns, to find out if they shared my joys and frustrations. Why only public courses? For one thing, I wanted the flexibility to choose courses on the spur of the moment as I traveled, something that would have been impossible while trying to arrange rounds at private clubs. More important, though, is the fact that public courses, with their crabgrassed fairways and sun-baked greens, are where the vast majority of America's twenty million golfers play out their dreams. The lush, carpeted fairways and silky greens of Augusta National or Pine Valley are as remote to the average golfer as a date with a movie star. When public courses are celebrated at all, they are usually lauded for the degree to which they do not seem to be public. The more they resemble a private club, the better their reviews. But it is the very openness of public courses that has always appealed to me. I like being able to show up, pay cash, and not have anyone know who I am, if I so choose. A public course, like a great city, offers anonymity when you want it. I like knowing I can play a particular course once, or five times, or never again, without entangling myself in obligations to a membership committee. Don't get me wrong. I've enjoyed rounds as a guest at private courses. My parents even joined one (after I left home, or I'd be a better golfer). Assuming I have the money I might even join one myself one day, when some final, unruly mob at a starter's stand, or some jerk leaving divots in the green finally pushes me over the edge. But there's something given up in exchange for the comfort of a private club, where behavior is governed by a rules committee and members go out of their way not to offend. Public golf courses possess a certain raw vitality that comes from constantly swapping genes with whoever happens to show up. There's an excitement, a randomness about public golf that ties into the great traditions of America, forever churning, struggling, reinventing itself. Public courses lay themselves out for general inspection, flaws and all. In return they are endlessly forgiving of a golfer's flaws. To borrow from Robert Frost's definition of home, a public course is a place where, if you have to play there, they have to let you play.

As the idea for my trip grew, I naturally began to ponder what route I should follow. One day as I sat poring over maps and golf guides, Route 1 practically leaped out at me. This fabled old road runs the entire length of the East Coast, from the tip of northern Maine to the last sandy outpost on the Florida Keys. I traced its path with a forefinger and noticed it bisects such hallowed golfing grounds as Pinehurst, North Carolina, and Augusta, Georgia, and the entire sun-splashed Gold Coast of Florida.

The road slices through the heart of America's most densely populated cities, the Northeast Corridor from Boston to Washington: meaning city golf and city people in New York, Philadelphia, Newark and Baltimore. But Route 1 also runs through long stretches of rural America, from the potato fields of Maine to the cotton fields of Georgia. Route 1 has long since ceded to Interstate 95 its function as a convenient way to travel any great distances. But for the traveler with a little time on his hands, it offers the incomparable advantage of forcing you to travel at the speed of your surroundings. For a golfer, Route 1 is almost heaven. It's not just the countless courses on or just off the highway. The road is a mobile support system for all a golfer's worldly needs. Need work on those long iron shots? Don't worry, there is a driving range just around the next bend. Snapped your putter in frustration? That strip mall on the left is bound to have a golf outlet store. Route 1 isn't America's prettiest strip of tar, but it may be its most functional. Cheap lodgings and fast food abound, and some zoning law seems to have ordered there to be a doughnut shop every half mile. Assuming homesickness and expenses didn't get the best of him, a man could cruise its 2,200 miles indefinitely, secure in his own insulated biosphere of golf.

The road has personal appeal to me as well. Though I'd never given Route 1 a lot of thought, it occurred to me now that the old highway forms a sort of charm bracelet of my life. Summers in Maine as a youth, winter visits to my grandparents' home in Florida, growing up near Boston, working in Richmond, marrying a girl from Norwalk, Connecticut—most of the defining moments and stages of my life have taken place a gimme putt from Route 1.

A few months before I was scheduled to leave, we learned that a second child was on the way, and due at the end of the summer. Barbara and I had longed for this news for years; now it came unexpectedly, when we had begun to lose hope. Should I call the trip off? Barbara, bless her, said go ahead, get it out of your system. Not long after my thirty-sixth birthday I loaded up my seven-year-old Pontiac Grand Prix. I gave her new front tires and a new electronic cluster for the failing instrument panel, and hoped she'd make the long haul. I loaded a large cooler with bottles of spring water, various crackers and breakfast bars, and two large packs of sardines, each containing about eight cans. I hadn't eaten sardines in a decade, but somehow, with their neat little tear-away containers and ready-to-eat fishiness, they seemed like essential road food. I packed every stitch of underwear, sports socks, shorts and golf shirts that I owned, a cellular phone that failed me about five miles out of town, maps, notebooks, pens, a point-and-shoot camera, an address book, tape recorder and assorted other odds and ends.

My irons were a brand-new set of Wilson Staffs, purchased out of the trunk of a man's car a few weeks before I left. The purchase was necessitated when an airline the previous autumn "lost" my clubs on a nonstop flight from Richmond to Boston (quotation marks for the benefit of the baggage handler who is probably swinging my sweet Big Bertha at this very moment). The check from the airline had dwindled away on other expenses over the long winter, and now I needed some good, cheap clubs. Fast. I was browsing in a secondhand sports store in Richmond with my daughter, Natalie, when an unshaven man sidled up close and whispered hoarsely, "You don't want any of these."

"I don't?"

He shook his head. "I got a set of Wilson Staffs in the car I'll let you have cheap. Brand-new, too, not like this stuff. Come on out to the parking lot."

I followed the man out to his beat-up old Buick sedan, certain that some vice squad would descend at any moment to arrest me in front of my five-year-old daughter. He popped the trunk, revealing at least three complete sets of irons, and lifted out the Wilsons.

"Why are you selling these?" I asked stupidly.

"My son gave them to me. I don't need 'em."

"I see."

He asked $250. They were good clubs. I offered $200. We settled on $225.

"Is he a nice man?" Natalie asked as we drove to a nearby cash machine, the man following close behind.

"I'm sure he's very nice."

I counted out $225 in crisp bills from the cash machine. The man folded them into his breast pocket and smiled.

"You'll love them clubs. You won't ever get a better price than that, I guarantee." Then he drove off into the afternoon, in search of another customer for some more clubs given to him by his son.

I completed the set with old steel MacPherson three- and five-woods, on loan from my father-in-law. These must have been among the first generation of nonwood woods, because they were painted a guilty, apologetic black to make you think you were using a real wooden club. Nowadays, manufacturers paint their synthetic woods nuclear-fallout orange to emphasize the use of space-age materials. My driver was a Daiwa with a graphite shaft and a titanium head, a castoff from my father. A perfect length for my father's lanky, six-foot, four-inch frame, the driver was too long for my six feet, but on the rare occasion when I hit the sweet spot, the ball traveled a mile.

I arranged these clubs in a nylon bag I'd bought at the Price Club for $49.95. The bag was a piece of junk, but it was light and stood on collapsible legs—crucial considerations since I planned to walk every round I could. I filled the bag with a couple of dozen new Maxfli X-outs I'd bought at a local sporting goods store, along with assorted other stray balls and about a thousand wooden tees, none of which I could locate when I needed them. I found myself buying bag after bag of replacement tees in pro shops all along the way. Strange thing about tees; they show up everywhere in a man's stuff—his change drawer, his lint, his dirty underwear pile. But try to find one when you're standing on the tee box with a ball in your hand and three partners waiting for you to hit.

On the day I left, I kissed Natalie and Barbara good-bye and drove off feeling like a cad. The feeling lasted about four miles, then dissipated under the strains of a Tom Petty song from my tape player and the hum of my tires, not to mention the thought of my shiny new irons smacking a golf ball. I love motion, travel. I love airports and train stations. It was one reason I chose the transportation beat at my paper. Now I felt the restorative powers of the road.

And that was how I came to be standing on the first tee at the Fort Kent Golf Club on a sweet Sunday morning in June. I saw the pin flag waving from a green 406 yards away. A wide fairway spread before me. I lifted my three-wood slowly out of my bag, almost trembling with the import of this, my first shot. I teed up a Maxfli X-out. I lined up my feet, waggled, took a nice, slow backswing, and hit a mediocre shot into the right rough bordering the practice range. How quickly and brazenly reality intervenes on a reverie. On my second shot, a four-iron, my club face caught a clump of grass and dirt, and the ball skipped thirty or forty yards and came to rest back in the fairway. Next I hit a decent six-iron that landed just short of the green. I hit onto the green in four, then three-putted for a 7. Presto, I had started my grand adventure with a triple bogey.

The first two holes (I bogeyed the second) at Fort Kent serve mainly to get you up a hill, where the personality of the course begins to assert itself. I breathed heavily after carrying my bag up the two inclined holes. But when I reached the third tee, fringed with blossoming apple trees rustling in a gentle breeze, and looked back down, it seemed that all of northern Maine had laid itself out for my approval. Far below, the clubhouse shimmered in the sun. Woodlands and farms rolled off in the distance across the valley. The hills beyond were covered with forests.

On the third hole, a par three, I hit a seven-iron straight, but I aimed it badly, and the ball landed to the right of a bunker next to the green. I chipped over the bunker and two-putted for another bogey. I also bogeyed the fourth hole, a sharp dogleg to the right that led back down the hill aways. Again I had pushed my tee shot to the right but was able to place a nine-iron over some trees to land just short of the green.

Two young guys had started behind me. When I had to wait for a slow foursome at the start of the fifth hole, I asked them to join me. They were big, square-jawed French Canadians named Yves and Mario. Mario wore Laguna shorts, black socks and a Montreal Canadiens hockey jersey and looked as though he could join the roster as a defenseman. They were in their late twenties or early thirties. Yves had a goatee. They spoke almost no English, although I gathered from our halting sentences and sign language that Mario was from Clair, the little New Brunswick town just across the river. Yves, his brother-in-law, was visiting from Quebec.

The French influence in northern Aroostook County dates to the earliest days of European settlement. The first European arrivals were French Acadians pushed out of New Brunswick by the British. They found a safe haven up the St. John, past non-navigable waterfalls, too high up to be touched by the long arm of the British navy. In 1840 Maine, New Brunswick and Britain (in support of the Canadians) all sent troops to settle a dispute over international boundaries and rights to the rich forests of white pine, cedar and spruce growing thick through the St. John Valley. It is one of the more obscure episodes in American military history, dubbed "the Bloodless Aroostook War." The lone casualty, according to local historians, was a cow felled by a stray warning shot. A treaty drawn up in 1842 established the current U.S.-Canada border.

In a sense, the Bloodless Aroostook War is still being fought here in a battle of silence between the Mainers of English or Irish descent and the French-speaking Canadians, a silence as old and permanent as the ponderous wooden fort that was built during the crisis in 1840, gave the town its name, and still sits at the confluence of the St. John and Fish Rivers just off Route 1. They live within a couple of miles of one another and cross the border to shop, to eat, to play golf, yet quite literally are unable to give each other the time of day. Bilingual Mainers descended from those first Acadian settlers provide a sort of buffer. They dominate the culture in Fort Kent and in smaller communities with names such as Frenchville and Lille. Driving through town, I thought some wildly successful entrepreneur named Ouellette lived nearby. Half the business signs bore his name. The local phone book later revealed an entire page of Ouellettes.

Before starting on my trip I had constructed a game plan that I felt would put me on a steady road toward improvement. I shortened my swing, replacing my erratic roundhouse with a moderate backswing that came back only about shoulder high. In the early days, at least, I would concentrate on keeping the ball in play, taking easy, relaxed swings, forgetting about distance. I would learn the game all over. I had all summer to improve; I did not need to be rash. I would play the white tees, not the blues, and on some far distant course in Georgia or Florida my game would come together.

That was my plan, anyway. Then on our first hole together, Yves pulled out a driver the size of a street lamp, took a huge swing, and whacked the ball out of sight. Mario did the same. They grinned pleasantly at me. Your turn.

How could I explain my carefully devised strategy to these smiling Canadians who didn't speak my language? Pull out a three-iron after their monster drives? They'd just think I was a wuss. I was suddenly faced with an international crisis, and my only diplomatic weapon was a stick of graphite topped with a titanium bulb.

I moved to the back tee, reached into my bag, and withdrew my driver, a club that yielded a ratio of one long, straight drive for four or five slices. I drew the club back, hoping something good would happen. *Please, golf gods, send down one of those 290-yarders.* The golf gods can smell hope and fear and are generally intolerant of either. No sport is more pitiless to a pleading heart. My mighty swing clipped the top of the ball. It whizzed off to the left rough, a few yards short of the women's tee.

One of the quainter customs in American public golf is the "dick out" rule, stipulating that a man whose drive fails to reach the women's tee must unzip his fly and play the remainder of the hole exposed to the world. I've never seen a golfer actually forced to whip it out, but the "Dick out!" howls from other members of the foursome are bad enough. I half expected Mario and Yves to yell "Deek out!" but either the custom hasn't crossed the border or they were too nice. They only uttered a sympathetic "Oh."

I followed with a good five-wood that partially compensated for my dismal drive. "Nice shot," Mario and Yves called. My third shot went off to the right rough, near some trees. Mario, who was starting to feel sorry for me, called "Okay?" to see if I needed help. I stumbled through the rest of the hole for an 8.

The seventh hole crests the hillside. As we marched along the fairway Mario pointed below and said something to Yves. I had been trying to understand snippets of their conversation, using the ragged remnants of my high school French. But the Canadian French sounded quick and clipped, nothing like the language imparted to me by Madame Meyer in twelfth grade. I asked Mario through hand gestures what he was pointing to.

"Clair," he said. The tops of white houses and churches glinted in the sun across the river in the valley.

On the seventh green, Mario left his putt well short.

"Cheekin! Cheekin!" Yves cried.

There comes a point in a bad round of golf when you pass the point of no return, the illusion of resurrection has been shattered, the bag begins to drag like a sack of wet sand, you are no longer playing golf but merely wandering futile fields banging an intransigent white rock. I was grateful that the ninth green was under repair and I didn't have to putt. I finished with 56 for nine holes. No room for anything but improvement. Mario and Yves wandered off with a smile and a wave. I grabbed a couple of hot dogs and an iced tea in the empty clubhouse, hit a bucket of range balls in a futile attempt to get some consistency, then got in my car and headed down the road.

A high-pressure system had warmed Maine for days while states hundreds of miles south wallowed in cold rain. Roadside towns such as Frenchville and Grand Isle glinted like white-washed stones in the sun. Residents, astonished by this meteorological gift so early in the season, played in their front yards, rocked on porches, fired up grills. Two teenage girls in bathing suits soaked up the sun on the hood of a car. Road signs for each hamlet said *Bienvenue* and Welcome.

At Van Buren, the road diverges from the St. John River and cuts due south into the heart of Maine potato country. The hills rolling away in every direction for miles were scarred with the same distinctive furrows, as if some great beast had raked its claws over the earth. Farmers plant seed potatoes a couple of inches into the loamy soil of the ridges. The deep troughs on either side make for easier harvesting.

The land in Aroostook County given over to potatoes has shrunk from 300,000 acres at midcentury to around 75,000. Even the Maine Potato Board (mascot: Spuddy) concedes that changing American tastes and competition from Idaho have made a dent. Farmers have begun raising broccoli, the young move off to Bangor or Portland in search of better opportunities. But the potato still dominates the landscape. In July, these scarred fields erupt in white and pink blossoms and Aroostook County holds its annual Potato Festival and crowns a Potato Blossom Queen. Then in mid-September the serious work begins. Harvest time. Schools still let out for a month in the fall here. It's one reason high-school football is practically nonexistent north of Bangor. As I pulled in to the Presque Isle Country Club, "public welcome," a sign announced an annual tournament coming in late July: The Spudland Open.

Presque Isle, with about twenty thousand residents, is the largest town in Aroostook County. If all you know about it is the name, you probably imagine a coastal town with rocky outcroppings jutting into the Atlantic. But Presque Isle is nowhere near the ocean. The name comes from a network of smaller rivers winding through the area, rendering the town "nearly an island." In the clubhouse, the starter immediately hooked me up with a threesome. Here, at a busy course on a summer Sunday afternoon, my Single Golfer Rule worked with reassuring ease. Unlike single diners, whom restaurants see as low-revenue space wasters, single golfers are nearly always welcome at a public course, even on the busiest days. For golf course managers, sending out a threesome or a twosome is the equivalent of flying an airliner with empty seats—lost revenue that won't ever come back. Single golfers, far from being a nuisance, are a beneficial organism in the golf course ecosystem, like those sucker fish who clean algae off the bellies of sharks. The Single Golfer Rule says you can show up alone, without a tee time, at virtually any public course and be guaranteed of playing golf within a short time, even on days when unannounced foursomes are being turned away. Presque Isle, busy but not jammed, was a good place to run the Single Golfer Rule through its paces. I'd be relying on the rule as I made my way down through the dense cities of the Northeast Corridor. But there is another component to the Single Golfer Rule, one that has less to do with practicality and more to do with the ease of making new friends on the course. Simply stated—the best way to make new friends on a golf course is to show up alone. Golfers who arrive in groups spend their entire round in the cocoon of their established friendship. The same holds true when two twosomes are put together. I've gone out with my father, or a friend, and spent five hours paired with another twosome, without exchanging anything beyond surface courtesies. But if you arrive alone, without ties, you will fit into any group. Threesomes will pity your solitude and take you under their wing. A single golfer is never threatening. Other single golfers will reach out. Show up alone, and you open yourself to the possibility of making friends.

My partners on the first tee were Stacey Kelly, Larry Nadeau and his brother, Jason Nadeau. Jason, twenty-three, was a part-time student at the University of Maine's branch in Fort Kent. Larry, twenty-seven, worked for a company that made packaging materials.

At thirty-four, Stacey Kelley was the unofficial leader of this trio: the oldest, the tallest, the most gregarious. The son and grandson of lumber men, Stacey lived in Allagash, a small outpost near the very end of the road in Maine, a few miles from Dickey, the last town on Route 161. His father retired after a falling tree cracked three of his vertebrae, leaving him unable to work but not paralyzed. Stacey had a wife and two young sons. Like other loggers (nobody in these parts uses the term *lumberjacks*), Stacey worked six months on, six months off. I was surprised to learn that the season stretches from autumn through the bitter Maine winter. But logging in the summer would mean building sturdy, expensive gravel roads deep in the heart of the forest, Stacey said.

By late fall, even the most rudimentary roads are frozen hard enough to support the enormous weight of a logging truck. For most of his career Stacey was a skidder, operating a tractorlike machine with a winch, used to haul the freshly cut fir and spruce trees from the forest to the road, where they were de-limbed and loaded on trucks. But newer machines called "processors" could cut a tree down, strip its limbs and cut the trunk into uniform logs right on the spot. Canadian woodsmen, willing to work the Aroostook forests for a relatively low wage because of a favorable dollar exchange rate, were filling most of the remaining jobs, Stacey said. Stacey had just put a down payment on a truck. Lumber companies would always need trucks to haul the timber out, he figured. That is, as long as the timber itself holds. To a casual observer on Maine's highways the supply of trees seems endless. But Stacey said, "Most of the big wood is gone."

During the long off-months, Stacey had picked up golf. He'd driven past the public course in Fort Kent for most of his life. One day in his twenties he'd decided to give it a try. Today Stacey Kelly may be the northernmost eleven handicapper in the continental United States. It was about four in the afternoon when we teed off, the sun hanging high over the potato fields. I was looking for improvement after my miserable showing that morning. Stacey hit a booming drive that screamed far left into another fairway. I hit a cautious three-iron that hugged the right rough. Then Stacey recovered with a shot to the green. It was both the best and worst time to be golfing in northern Maine. In early June, the weather was glorious. But the course was in spotty shape, with patches of winter kill on the fairways and greens. And the mosquitoes were so big and hungry that they almost made us forget about the blackflies. I swatted enough mosquitoes to fill a bushel basket, but still they came. My wife had given me a plastic jar of some stuff called Skin So Soft, which had a strong perfume smell that was supposed to keep the bugs away. The top leaked, and soon my entire golf bag smelled like Eva Gabor's boudoir. Not that the Skin So Soft did much good against the mosquitoes.

They seemed to like it. I soon began to suspect that Skin So Soft was not the name of the product so much as a mantra being chanted by the mosquitoes:

"Hey, fellas, check out this guy. His skin's *so soft*."

"Yeah, smells nice, too."

I started steady but deteriorated amid the heat and bugs and my own incompetence into a procession of sorry shots and still sorrier ones. My tee shots veered off to the woods like pine-seeking missiles. When Stacey, Larry and Jason asked what brought me all the way up to Presque Isle I told them about my trip and the book I planned to write about my travels. On the ninth hole I hit a perfect sand wedge—sky-high and sixty yards. Unfortunately, I was using my driver at the time and aiming 280 yards down the fairway. Stacey, ever cordial and polite, watched the ball, then turned to me and said, "I take it this isn't a golf instruction book you're writing."

No, it wasn't. In fact, I was already having my own doubts about the whole affair. I never had any illusions about being anything other than a weekend duffer. But a duffer was two or three leagues above the way I was playing on this, my first day out. The clubs felt like garden rakes in my hands. I might as well have snapped off a birch sapling and taken a few swings with that. And I'd spent enough time in the woods to have a good choice of saplings. Rotate my hips and bring my arms back smoothly? I might as well have commanded my body to skip across the stage with the New York City Ballet. I asked myself: I'm going to do this all the way to Florida? I'm going to write a book about golf? Just now it seemed that golf was writing a book about me, and the working title was "You Suck."

Fortified with big, cold drinks, we pressed on to the back nine. Presque Isle proved to be a better and more interesting course on the back nine than the front. The opening holes had been fairly crowded, flat and open. But on the back nine the holes stretched out and meandered in unhurried isolation. Before long I had the feeling of being miles from the clubhouse, miles from everything. Much is made in golf of the fact that no two courses are alike. More mysterious and compelling to me is the way that no course is like itself through eighteen holes. A round is long enough and a course large enough that a round of golf rarely begins as it ends. You may start in darkness and end in light, or start in light and end in darkness. Heat gives way to a chill; flat ranges yield to hills, seascapes to forests, rains end or begin, fogs lift. You live a whole lifetime in a round of golf. The promise of youth on the first tee yields to the dreary, hard-earned lessons of middle age around the ninth or tenth, and, if you're lucky and persistent enough, perhaps you find a moment of redemption here and there before you're through. By the end of the round you try to recall the first shots of the day, but they seem to have taken place on a different day altogether, maybe even in a different year. Those first few holes seem as distant and naively optimistic as your smiling face in a high-school yearbook photo.

The twelfth hole is a monster par 5, 629 yards from the championship tees, a still-long 525 yards for us from the white tees, with a dogleg left followed by another to the right. I hit a poor drive off to the left that left me in some nasty tall grass. Larry, standing near me when I found my ball buried in the grass, suggested I use a "foot wedge" to improve my lie. I resisted the temptation, hitting a five-wood that sailed straight but wound up in hillside rough to the right of the green. I felt as though I might begin to turn myself around here, but every promising development was quickly answered by failure. It took me two approach shots to reach the green, and I three-putted for a double bogey. Tired, sweaty, hungry and despondent, I was playing out the remainder of this course like a sentence.

Then came an unexpected gift from nature. On the fifteenth hole, a dogleg to the right, I hit a passable tee shot to the right rough and walked down a gentle slope. When I reached the bottom a rush of cool air swept by me no higher than waist level, as though I were wading in a trout stream. The coming dusk had taken the edge off the heat, but this trough of air was too narrow and defined for that. I wondered at the source until I passed a stand of trees and found the right side of the fairway bounded by a large, freshly dug potato field. The exposed troughs were like the coils of nature's own air conditioner. Every time the wind blew over the field, it carried with it the stored-up coldness of the Maine winter. I pretended to tie my shoes and dropped to my knees to savor it.

Darkness embraced us as we walked up the final fairway. The only light came from a dim street lamp and the pale dying halo of red and pink on the western horizon. All the other golfers were long gone; even the staff had closed shop. We were alone on the last green at the end of the earth.

"I love golf," Stacey said a little wistfully as we headed toward our cars. "I love the challenge, I love the courses. But the best thing is the people you meet."

I took a picture of these newfound friends of mine whom I would probably never see again. We shook hands and said good-bye. I made my way back to Route 1 and retraced my steps to a motel I had passed in Caribou, just north of Presque Isle. The evening was dry, clear and cool. Perfect sleeping weather, except that somebody had left the thermostat in my room up around sti-fling. I was too tired for an encounter with the night manager, so I cranked the air conditioner—on the most beautiful night in the world I used an air conditioner to counteract the effects of a heater. I fished some crackers and breakfast bars and warm spring water out of my cooler and phoned home.

Barbara asked me how my day had gone. She'd asked me that a thousand times before when I came home tired at the end of another workday. Only now, instead of railing at the intransigence of some assistant city editor in the newsroom, I spilled tales of hooks and slices and missed putts, and of cool breezes blowing off potato fields. She listened politely, offering vague reassurances and condolences, not sure what her responses were supposed to be now that my golf game had somehow been elevated to the level of a professional concern. I asked her about her day, searching her cheerful recitation of daily events for a sense of how things were really going on her end of my adventure. So far, so good.

Natalie got on next. She asked me where I was and when I'd be home and accepted my explanation without comment, shifting the subject to whom she'd seen that day and the gifts she was making for my return. Her voice was indescribably sweet and made me wonder what I was doing a thousand miles away from her. It may sound disingenuous for a guy who has wangled the golf trip of a lifetime to question his good fortune, but I suddenly wished I were on a bona fide business trip, selling computer software or casualty insurance, something sober and sturdy and irreproachable, something commensurate with my wife's forbearance and my daughter's trusting voice. I hung up the phone and collapsed on the bed. Sleep came within minutes.

2

I Am Tiger Woods

I woke early, a Monday morning. My first thought: Better get to work. My second thought: This is not my bed, this is not my house. This has not been a dream. I must actually *be* in a motel in Caribou, Maine, with nothing on my agenda but another day of golf.

Houlton, Maine, proved to be just what I needed after my golfing debacle at Presque Isle. Houlton is a small town with shady streets, white houses and friendly people, located about a hundred miles south of Fort Kent and sixty miles south of Presque Isle. From this improbable spot Interstate 95 begins its mad rush to Miami, starting with little fanfare at a Customs checkpoint separating the United States from Canada. I asked a road construction worker along a residential section of Route 1 where I could golf. He told me to take a right, go past Greg's store, over the ridge and take another right, your second not the first, can't miss it.

I found the clubhouse of the nine-hole Houlton Golf Club surrounded by flowering apple trees and set snug against the banks of Lake Nickerson, a long, spring-fed trough that is more than a hundred feet deep in places, deep enough for lake trout. The clubhouse was built in 1926 around an enormous stone fireplace. To become a member of the Houlton Golf Club you buy a bond for $50, then pay a $280 fee for the entire season ($425 for a family) entitling you to unlimited golf. I paid $10 for nine holes, walking.

The past winter had been a particularly bad one for golf courses in northern Maine because it had produced little snow but plenty of sleet and ice. When ice forms on greens and fairways without a protective covering of snow, the result is winter kill, ugly brown patches of dead grass that make hitting from the fairways about like knocking a ball off your driveway. Greens roll with the reliability of the threadbare AstroTurf at a seaside miniature golf course. The problem comes during early spring when the sun's rays intensify but the ice remains. Without a protective layer of snow, the sun shines directly onto the ice-covered turf, triggering it to grow. But the fresh shoots quickly die in the frigid, airless cocoon. Hence winter kill.

I learned all this from Babe Caron, the Houlton pro, who told me I should really come back around mid-July and see the course in its full glory. Caron has been the pro at Houlton since 1973. A baseball player and boxer in his youth, Caron learned to golf in the Air Force in Okinawa during the early 1960s.

"One day a military transport landed at the base. A man got off the plane, and everybody was excited. They rolled out the red carpet for him, treated him like a real VIP," Caron explained. "I figured it was a politician or a movie star. Turned out it was a professional golfer. I liked the way he was being treated. I'd never swung a club before, but I figured I could learn." Caron started playing the base course in Okinawa, and by the time he left the Air Force a few years later was good enough to get jobs as an assistant pro at golf clubs. These days, he spends his winters as a pro at a course in Myrtle Beach and returns to Houlton each summer.

Determined to keep my driver sheathed until I gained a little consistency with my other clubs, I hit a nice, easy three-iron up the fairway on the par-four first hole, a 325-yard straightforward hole leading away from the clubhouse. The shot was not perfect, by which I mean to say that it lacked that satisfying *thwack!* when you can feel the ball compressing properly against the club face. I caught it a little fat, but it was straight and I couldn't complain. I next took an easy swing with a seven-iron and the ball sailed nicely and straight and landed just short of the green, in a gentle shower of sprinklers. Using the same club, I chipped up to within six feet of the hole. The putt for par scraped across the still-ragged surface of the green and sank into the cup. A fine way to start.

My next hole was a 475-yard par-five. Again, I hit an iron. I don't know what an instructor would say about that. I could envision the late Harvey Penick, author of the famous little red-and-green books full of golf wisdom, sitting in his cart in his dapper cap and tartan sweater watching me with quiet disapproval as I picked my three-iron out of the bag to tee off on a par-five hole. It would probably earn me a spot in one of his immortal notebooks: "Whenever I see a young fellow select a three-iron instead of a driver in order to play it safe," he would write, "I ask myself if this fellow understands what the game of golf is all about. If he can't bring himself to use the proper club, he will always be second-guessing himself when it counts most. He will never have the confidence to choose the big club when he needs a big shot." Or something like that.

But you can find a maxim to support just about any position you take. For every "nothing ventured, nothing gained" there's a "slow and steady wins the race." I went with the latter. To begin to put decent rounds together I would need to keep the ball in play. I struck my three-iron well. The ball stopped about two hundred yards down the fairway. My second shot, a four-iron, pushed right, but not nearly so much as if I had taken a big swing with a fairway wood. The ball stopped in the right rough, with a tree between where I stood and the green. I lofted an eight-iron over the tree but it landed short of the green. I chipped up and two-putted for a bogey six. I bogeyed, double bogeyed and bogeyed the next three holes. On the fifth, I played smart on a hole that normally would have spelled big trouble for me. It was a downhill par-four, and I hit my three-wood off the tee and sliced it right into a patch of gnarly rough with no view of the green. Instead of trying to hit over the trees to the green I pitched back onto the fairway, then put my next shot onto the green and saved a bogey. Smart golf. Next, I put together a string of three pars and felt my spirits lift with each one. I swung easily, comfortably, not worrying about where the ball was going or trying to steer it. The new me was having fun. I stopped from time to time to enjoy the scenery, the blue sky, the pines, the air sweetened by apple blossoms, the quiet.

The eighth hole at Houlton is a par-three that also doubles as a par-four seventeenth hole for the back nine (to play eighteen holes you play the course twice, with changes in configuration of the tee boxes). With no one around to ask, I mistakenly hit off the ladies' seventeenth tee, which is a 210-yard par-four. This meant I was playing a 210-yard par-three. It didn't ruffle me in the slightest. I laughed at the challenge. I pulled my five-wood from the bag and stuck my tee shot over a bunker and onto the green, about eight feet short of the pin. I just missed my birdie putt and tapped in for par. So THIS is how golf works. I bogeyed my last hole for a nine-hole score of 42. Figuring an eighteen-hole score by doubling a good nine-hole score is a time-honored act of self-delusion among golf hacks. I would have had an 84. In reality, it's infinitely harder to carry a hot streak across eighteen holes than nine. The ability to do so is precisely what separates real golfers from pretenders. But what the hell. I drove away from the Houlton Golf Club loving Houlton and apple blossoms and Babe Caron and springtime and golf and life.

The road from Houlton runs through deep pine forests, and then along a crest with spectacular views. To the west I saw the snowy cap of Mt. Katahdin. To the east, just below my window, were the ice-blue waters of Grand Lake, surrounded by immense forests of pine and birch. At Danforth, a mournful-looking hillside town of old wooden buildings, like an Appalachian hill town transplanted from eastern Tennessee to northern Maine, the road made a sharp dogleg left, cut through a series of Passamaquoddy Indian villages and then ran south and east through the mill town of Woodland and into Calais. Calais, pronounced Callus, shares an international border with St. Stephen, New Brunswick, over the St. Croix River.

I'd heard there was a driving range in St. Stephen, on a street with the wonderful name of Happy Valley Lane. Something about going international to hit a bucket of balls appealed to me. I crossed the St. Croix into Canada, turned right along Main Street in St. Stephen, past duty-free shops and businesses on the left and the river on the right. Then I turned left on Canada's Route 1 and followed it for a couple of miles to the edge of town. Near a crossroads of Route 1 and Route 3, I found Happy Valley Lane, which turned out to be little more than a dirt path. I followed an arrow pointing down the path, past a farmhouse to a scrubby field that looked as if it had been a driving range long ago. There were no signs, just a forlorn white shack. I parked my car and walked down toward the range. There were a couple of AstroTurf tee boxes; the rest were packed dirt and dried mud. The field was covered with dandelions and wildflowers. The shack looked deserted. I was about to leave when something in the shack moved. I walked to the window. A pretty young woman with brown hair and brown eyes smiled at me.

"Are you open today?" I said hesitantly.

"Yes."

"I'd like to hit a large bucket."

"Sure."

I took my $3 bucket over to what looked like a tee box. The sun soaked my back. The range spread before me in a gently sloping Andrew Wyeth landscape of wildflowers and tall grass. A stiff fresh breeze pushed straight out. I was the only customer. I slowly tied my shoes, stretched, placed a ball on a wooden tee from my bag, and hit some seven-irons far out into the daisies.

After a while a man pulled up in a Buick sedan. He was about forty-five years old and prosperous looking. He spotted my license plate and called out, "Coming from Virginia, I guess this seems like cold weather to you, eh?"

"Actually, I spoke to my wife yesterday," I said. "It's hotter here than in Virginia. They've been getting nothing but cool air and rain."

He considered for a moment. "My wife and I are supposed to go to Virginia Beach next week."

"I'm sure it'll be sunny and hot by then."

He was from St. Andrews, a seaside village of tidy homes and carefully tended gardens about half an hour from St. Stephen and Calais. During the brief growing season, yards explode with color. The town is dominated by a turn-of-the-century hotel, the Algonquin, one of those hotels that railroads used to build in order to give passengers a reason to buy train tickets. Now owned by the Canadian government, the Algonquin looms in feudal graciousness over St. Andrews, high on a hill overlooking the Bay of Fundy, where the tidal changes are the highest in the world. I had proposed to my wife in the lush gardens on the hotel grounds. I thought about returning there for a round at the hotel course, but St. Andrews lay too far off my path.

I returned the empty bucket to the young woman in the shed.

"Must be a pretty lonely job here," I said

"Uh huh. It should pick up in a little while. It's still early."

I saw a sign for Cokes for a dollar and asked for one. She reached into the cooler. I handed her a $20 bill. She fumbled over the money and handed me back about ten singles.

I pointed out the mistake. "Tell you what," she said cheerfully. "Here's your twenty back. You can have the Coke. I can never figure American money out. It all looks the same."

I drove back to the border to Calais, where a slender bridge crosses the St. Croix River just short of the fall line.

The U.S. customs officer regarded me with a sort of impassive suspicion.

"Where do you live?"

"Richmond, Virginia."

"And what was the purpose of your visit to Canada?"

"I went to the driving range to hit some balls."

"You drove up from Virginia to go to the driving range."

I wondered whether I was going to wind up explaining my whole golf trip. "Well, no," I said. "I'm traveling through the area, and I heard there was a driving range there, so I decided to hit some balls."

"Are you bringing anything back with you?"

"Just a Coke."

The officer peered into my car, at the jumble of maps, spent soft-drink containers, and assorted other road flotsam. Though I had nothing to hide, I had the strange feeling under inquisitive eyes of being a smuggler. He paused as if considering how deeply to involve himself in my life. He smiled, shook his head, and waived me through.

Calais is a working-class town of about three thousand people. I know Calais well. In a sense, we'd grown up together. When I was a boy my family spent summers in an island cabin we owned on nearby Meddybemps Lake. We drove seven hours north from Boston to sleep in a cabin with no electricity or running water, no telephone. We drank the lake water and slept on army cots with sleeping bags. We fished and swam. On cool nights the cabin filled with laughter and wood smoke. The town of Meddybemps has but one place to shop, Palmeter's General Store, so supply runs for us meant trips into Calais. As Calais grew, the homogenization of America left its stamp. I remember when the first McDonald's came to town, planted like a Day-Glo jelly bean amid the weathered whites and greens of Route 1, Main Street, heading into downtown. My parents greeted this development with sadness, as if the world they longed to escape had found them even here. At thirteen, I found Big Macs oddly reassuring in this place that seemed like the far end of the earth. Burger King, Dunkin' Donuts and Hardees followed, and soon the small restaurants catering to loggers and truck drivers, the places with stained coffee mugs and signs for *ho-made* blueberry pie, started going out of business. Then a Kmart clone set up in a strip mall on the edge of town and that was the beginning of the end for the local hardware stores, including the world's best hardware store, Todd's, on Main Street. Todd's had wooden floors and that heady hardware smell of fuel, leather, wood and fertilizer all mixed together. You could get anything at Todd's—a Daredevil fishing lure, tackle, licenses, just the right-sized screw, a length of boat rope, a sturdy hammer, a balsa wood glider, washers, a pump handle, boots, and a gas can, a gutting knife, batteries, a high-powered flashlight that would send beacons across the darkened lake, and gum, nuts and bolts, chains and just about anything else. The merchandise at Todd's seemed not to have been brought in by outside suppliers at all, but to have grown organically onto the shelves. The clerks were ageless, stoic, and solemn as judges in their dark green Dickies. When you bought hardware from Todd's you searched their eyes for signs they approved of your choices. On this return visit to Calais I noticed with a sort of wistful satisfaction that the Kmart clone that had put Todd's out of business had itself closed down, the victim of a new and even bigger retailer, a Wal-Mart.

Just south of downtown, Route 1 winds along the St. Croix, past a small historic district of nineteenth-century homes built by prominent merchants and shippers. Just beyond is the St. Croix Country Club, a public golf course not just on Route 1, but actually bisected by it. The first hole and holes six through nine are on the north side of the highway, sandwiched between the road and the river, while two through five run through woods and hills south of the highway. According to the scorecard, "the grass-covered portion of the highway, though not belonging to the club, is in bounds." Say what you will about the Amen Corner at Augusta or the eighteenth hole at Pebble Beach. You have not tested your powers of concentration until you have chipped a ball back onto the green from a grassy highway embankment, trying to forget about that fully loaded logging truck bearing down on you. In addition to being split by the highway, St. Croix Country Club also has the distinction of being the easternmost golf course in the United States. So if you are ambitious enough to rise early and tee off at sunrise, you might lay claim to being the first golfer in the nation that day.

I resisted that temptation, and at midmorning hooked up on the first tee with Sue Gordon and her son, Ross, graduating that day from Woodland High School. Ross had started playing golf in eighth grade when the high-school golf team, to encourage more kids to play, allowed eighth-graders to play practice rounds with the team. Later, he played on the high-school team. His mom picked the game up a couple of years later, in part as a way to spend time with her son. They were fitting in a few holes of golf before meeting up with Ross's dad for Class Day ceremonies. Ross had enrolled for the next year at Maine Maritime Academy in Castine, a resort town on the southern coast, where he planned to study international business.

"Going to focus on U.S.-Canada?" I asked.

"I think he may go farther than that," Mrs. Gordon interjected.

Ross, who had looked across the river at Canada every day of his life, said, "I'm interested in Asia."

The first hole is a par-three heading straight out from the clubhouse to Route 1, 165 yards away. Ross and I both put our tee shots onto the green, a nice way to start, especially with a foursome behind quietly watching. I three-putted for four, while Ross sank his in two for a par.

Across the highway you tee off at the 520-yard par-five second, which leads up a gentle slope and narrowing fairway to the green and is the hardest hole on the course. "*Mmmm*, smell the apple blossoms," Mrs. Gordon said. Only women can get away with saying stuff like that aloud on a golf course. Ross swung his club with the abandon of an eighteen-year-old on the day of his high-school graduation. He mishit his drive but hit a fine second shot and a third that stopped about forty yards shy of the green. My own drive curved to the left, the worst spot to be on this hole; I found myself in some woods on the far side of a ravine, punched the ball up the fairway and after a couple of more poorly struck balls was on my way to a disheartening 8. Ross, meanwhile, hit a wedge from forty yards that ran up the fringe of the green and plunked into the hole for a birdie.

"I am Tiger Woods!" he cried, mimicking the Nike commercial of that summer.

On the fifth hole, a 415-yard par-four, Ross hit a monster drive. "I *am* Tiger Woods!" he repeated.

After six holes the Gordons left for Class Day. I finished the last three holes myself. The seventh, a short par-four, is the most interesting hole on the course, tucked in behind a bend in the river. You tee off from an elevated tee box, over a brook and between two stands of trees. The hole doglegs sharply back to the right, to a green protected on three sides by trees and traps in front. A family of bald eagles had nested in a tall pine looming over the green and spent their time gazing sternly down on human folly. The inevitable clubhouse joke was that the only eagles you'd ever see on that hole had wings. I hit a great four-iron off the tee, putting myself in perfect range for a short pitch to the green. Then I fluffed my second shot, and my third, and my fourth. I later learned that the area in front of the turf had just been resodded and was well-nigh impossible to hit out of. I felt only marginally better.

At the next hole I bought some lemonade from two girls who had set up a stand in their yard running down the right side of the fairway. They were also selling found golf balls, for 25 cents apiece, back to the golfers who had knocked them out of bounds a day or two earlier. I bought a couple of bucks' worth. A dog and a cat lurked nearby. Some regular golfers told me later those two beasts were famous for assisting the youthful entrepreneurs in building their inventory, sometimes plucking balls from the fairway. Armed with eight new (or, near-new) balls and the sweet residue of lemonade still on my lips, I finished out the last two holes for a 48 on an easy course. A pair of 8s killed me.

Later, in the pine-paneled clubhouse, I sat over a beer with Duane Ellis, an elementary-school teacher in Calais who doubled as the course pro, and Jan Ellis, his wife and the club's manager. The course was built by some prominent citizens in the 1930s on the site of an old farm. The farmhouse, a simple, white frame structure backing up on a bluff overlooking the St. Croix River, is now the clubhouse. Over the years, extra rooms have been added, but the original structure remains the core. The Ellises live upstairs during the golf season and, during the winters, across the river in St. Stephen, Jan's hometown. Nearly half of the course's regular golfers are Canadians.

"I love the course," Jan said. "It's beautiful. I love being outdoors. But I find life frustrating enough without trying to knock that little ball around and stuff it into that hole. So I don't golf."

The son of a storekeeper and a schoolteacher, Duane Ellis grew up in the southern Maine town of Monmouth. Monmouth was dominated by a hilltop resort that, in the stratified social order of the 1950s, catered to wealthy Jewish vacationers who were not welcome at the WASP resorts. Like many excellent golfers from modest backgrounds, Duane Ellis learned to play by caddying, an occupation that has all but vanished in the tire tracks of the motorized cart. Each morning, a truck from the resort would drive down from the hilltop to fetch local boys, after unloading the previous day's hotel garbage as slop for the local pig farms.

"I will never forget that smell," Ellis said. "It was only a couple of miles back up the hill, but I can still smell that smell."

But he learned to golf and learned to love the game.

"I'd always dreamed of being a schoolteacher, like my mother, and then in the summers I thought it would be great to be a golf pro somewhere," he told me.

When he graduated in the mid-1960s from a state teachers' college in Machias, Ellis was about to accept a teaching position in Auburn, a small city about thirty miles north of Portland in southern Maine. At the last moment an insurance company looking for bright young graduates offered to double his $4,200 starting teacher's salary if he'd take a job selling insurance in the Calais area. He took the money but soon regretted it.

"It's a tough racket. You can't just have a conversation, you're always sizing people up," Ellis said. "If I was sitting here talking with you I'd be having a conversation but I'd be thinking to myself, *hmmmm*, he looks pretty healthy, I wonder if he's covered. You've got to think that way in that business. It wasn't me."

After ten years he switched to teaching. Ellis had joined the St. Croix Country Club and won some tournaments. When the resident pro announced one day he was leaving, the job more or less fell to Ellis. It was going to be temporary. That was in 1987.

"It's funny, but I got my dream after all," he said with a smile. "Here I am, teaching school, and I'm a golf pro."

It was nearing dark when I left the Ellises, dinner now central in my mind. Calais, located near the mouth of the St. Croix River, marks the geographic spot at which Maine breaks off from New Brunswick and faces the cold waters of the North Atlantic. That means the start of lobster country. Up here even McDonald's serves lobster sandwiches. I headed down Route 1 toward a place called the Crossroads, where I remembered they serve a lobster roll piled in a pink mountain on a hot dog bun. The Crossroads sits on Route 1 near the crossroads town of Robbinston. In the disappearing sunlight, off to the left, the St. Croix widened out to meet the Bay of Fundy. I expected a fifteen- or twenty-minute drive to the Crossroads, but as the road wound into a gathering darkness and I plodded along the two-lane highway behind a logging truck, I fell victim to an old truth about driving in Maine—whenever you think you're there, you're still forty-five minutes away. Maine may not be as big as Texas, but for an East Coast equivalent it will do. It's a huge state, more than 33,000 square miles, most of them rural. In sheer mileage, nearly a quarter of my trip on Route 1 down the East Coast would be spent just in Maine. By the time I reached the Crossroads the windows of the restaurant were as dark as the night sky. My hopes of an overflowing lobster roll, cold beer and a wedge of pie dashed, I drove on to a country gas station, filled my gas tank and bought a bag of Oreos to go with the can of sardines beckoning from the trunk of my car. Hungry and disappointed, I turned right on Route 214 and wound through more pine forests toward the family place at Meddybemps Lake.

My parents had held on to the island cabin but in recent years had built a larger and more comfortable cabin on the shore. It was still bare-bones, with two simple bedrooms and a large, sparsely furnished kitchen and living room. But it offered several amenities the remote island camp lacked—running water, electricity, a telephone and proximity to the village of Meddybemps. These were crucial considerations for my mother, because they gave her the independence to begin coming to Maine alone when my father was working or traveling. We had spent some of our happiest times as a family on that lake, but my mother's heart holds the largest share of Meddybemps. Her family connections had started us coming to the lake in the first place. Some relatives, the Paxtons, owned the largest island on the lake. My parents spent their honeymoon in a stone cabin on Paxton Island. A man who owned several islands on the lake took a liking to the honeymoon couple and gave them the tiny, windswept island upon which years later we built that first cabin. From the start my mother insisted on simplicity and spareness, unfinished walls with nails for hangers, army cots and sleeping bags instead of beds and sheets—anything to distance her and us from the trappings of our home in suburban Boston. Now that we kids have grown up, she speaks sometimes of loneliness that permeates the house in Boston on cloudy days. Yet she can spend days or weeks in the voluntary solitude of Maine, regardless of the weather, without feeling a pang.

I pulled off the two-lane highway just before reaching the village. As my car bumped and jiggled along a dirt path, the headlight beams danced off pine trees, piercing a darkness so complete I might have been a submarine captain searching the ocean floor for sunken treasure. After a few hundred yards I pulled up in front of the cabin. I trained my headlights on the steps and walked up to the porch, found a hidden key and let myself in. It was a windless, starless night, and chilly. The quiet and darkness, more than the cold, made hairs rise on the back of my neck. I flipped a light switch. I tore a year-old copy of the *Bangor Daily News* into strips and laid them in the fireplace under some kindling. When the fire took, I added a couple of aged birch logs from a woodpile on the porch. The chimney drew well, allowing just a faint aroma of wood smoke to spread its rustic cheer around the cabin. I ate my dinner, such as it was, then sat in a rocking chair by the fire and jotted greetings in a communal journal my mother had left prominently on a bookshelf. I spent the next morning organizing notes from the courses I'd already played and poring over maps and golf guides for the road ahead. It was too early in the summer for a swim, so I walked down to the lake and hiked over rocks, roots and fallen trees along the shore. In the afternoon I walked back up the dirt road and crossed the highway to the house where Cecil Ward lived with his wife, Helen. Cecil was a small, slender man with weathered, leathery skin covering delicate features. Like his father before him, he plied the lake for a living, serving as caretaker for the cabins he'd built, doing repairs in the off-season, changing propane tanks, resetting docks displaced by winter storms. He had built our island cabin and, though by then retired, helped oversee construction of the shore place. But he was always much more than a builder and caretaker to us. With the exception of a stretch in Burma during World War II, Cecil had lived his entire life in Meddybemps. He spoke of Portland and Bangor as if they were major cities. And yet in his own environment Cecil Ward possessed an undeniable genius. By turns electrician, carpenter, roofer, architect, and mechanic, Cecil could do anything. At least that's the way it seemed to us, and our faith in him was never disappointed. He embodied our conception of the ideal Maine outdoorsman, skillful and self-reliant, with a wry sense of humor. He moved with the precision of a cat, hopping from his boat to a dock, sticking out a foot just in time to keep the gunwale from scraping the wood, as always happened with our own boat.

I sat in Cecil and Helen's small, comfortable kitchen for the first time in several years. They asked me about my golf trip, brought me up-to-date on happenings around the lake. Cecil was by now in his late seventies; his health had been failing in recent years. He looked frail, but his eyes still sparkled. He seemed eager to reminisce, as if making a conscious effort to sum things up.

He said, "Your father was always an easy man to work for. As far as he was concerned, everything was done right."

"Well, Cecil," I said, "that's because everything was done right." He smiled warmly. I will always be glad I said that. A few weeks later, I was sitting in a motel room somewhere in North Carolina, cooling down after a round of golf, when my wife passed along the news from my mother. Cecil had died in his sleep of a heart attack.

3

Shank Happens

I left Meddybemps around sunrise, picked up Route 1 and rolled down the coast. At Machias I stopped at the Bluebird Ranch Café, where a waitress named Dottie filled my cup, called me "dear" and took my order for blueberry pancakes, bacon, home fries and orange juice. I was now in Washington County, home to most of Maine's 65,000 acres of blueberry barrens. Instead of the orderly furrowed ridges of the potato fields, the hills were marked by scrubby, irregular fields, many of them scorched black. The practice dates back centuries. Indians discovered that burning the bushes every other year, in rotation, yields a plumper berry and more berries per bush. Burning also kills off other plants that might choke the low bushes. Blueberry bushes, which lie 70 percent buried, easily survive surface burning.

A truism among Mainers holds that blueberry bushes cannot grow unless the seeds first pass through the digestive system of a bird. Therefore, the reasoning goes, it's impossible to plant a blueberry seed by hand. I'd heard the same thing repeated by many people over the years, that some enzyme in a bird gut acts as a catalyst for the blueberry seed.

"It's not true," said Dell Emerson, director of Blueberry Hill Farm, a research station run by the University of Maine. Shortly after breakfast, I'd spotted the farm's white administration building on Route 1 just south of Machias and pulled off the road to get the lowdown on the birds and the berries. Emerson, a tall, thin, ruggedly handsome man in his fifties, wearing a Red Sox baseball cap, shook his head and laughed when I repeated what I'd heard. Birds, like bears, small mammals or humans, do perform an important digestive function of separating the blueberry skin from the seed, Emerson explained. A seed mummified in its own skin won't grow. But a seed stripped with an X-acto knife will grow just as well as one expelled by a bird. The reason the plants aren't sown and cultivated like squash or potatoes is economic rather than biological. It takes eight years to bring a bush from seed to full maturity. "The investment just isn't worth the payoff," Emerson said. "Better to let Nature do her thing."

Somewhere between the coastal towns of Machias and Ellsworth there is an invisible Maginot Line of tourism. North of the line, there are fewer hotels and motels, fewer out-of-state license plates on the road. You are more likely to be stuck behind a logging truck than an RV. The houses hunker lower to the ground, intent on fending off the winters rather than presenting a sort of idealized vision of Yankee quaintness that people from Boston and New York expect.

South of this line the state becomes acutely and obviously aware of its own value as a tourist attraction. Real estate prices jump by $100,000 or more; the shops cater to people with more money and less need for socket wrenches and tarpaulins. The churches seem to point a little straighter at the sky, picket fences stand a little more smartly at attention and everything seems to have been covered with a new coat of white paint.

By the turnoff for Bar Harbor, the transformation is complete. Maine is still Maine, but now it is also what other people wish Maine to be. Here the state tips its hat to the legions of Volvo-driving Massachusetts vacationers (Mass-holes, as they are sometimes called) and other out-of-state visitors who are at once needed and disdained by the local population. My family had been from Massachusetts, but Meddybemps was too far north and too far off the track for us to feel the sting of that epithet. The summer people on Lake Meddybemps seemed to gain some measure of respect in the eyes of locals for having come so far.

I turned left at Ellsworth and followed a winding road into Bar Harbor. Bar Harbor, which from the late 1800s through the 1920s was the preferred summer spot for America's superrich, sits at the northern end of Mount Desert Island, a mountainous circle of land hanging like a Christmas ornament off the Maine coast. When the rich moved on, they left behind 33,000 acres of donated land that became Acadia National Park, a few magnificent homes not destroyed in a series of devastating fires, and a golf course, Kebo Valley.

Built in 1888, Kebo Valley sits in a wooded valley surrounded by the peaks of the national park, softened by red spruce, firs, jack pines, beech and aspens. The course was built under the direction of men with names such as Ogden Codman and DeGrasse Fox. They called themselves "rusticators" for their love of the rustic life on the Maine coast, but their definition of rustic was sufficiently flexible to include "cottages" with fifty rooms and servants' quarters. The layout of the course itself remains largely as it was in the days when Fords, Morgans and Astors swung their mashies and niblicks here. In the early decades, budget tourists who crammed the lesser Bar Harbor hotels were as unwelcome on the course as local residents. But by mid-century the rich were moving on. A fire in 1947 that nearly wiped out Mount Desert Island took most of the grand old summer cottages. The fire also destroyed the rambling clubhouse. A new, far more modest one was built in its place. Membership today is open to anyone and costs $500 for a season of unlimited golf. Tourists, once despised by the rusticators, help keep the course afloat now by paying greens fees that are high by Maine standards. I paid $35 to walk eighteen holes. After the first of July the fee would jump to $50.

The course was virtually empty, so I paid up and headed out for a round by myself. Kebo Valley is perhaps best known for a single hole, the par-four seventeenth, featuring the Sand Trap. This was not just a big trap, not just a challenging trap, but the entire side of a hill, thirty-five feet of hell with a green at the top waving its pin flag like a taunt. William Howard Taft, known elsewhere for being the fattest president in American history, is famous in Bar Harbor as the man who one summer day in 1911 shot a twenty-seven on the seventeenth hole at Kebo Valley. The best that can be said of Taft's performance that day is that he waived all offers of executive privilege and gamely finished the hole, counting every stroke.

I was having a decent round, enjoying the early summer air and the views of Cadillac Mountain. A 10 on the par-five fifth hole marred what was an otherwise fair round going into the later stages. I had parred a number of holes in succession and felt confident heading toward my date with the Trap on seventeen.

On the tee at seventeen I surveyed the hole ahead with the calmness of Patton looking over a battlefield in North Africa. It was a short par-four, just 349 yards from tee to pin, with an open bowl of a fairway. This called for smart golf. I left my woods in the bag and pulled out a three-iron. Placement was everything on this hole. I teed my ball low and struck it smartly down the middle of the fairway. So far, so good. All that remained was a soft nine-iron to the green. The trap is said to be thirty-five feet high, but as I walked to my ball it seemed much higher. It ran the width of the fairway like a grin. No problem, I told myself. It's no different from any other hillside. The trap doesn't exist if you don't hit it. Take that trap *out of play*, I told myself. I lined up my shot thinking *I will not hit the sand trap, I will not hit the sand trap, I will not hit the sand trap.* Only in real life is one allowed to be this predictable. The ball found not just the trap, but the center of the trap. If that trap were the continental United States, my ball was in Kansas. It came to rest in a foot crater so large and deep I was sure it was the fossilized imprint of President Taft's left shoe. More depressing was the way I had gotten there. A shank. The ball whistled low and ugly to the right, ricocheted off a railroad tie and whizzed into the sand. A shank is the nakedest shot in golf, and you don't need spectators or playing partners to feel humiliated. There is no absolution for a shank. It is infinitely more damaging to one's psyche than a run-of-the-mill hook or slice. It is worse even than a complete whiff, which at least can be joked away—"There's my practice swing!" A shank happens when the club strikes the ball not squarely with the face but at the place where the shaft and the face meet, known as the shank of the club. The ball squirts off to the right at a grotesque angle. It can happen because you are standing too close to the ball, or because you are standing too far away. Once you have developed a shank, it may well be the only golf shot you can hit with consistency. Golfers will openly commiserate with you on just about any swing malady you can name: Sky hooks, wicked slices, misread putts. But nobody wants to talk to you about your shanking problem. It might be contagious. Slice and the world slices with you; shank and you shank alone.

It took me four shots to work the ball up over the top lip of the trap.

"Why didn't you just hit back down the hill and try another wedge over the trap?" someone asked me when I described the cursed hole a few days later. It was a reasonable question to which I could only reply that it hadn't occurred to me. Why don't men ask for directions when they're lost?

I finished the hole with a round-killing 10, my second of the day, which pushed my score over the century mark to 103. I was particularly frustrated because I felt I had been playing well on a difficult and challenging course, parring a string of holes, showing improvement. The fact that I had beaten President Taft by seventeen strokes on the seventeenth hole did not move me. I trudged up to the clubhouse, hot, tired, thirsty, and depressed.

"How'd you make out?" a man called from the clubhouse deck.

"I was doing okay until the seventeenth," I said. "Whose idea was that sand trap?"

The man offered a sympathetic smile.

"I hope you teed the ball up and grounded your club in there," he said.

"Why? Is that allowed?" Teeing up your ball in a sand trap, and grounding your club by pressing it into the sand behind the ball, are normally forbidden.

"Sure," he said. "It's impossible to get out of there otherwise. Except during tournaments, it's impossible to keep that huge trap properly raked. Once the ball gets rolling back down the hill it's bound to stop in a footprint."

"I noticed."

The man nodded. "It's a club rule. You're allowed to tee the ball up and ground your club. The only way to get out of there is to get under the ball. A conventional sand shot is useless." I later chatted with the head pro, Gregg Baker, who confirmed the unwritten rule, saying it was instituted to keep play moving. A hole where golfers routinely shoot in the double digits can clog a course like a jackknifed truck on the Interstate.

"I wish you had been out there with me," I said to the man on the deck. "You could have saved me some aggravation."

I found a good, clean, inexpensive motel, the Acadia Inn, on the outskirts of town. My cardinal rule in looking for lodgings was to inspect the parking lots for large, late-model American sedans. A string of pastel Caprices and Bonnevilles means one thing—old people. And old people have an unerring eye for accommodations that are clean, cheap, and that toss in a complimentary breakfast. Acadia Inn was just such a place. I settled in my room, showered, changed, then headed into town for dinner. Downtown Bar Harbor is a curious mixture of tourists, students, locals, fading hippies in tie-dyed shirts and sandals, biker dudes and dudettes, and trail-weary hikers with immense backpacks, bulging calf muscles and hungry eyes. The shops cater to all types—folksy knickknack shops press up close to rowdy-looking bars. I found a clean, well-lighted restaurant on Cottage Street called the Island Chowder House, offering a boiled Maine lobster dinner for under $10. I ate slowly, letting the sweet meat bathe in the cup of melted butter. I ordered a bottle of a locally brewed ale infused with the juice of Maine blueberries. It didn't taste bad, except my taste buds couldn't decide whether I was having pancakes or a cold beer. I wouldn't want to deal with a blueberry ale hangover.

After dinner I walked down to the waterfront and had a beer without berry juice on the deck of a restaurant overlooking Frenchman's Bay. Then I strolled through a little park where honeymooners held hands on benches and a young woman sat cross-legged on the grass earnestly strumming a sitar. It was a beautiful cool evening, dry and clear, and the air smelled of the sea.

On my way back to the motel I pulled off the road at the Turrets, one of the grandest of the old cottages and one of the few not destroyed by the 1947 fire. Built for a soap magnate named J.J. Emery, the Turrets required a hundred laborers and two years to build. When the age of the rusticators passed, the cottage was converted to a hotel, and, later, a monastery. In 1973 a new college, the College of the Atlantic, turned the imposing structure into its administration building. I parked in a lot not far from the cottage and wandered the deserted grounds. This was post-graduation and barely a soul stirred. The front door to the Turrets, under a heavy portico, was unlocked. As I stood in the soft evening air, I tried to imagine the smartly dressed guests who must have pulled up to this door in carriages on summer nights just like this a century ago, the ladies in long dresses, the men in stiff collars and ties. The main hallway was an overwrought affair with molded ceilings and intricate, hand-carved woodwork.

The College of the Atlantic, with its emphasis on environmentalism, attracts a student body of budding activists. The front hallway was filled with fliers, free brochures and notices announcing rallies against this and boycotts of that. Earnest, badly printed posters urged students to avoid such capitalist products as Pepsi, Coke, meat and nonorganic coffee. The Student Environmental Action Committee planned to observe September 25 as the National Day of Action Against Corporate Greed. I wondered how many students here appreciated the irony as they tacked up these notices on lovingly crafted woodwork in the entryway paid for by J.J. Emery the soap king. And just beyond that entryway were hundreds of pristine acres of Acadia National Park, the only national park formed entirely from private land, donated by soap kings and cereal queens and assorted other scions of corporate greed.

South of Bar Harbor, the Northport Golf Club in Northport, Maine, lies eight-tenths of a mile off Route 1, according to a little blue-and-white roadside sign. The morning was cool and clear, the pines poked crisply into a blue sky and the entire world seemed to have been washed and hung on a taut line to dry. Little towns with a single white church and red brick buildings built right up close to the road popped up like a memory and disappeared. I had planned to make it farther along the coast before stopping. But when I spotted the Northport sign I hung a U-turn and headed down a narrow country road. Maybe this course had a driving range, and I could hit a bucket, then move on.

The large wooden clubhouse, with its dark green paint and broad, shaded verandah, looked like a hunting lodge.

"Are you open to the public?" I asked the woman behind the counter.

"Yup."

"Do you have a driving range?"

"Yup."

"May I get a bucket of balls?"

"Yup. Ask me a hard one."

Her name was Eileen Estes. She and her husband, George, managed the pro shop in their retirement.

I asked her when the course had been built. She pointed to the club charter, framed on the wall. A wealthy Bostonian named Ira Maurice Cobe in 1916 donated the land and posted a quarter of the $975 put up by a small group of founders to get things started.

The original clubhouse, a cavernous barn with a steepled roof, still serves as the club's social hall. A modern structure has been added on to the front as the latter-day clubhouse, pro shop and snack bar. When Eileen Estes was a girl, the golf club was the social center of town. The highlight of each year was the Fourth of July dance. Eileen led me back to the old building. She gazed up at the angular ceiling and recalled a summer night fifty years earlier when a big band played and she was sixteen years old and wore a lavender gown to the ball.

"I can remember that just as plain . . . ," she said, letting her voice go quiet as if to recapture the strains of some forgotten melody. "'Course those balls ended years ago. Times got modern."

Clutching a $3 bag of balls, I followed Eileen's directions down a steep slope between the first tee and the ninth green to a driving range with grass tee boxes. The range and the course lie in an open valley, a wide, flat bowl bounded by thick woods of pine and birch. The Eastern Maine Conference of Churches a hundred years ago used this idyllic spot for open-air religious meetings.

I stretched my road-weary muscles and took a few practice swings. I lofted some lazy seven-irons and looked out onto the marvelously uncrowded course. Who the hell was I kidding? I finished the bag in a hurry, marched back up the hill, and handed Eileen $14 for nine holes, walking.

"Changed your mind, huh?"

As I approached the first tee, an older man was just moving off down the fairway dragging a pull cart. I figured I'd catch up with him in no time. But the man was gone from the first green before I knew it. The first hole is a nice, short opener with a wide-open fairway from a hilltop tee box to a level green 290 yards away. I topped my three-wood. It rolled about seventy-five raggedy yards to the rough just before the beginning of the fairway. I followed with a nice, easy five-wood that zipped down the left side of the fairway and rolled onto the edge of the green, about forty feet from the hole. Keep the ball in play. Get in trouble, get out of trouble. No problem, golf is simple. The greens were dry and fast. My first putt rolled way past the hole and I two-putted from there, for a shaky bogey. As I teed up for the second hole, I saw the old man in the red shirt charging off into the distance toward the third tee. If I was going to hook up with him, I would have to speed up.

He had teed off on the par-three third while I worked my way down the second fairway.

"Want a partner?" I called.

He paused for a moment.

"Yeah, all right," he said. "I'll wait for you on the green."

I finished the second hole as quickly as I could and made my way to the third, a straightforward 157-yard par-three. The man with the red shirt was standing on the green. He waved me on. Sticking with my shortened backswing experiment, I took out a six-iron instead of a seven or eight. I caught it fat and it landed just shy of the green. I chipped up, two-putted for a bogey, and shook hands.

His name was Joe O'Neill.

"Golf here often?" I asked.

"At least four times a week," he said. "Sometimes five. Every day except weekends. Weekends I leave the course to the guys with jobs."

He was a native of New Jersey, born in East Orange. He'd raised four sons and a daughter in South River, helped coach his son's Pop Warner football team, whose star player was a kid named Joe Theismann, and spent a career as a distributor for an oil filter manufacturer. After his wife died in 1991, Joe found life at his retirement community in New Jersey confining. In 1995, at seventy-three, he had moved to Northport to live with his married daughter.

"I had to get away from the casserole army," he said. "It was after my wife passed away that it started. Every day another lady showed up at my door with a casserole. My refrigerator was jammed with 'em. So you go out on a date with one of the ladies. Another night you date another. Then the first one asks, 'Why'd you go out with *her*?' It's just like high school."

"Now, when I go back to visit I date whoever I want," he said. "Let 'em talk."

Now, Joe's days were filled with golfing in the summer, bowling and traveling in the winter. He'd found new friends at the Widow's Tooth, a local tavern, and blessed peace.

We teed up together at the par-four fourth hole, an easy-looking 310 yards away. Even though I topped my three-wood off the tee, I was in reach with a four-iron. I swung well and watched with pleasure as the ball sailed straight at the green. My satisfaction turned quickly to dismay when the ball returned to earth and kicked up a splash. I turned to Joe.

"I forgot to tell you," he said with a mischievous smile. "There's water on this hole."

The Northport course is harder than it appears, and the fourth hole is a prime example. The little stream that bounds the front of the green is invisible from the fairway. You can't perceive even a slight line or break in the grass until you're right on top of the water. The regulars treat this as the initiation hole for first-timers. Everyone gets his chance to be surprised. Now I'd been duly initiated.

As I walked along with Joe I could see why I'd had trouble catching up with him. Joe was not especially tall but was big and powerful, with a barrel chest and thick freckled forearms.

"In the Navy they called me Red," he said, lifting his hat with a laugh to reveal wisps of white hair and a few last stubborn streaks of auburn. I pictured this stout, white-haired widower fifty-five years earlier, as a tough, twenty-year-old Irish kid from East Orange, the kind of guy who took shit from nobody.

In the war, Joe had been a boatswain's mate aboard the USS *Claxton,* a destroyer that saw action in both theaters of World War II. The *Claxton* was in battle in the Philippine Sea in 1945 when a kamikaze pilot slammed into the side of the ship. A sailor standing a few feet above O'Neill was decapitated by the plane's wing. O'Neill wasn't scratched. Moments later, another ship in the squadron was sunk by a kamikaze. O'Neill and two other sailors jumped into a small boat and rescued several sailors. At home, he was building a three-foot-long replica of the *Claxton.*

Joe used his driver on the tees and fairways. What he'd lost in distance he compensated for with steady shots that stayed in play. My own game was terribly inconsistent. The eighth hole, another short par-four, turns almost ninety degrees to the right. One Sunday morning a few weeks earlier a foursome playing in a club tournament turned the corner and discovered a bull moose standing placidly in the middle of the green. The golfers waited a few moments for the moose to move on. It didn't. The golfers hit up to the green anyway, probably having agreed in advance upon a casual moose rule, should their lies wind up under a few thousand pounds of animal flesh. No need, though. The moose finally sauntered off under the hailstorm.

The last hole is a pretty par-three with the green at the base of a benevolent hill that corrects tee shots pushed right, by rolling them back down onto the green. Mine landed about midway up the hill and trickled down, gaining momentum. It spilled onto the green and came to rest about twelve feet from the pin. I two-putted for a par. Later, Joe and I sat on the verandah. Before we parted, he mentioned a place he'd played in February in Florida, called Key's Gate, right at the entrance to the Florida Keys, just off Route 1.

"Go there," he said. "At the end of your round you get a free beer."

The Florida Keys, all palm trees and flat tropical lowlands, lay more than two thousand miles from this eighty-year-old course scratched out of the hilly, rocky Maine coast. I would take Joe O'Neill's advice. I thought, that's one beer that will go down well.

Back on the road heading south from Northport, I cruised through the gentrified town of Camden, past the bay with three islands that Edna St. Vincent Millay immortalized in the opening lines of her most famous poem, "Renascence":

> *All I could see from where I stood*
> *Was three long mountains and a wood;*
> *I turned and looked the other way,*
> *And saw three islands in a bay*

A few miles farther on I arrived in Rockland. Rockland is like many other picturesque New England seaside towns, with a tidy downtown of shops and restaurants and weathered old homes. But it also has a grim, Gothic state prison looming over the highway. If this building wasn't the model for Stephen King's fictional Shawshank Prison, it should have been.

The Rockland Golf Club, which I'd seen listed in a Maine golf guide as a fine old course, lies well in from the sea, amid converted woods and farms. I paid my greens fee and walked across a little road to the first tee, where the starter hooked me up with a couple of guys taking their practice swings. They stood on the back tees. I had a moment of decision. My shaky game wasn't ready for the added challenge of the back tees. But I imagined a round of waiting while these guys teed off, then waddling up to the whites. It was Mario and Yves all over again. I joined them on the blues. This may have been a mistake, though I don't know whether anything could have improved my game on this day. It was a fixed commodity from hell. I started, if not promisingly, at least not disastrously, with a moderately sliced wood that came to rest somewhere in the right rough. I hit an iron out and then reached the green in four (it was a par-five) and three-putted for a double bogey seven. I flubbed my way to a fifty-one on the front nine. It wasn't so much the bad score as the feeling that I couldn't remember what I was doing out there. Where was my budding confidence? Where was that reliable five-wood from the fairway or rough? What was going on? And the worst was yet to come.

My playing partners were a pair of young orthopedic surgeons from the Mass. General Hospital, on vacation in Maine. Steve Barr, who had grown up in Needham, Massachusetts, was a chief resident in orthopedics. He was in his early thirties, a couple of years younger than I. Lars Richardson, who had grown up in Hanover, New Hampshire, the son of a Dartmouth professor, was a resident at Mass. General, in his late twenties. Steve had an easy, natural swing and had obviously played some golf. Lars had picked up the game recently and was inconsistent but could give the ball a ride when he connected.

"I grew up in the country," Lars said. "When I moved to Boston, golf at first was a way of getting outdoors. Now, I'm hooked." He wore a New England Patriots cap, a souvenir from his recent season with the Patriots in an orthopedic training program. A pro football team is heaven's own salad bar to an orthopedic surgeon. Lars was thinking about going into sports medicine. Steve was preparing for a year in New Mexico, to treat patients on an Indian reservation. Guys with plans. I had that special sinking feeling you get when you meet people who are younger than you are but who seem to have made important decisions on questions that you are still wrestling with. Such as, What am I going to be when I grow up? And here I was on another golf course, hacking it up. For what? Going where? Another few miles down the road to another golf course. When I played well this prospect seemed like bliss. But golf has a way of throwing into relief one's most closely held beliefs about oneself, both good and bad. Play well and you feel as if your life is falling into place. Knock a few into the woods, and that forlorn stumble through the underbrush in search of a lost ball becomes a metaphor for one's deepest doubts.

If my front nine had been poor, the back was abysmal. The scorecard contained enough 6s and 7s to start a fleet of Boeing's larger jets. There was also a disastrous 10 on the par-four thirteenth hole, a dogleg to the left over a hill, that started with me topping my drive into a creek lined with gnarly grass.

"One thing about this trip of mine," I told Lars and Steve as I trudged along another fairway of defeat under a merciless sun. "I'm not intimidating anybody with my golf game."

The last hole at Rockland is a par-three requiring a tee shot over a bottomless pond formed from an old quarry. It should have been a fun hole. But I topped my four-iron and sent that doomed Maxfli to a watery oblivion, down where some last stonecutter hauled out the quarry's last, deepest slab. Just to keep it company, I sent another one down. Then I hit a poor shot that at least cleared the water. I lay six and was still well off the green, about sixty feet from the hole, in the rough. I chipped the ball onto the green and it rolled and rolled, breaking slightly to the left, and dropped into the cup. But it was too late for my good fortune to serve as anything but comic relief. We all spontaneously cracked up. For the round: 110. I was not progressing, I was going back to where I came from. In my address book Steve drew a picture of a stick-figure golfer, me, sinking my improbable chip on the eighteenth.

There was nothing for me to do but find another course. I could not stop now. There was always another course, always another chance, no excuse to wallow in misery.

Route 1 followed the craggy coast south and westward, occasionally darting inland for a few miles, only to return again to the sea. It was late afternoon when I crossed a bridge into Bath, a working-class town of brick buildings on the west side of the Kennebec River. Cranes and factory buildings of the Bath Iron Works, the state's largest private employer, loom over the town. Bath has less tourist polish than other coastal communities and more of the gritty feel of a working town. I drove slowly past the haunting, Dickensian gates of the iron works, past a sign proclaiming "Through these gates pass the best shipbuilders in the world."

Bath has been home to shipbuilders for nearly four hundred years, since the first English ship captains stumbled across this spot, twelve miles upriver from the Atlantic. Here, explorers discovered, the broad, deep and navigable Kennebec River brushed the edge of an illimitable forest of prime New World shipbuilding timber—oak, birch, firs and tall, straight pines for masts. By the mid–nineteenth century, Bath had twenty shipyards and some of the nation's most skilled craftsmen. When the transition from wood to metal ships rendered proximity to forests irrelevant, it was the Bath Iron Works, founded in 1884, that kept shipbuilding alive here, and ultimately, become synonymous with the town itself. Amid the general decline of the U.S. maritime industry in the latter part of the twentieth century, Bath Iron Works has stubbornly hung on, finding new life as a subsidiary of the mammoth defense contractor General Dynamics, which bought the company in 1995. Today, behind these deceptively old-fashioned brick factory walls, Bath Iron Works is cranking out sophisticated Aegis-class guided-missile destroyers.

I was just passing the front gate at 3:30 sharp when a loud bell sounded and two workers burst through one of the doors, racing to the gate at a dead run. At first, I thought there was some emergency at the plant. But presently a few more workers appeared, then more, then a steady river of humanity. I realized these early ones were just the first of the 3:30 shift to leave the building. The dead run was an attempt to be among the first to reach cars or trucks or motorcycles and thus escape the traffic jam that was about to ensue. In a few moments workers were pouring out of every door and gate, like prisoners on furlough, not looking back, dressed in work boots, jeans, T-shirts. I crept through the town at about two miles per hour, an island in the stream of bodies. I had an idea that some of the workers might be heading out to the local golf course. So I asked a man watering a lawn, a friendly man with tattoos wrinkling along with the skin on his forearms, where I could find the nearest public golf course. He gave me some complex directions that I stopped listening to after the first sentence. All I needed to hear was the general direction.

I was getting to the point that I could *feel* the presence of a golf course, sense by some subtle but unmistakable signals when I was getting close. Driving along a country road I could perceive by the roll of the land, by the way the trees began to thin out, by the look of the drivers, that a golf course was nearby. On the rare occasions when my senses betrayed me, I had begun to be offended by likely-looking land that did *not* contain a golf course. Passing a rolling field that disappeared into some trees, I would imagine a pretty dogleg converging on a narrow, protected green. I could not pass a lake without gazing onto the island in the middle, judging the distance, and mentally transforming the mound into an island green, figuring what club I would use to reach it. Farmland seemed to me to be a waste of valuable golfing space. I headed in the general direction the man had pointed me, then started taking rights and lefts by the feel and look of the land, and, sure enough, soon wound my way along Whiskeag Road to the parking lot of the Bath Country Club.

Although the parking lot sported a promising bounty of pick-ups and the man in the clubhouse assured me that many of the ship workers did in fact golf there, the headlong rush to the golf course on this afternoon failed to materialize. I found myself hooked up instead with an engineer named Jeff, his son, Ryan, and Ryan's friend, Tommy. Ryan was fourteen, Tommy thirteen. The sky had begun to threaten and I hesitated. Perhaps I should just give this game a rest, I told myself. But the fairways called. It was afternoon, I was here at a golf course. Did I really have any choice?

The first hole is a tester, a par-four with the approach to the green over a pond. I failed the test, plunking two shots—my normally reliable seven-iron—into the water. Now I was even shanking my sevens. It was a disease, contagious from one club to the next. The third hole is an unusual par-five with a sharp dogleg to the left after an elevated tee shot. If you feel lucky or talented enough you can shoot straight over the pines and turn the hole into a par-four. Having nothing to lose, that's what I did, and sent a well-struck driver shot to the right side of the fairway. Tommy, who confided that he had designs on the PGA tour, also hit a fine drive, as did Ryan and Jeff. Then it began to rain. We finished the hole but as we putted lightning flashed in the distance, followed by an ominous peal of thunder.

"If it gets any closer, we're leaving," Jeff warned his son. Ryan rolled his eyes at the mortifying uncoolness of grown-ups. Imagine curtailing a round of golf for something as trivial as lightning. Ryan, who at fourteen was planning to live forever, suggested that his father leave but that he and Tommy would probably stick it out.

Dad said, "If I leave, you leave."

Rain began to fall steadily and the bruised sky grew darker. We held out a while longer, but it didn't look promising. On the fourth green a flash lit up the sky just over a bank of trees. The lightning was probably still several miles away, but it was one of those bolts that you see on the covers of science textbooks, cracking the sky like a windshield. It was followed by a clap of thunder that you felt in your molars. In the distance, carts scampered like June bugs for the shelter of the clubhouse.

Tommy, Ryan and I had been walking, but Jeff had a cart. All four of us piled onto the cart, and we made our way through the downpour to the parking lot. I shoved my bag into the trunk and, tired and wet, waved good-bye and wound my way back to the ramp leading to Route 1. A few miles later through the rain and thunder I stopped in Freeport and checked into a motel, then found my way into the little downtown, transformed by L. L. Bean and other retailers into an odd paradox: a quaint outlet-shopping mecca. I had been to Freeport on hot summer days when you could barely move down the sidewalks for all the thigh-slapping bags from Bean's and Lacoste and the Basket Barn and all the rest. On this early-season evening in a persistent drizzle, the town was almost deserted. I had dinner in a cozy tavern that served burgers and pints of ale, then afterward I wandered through the nearly empty caverns of L. L. Bean. In the hunting section I watched on a monitor as a bow hunter stalked and killed a buck, then stood grinning over his steaming kill while his buddies congratulated him. I bought a stuffed toy lobster for Natalie and matching shirts for Natalie and Barbara, and then headed over to the Ben & Jerry's ice cream store, where I spent an outrageous sum on four or five scoops that I brought back to my motel room. My room smelled like antiseptics losing their battle against mildew. The bed sagged. I flipped on the television and drowned my golf sorrows in heaping spoonfuls of Cherry Garcia and Rainforest Crunch.

4

I Love the United States of America

And then, inexplicably, wonderfully, the next day went like this. I woke up and headed toward Portland, the first city of any size through which Route 1 passes. As the city swells, the road becomes more obscure, transforming into a series of urban streets with ever-changing names. Bold signs every couple of miles urged me to reconsider my plans and pick up I-95. I had called a municipal course called Riverside in Portland the day before and asked for directions. Here, I ran into a problem I would encounter in cities for the rest of the journey. In small towns, where Route 1 is the major thoroughfare, getting directions is easy. But in cities, you meet only consternation when you offer that road as a reference point.

"Where are you coming from?"

"Route 1 from the north."

"Yes, but where are you coming from?"

"I'm just north of Portland right now, in Freeport."

"Oh, well, get on I-95 and . . ."

At Falmouth on the north side of the city the road led me across a bridge and deposited me in an older neighborhood of two-family homes and shops and restaurants with Asian names. I crept with the morning traffic around Back Cove along Baxter Street and into the financial district, past sturdy-looking banks and investment houses. I crossed another bridge into South Portland and came upon a spot where Route 1 converged with I-95. Here I had no choice but to cut back onto 95, also known as the Maine Turnpike, since I was already through the city. The toll booth attendant gave me directions, and I followed them until I came to Riverside Municipal Golf Course. I pulled up next to a clubhouse that was little more than a shack. The old man in the shack said he couldn't take my credit card. "They can at the other course."

This modest clubhouse was for the nine-hole course, which was empty and looked inviting. But I wanted to play eighteen, so I retrieved the bag from my car and walked to the other end of the parking lot. I must have looked confused when I got there because a couple of retired guys asked me what I was trying to find.

"The eighteen-hole course. The man in the shack said it was at this end of the parking lot."

"You can't listen to him," one of the men said, "the clubhouse is a half mile up the road. Tell you what, though, this is the second tee right here." He pointed to a chain-link fence. "You can save a lot of greens fees by startin' right here."

"Thanks," I said. "I'll drive on over."

It was a cool, overcast morning, one of the few sunless days since I'd started. A gauzy half-rain, half-mist coated my hair and shirt. I hooked up on the first tee with a man named John O'Malley. John offered me a seat on his cart, but I said I needed the exercise.

"I'd be walking, too," John said. "But I tore up my ankle running a couple of weeks ago." He pointed to a brace. "Lotta hills out here. You've gotta be part mountain goat on this course."

John was in his mid-fifties, of medium height, with a slender, athletic build and aviator-style sunglasses. He'd just taken early retirement from the telephone company. He'd never played much before retirement, just a social round here and there with a group from work, but in the past few months he'd caught the bug. He'd bought a $450 membership at Riverside that allowed him unlimited play on both the eighteen- and nine-hole courses. He'd worked his game to the mid-nineties.

"I want to break eighty this year. I don't know if it's realistic, but that's my goal," he said. "I wish I'd taken up golf twenty years ago."

The first hole is a short par-five of less than 450 yards, requiring a downhill tee shot, then an uphill second shot to the left. My first shot was long but pushed right into some rough. I hit a nice iron out and was within an easy chip of the green. Wouldn't it be nice to start the day with a par, or even a birdie! I took a nice easy swing but instead of the ball floating placidly to the green I shanked it to the right of the green. Now I was pin high but well off the green. I took another easy swing and *shank!* Now I was directly behind the green, but no closer to it than I had been two shots earlier. What's more, I was now in a sand trap, lying four. The green had transformed into an alien flying saucer with a force field to ward off my feeble missiles. I managed to scoop my way out of the trap, and the ball limped to the green. I two-putted for a disheartening double bogey. John got into some trouble and chalked up the same score. After that, though, we both settled down and started recording some pars and bogeys. The rain held off. It was now damp and cool. I wore a sweatshirt.

John had fallen in love with his seven-wood. "When I started using that club, I took my three- and four-iron out of the bag," he said.

I finished the first nine with a pair of pars and turned the corner feeling confident. This feeling continued when I hit another booming drive off the tenth tee, the longest hole on the course, a 534-yard par-five. I followed with a five-wood from the center of the fairway that flew straight and true and left me with a soft wedge to the green. The green beckoned like a swimming pool on a hot day. Dive right in. No problem. *Shank!* The ball skittered off sideways to the right rough. Head down, concentrate. You're not lost . . . *focus,* recover. I brought the club back slowly . . . *shank.* This second shank carried injury with insult because the ball whistled into some tangled bushes and trees and disappeared into a little pond or creek. Lost ball. It was as if some cosmic golf accountant was demanding payback for those first two perfect shots.

"You pulled right out of it," John said, shaking his head thoughtfully after my second shank. He made a swinging motion and jerked his head up to the heavens like a spastic batter trying to avoid a beanball. "Right out of it."

I was determined not to let the shanks push me into a tailspin. I would not fall prey to the old enemy of the Bad Attitude, which in varying degrees has dogged me my entire sporting life. Losing with grace has never been one of my strong suits. A half hour after a loss I am fine, it's forgotten, but while I'm losing in anything, tennis, cards, Ping-Pong, a black cloud spreads over me. Once, when I was losing in a tennis tournament at summer camp when I was fourteen or fifteen years old, I got so mad that a counselor stood on the veranda of the clubhouse with a megaphone and sternly directed the competitors on court four to refrain from using obscenities. The players up and down the lengths of the eight courts stopped while everybody silently counted the court numbers affixed to the wire mesh until their eyes stopped at court four, mine. My opponent, who had been silently enjoying beating me, rolled his eyes and stuck out his arms, palms up, as if to say *Don't look at me.* I've been working on it.

I was finding myself slower to anger as the trip progressed. At Rockland I had been able to see humor in my miserable play. And here at Portland I found myself able to move on after a bad shot, not carry it with me. Perhaps the endless procession of holes on my trip was having some effect, the knowledge that there was another opportunity just ahead.

John sensed what I was thinking.

"I used to be pretty volatile," he said. "One shot would ruin me for the entire round. Now that I'm playing all the time, I can let it go. Every shot's a new experience."

As we made our way up the fifteenth fairway, some guy coming down the parallel fourteenth, as if cued by our conversation, scrubbed an iron shot off the fairway and then suddenly pivoted like a hammer thrower in the Olympics and winged his club down the fairway with a scream. The club traveled farther than the ball. I thought: That idiot's not a good enough golfer to get that pissed off. Then I thought: I'm glad it's not me.

We were zipping along, up and down the hills of Riverside, when we suddenly became aware that there were no foursomes immediately in front or behind us. It was mid-morning on a Friday; the mist and clouds had begun to burn off. The course should have been packed.

"Usually is," John said. We'd hit one of those inexplicable air pockets you sometimes find on municipal courses. It enabled us to play at our own speed, leisurely but swiftly. And because we were moving quickly, we were relaxed. It's when you play slowly, with delays between each hole, that tension mounts.

"Unbelievable, this is great," John said. "This is the way golf should be played."

I shot a 93, which I took as an encouraging score after the disaster at Rockland. John and I had played eighteen holes in barely three hours. Afterwards, we ate a couple of Red Dogs (a Maine links-style hot dog in a red casing) in the clubhouse. It was still just a few minutes after noon. My bitter mood from yesterday was forgotten. The world was once again beautiful and full of unplayed golf courses just down the road. And the best was yet to come.

I hooked up with Route 1 again in South Portland, winding through the city's southern suburbs. I stopped at D'Amato's for an Italian sandwich. Italians are a specialty of southern Maine— ham, cheese, peppers, tomatoes, olives, pickles and oil folded into a soft sub roll with the consistency of Wonder Bread. You can buy them at just about any mom-and-pop variety store, but D'Amato's is a chain that serves up some of the best. Since there was no seating inside the restaurant I sat in my car, balancing the sandwich and the crackly butcher paper on my knees, savoring the sweet oil and the bite of the peppers.

Around 2 P.M. I came to the town of Saco. I had been thinking about those nagging shanks, trying to figure out what I could do to cure the problem. I need some practice swings, I told myself. And within three or four minutes, a driving range popped into view.

I took a wedge, a nine-iron and a three-wood from my bag, bought a large bucket at the little shack, and headed over to the range. The range had a video set up and for a fee you could get someone to capture your swing. But there were no takers just now, and I certainly didn't want my swing recorded. Concentrating on my shanking problem, I figured out by trial and error that I was simply standing too close to the ball on the short irons. It was as simple as that. My arms, instead of hanging straight down from my body, pointed inward between my knees. So on my downswing the shank rather than the face was meeting the ball. I took a half step back. For a moment the ball seemed unnaturally far in front of me, but when I flexed my knees a little everything came into place. I pulled my nine-iron away from the ball, swung and *Voilà!* no more shank. The ball lofted perfectly, flew straight. I tried the same thing with a wedge. Same result. I had been golfing enough by now to know that the *Voilà!* factor in golf is at best transitory and at worst cruelly deceptive.

There are no permanent cures for your game. Bad tendencies simply go into remission. When you figure something out you have a sort of grace period when everything falls into place like the last page of a mystery novel. *Voilà!* Then, of course, your body finds ways to betray you again. Usually it does this by exaggerating whatever cure you have devised, until the cure itself becomes the problem. For example, if you step back because you have been standing too close to the ball, your mind will fixate on standing far away from the ball. Eventually, you will line up so far from the ball that you must bend forward and reach. This leads to a whole new set of disasters, which are inexplicable to you because, after all, you already *cured* the problem. And then some pro or friend tells you to move in toward the ball. So you move a half step in and *Voilà!* your problem goes away and the cycle begins again. But for now I was just happy to be rid of the damned shanks. I hit about two-thirds of the bucket just with the wedge and nine, then grabbed my three-wood. The confidence translated to the wood. I hit shot after shot straight out to the farthest point of the range.

There was a nice-looking public course nearby, Biddeford-Saco Country Club, just a mile or two off Route 1. But I decided to press farther on down to the rarefied summer haven of Kennebunkport and Cape Arundel Golf Club. Cape Arundel, built in 1901, is the home course of George Bush. His grandfather, George Herbert Walker, had been president of the club, president of the United States Golf Association, and founder of the Walker Cup, the international amateur tournament. The president's father, Prescott Bush, also was president of the USGA. As I wound past gracious summer homes I had hopes of an impromptu round with Bush. He would zoom up to the first tee just as I was paying my greens fee. He'd spot me and say, in that nasal, patrician voice that decades in Texas could never erase, "Why don't we hook up, young man? If you don't mind playing with an old duffer." Then we'd proceed around the course, under the gaze of a couple of Secret Service agents in bad golf shirts, and the former president would show me the lay of the land and divulge fantastic stories of international diplomacy and the Gulf War.

The Cape Arundel clubhouse is a single-story building with a porch and large rocking chairs overlooking a branch of a river that meanders through the course. The greens fee was steep for early June in Maine, $35, but reasonable in comparison with other resort-level courses.

"Is the president golfing today?" I asked the man in the clubhouse.

"He was in here yesterday," the man said. "And the day before. But he's taking today off." He added, "I usually don't send singles out alone. But there's a threesome that went off about thirty minutes ago. You can catch up with them."

It was a cool afternoon. The clouds that had produced that light mist at Portland had gathered strength and now hung heavy and threatening over the course. I wore long pants and a sweatshirt. I bogeyed the first three holes and parred the fourth, thinking they might be the only four holes I'd be able to play. Thunder rumbled in the distance. The course was in fine shape, immaculately maintained, the fairways so smooth they looked painted on. With soft rolling berms and hills, Cape Arundel was a compromise between a British-style links course and a traditional American course with tree-lined fairways. The rain held off. As I approached the fourth green the threesome ahead, standing on the fifth tee box, waved me up to join them.

Playing well alone is much easier than playing well with other people. And joining a group after a promising start is the surest way to kill a streak. The fifth hole, moreover, had plenty of places to get into trouble. It was just 350 yards long but ran down into a sort of gully, taking a sharp dogleg left over a stream. I shook hands with Patrick, Jeff and James. My first shot, a three-iron, wound up in some rough below the green and to the left. My second shot, an eight-iron, was a good one, to the fringe of the green. I chipped close enough to the hole to sink my par putt. So far, so good. The next hole was a par-three, just 118 yards downhill, but over a pond. I realized I'd left my pitching wedge and nine-iron in the trunk of my car, having removed them from the bag to practice at that driving range in Saco. Against my better judgment, I lifted my eight-iron out of the bag, figuring I'd hit a nice soft eight to the green. It was a bad idea, and an even worse shot, a low slice that started left and curved right toward the green, stayed just a few feet off the water, bounced before the green and rolled up about twenty-five feet from the pin.

I said something like "better lucky than good" and hurried off the tee box. I two-putted and had now parred three straight holes. I was within shouting distance of the parking lot, so I excused myself and ran to retrieve my missing clubs. Hoping the spell hadn't broken, I lined up another three-wood on the 381-yard par-four seventh. The ball sailed 250 yards and came to rest just right of center in the fairway. My next shot, an eight-iron, landed on the right side of the green. I two-putted for another par, my fourth straight, and my third in as many holes with my new friends.

Since they had no prior experience with me they took me for a golfer. I could feel their respectful gaze on my back as I lined up a shot, and could tell in their quiet rather than surprised praise when I hit a good shot that they assumed I was someone for whom a 250-yard shot down the middle of the fairway was no big deal. The oddest thing about playing with new partners every day was the opportunity constantly to reinvent myself. A day earlier I had relied on the kindness of strangers to help me laugh off a miserable round at Rockland. Now, on a more difficult course, I was a serious golfer, a player. I double-bogeyed the eighth, but only because I hit my approach iron so crisply that it overshot the green by a few feet and bounced into an impossible lie. It did nothing to shake my confidence. Something had clicked. I could not miss. I was also getting good luck to go with my good play. Balls that might have bounced out of bounds stopped inches from the markers.

By this time I was getting to know my playing partners. James Drumstas, compact and powerfully built, with a military-style buzz cut, was a police officer in York, Maine, just a few miles from Kennebunkport. Jeff Larocca, slender and dark haired, worked for a bank in western Massachusetts. Jeff's wife and James's wife were cousins, and the Laroccas were visiting the

Drumstases in York. Jeff and James golfed about the way I usually did: the good, the bad and the ugly all mixed together. James, the police officer, was playing as a sort of physical therapy, to repair a shoulder he'd torn up while helping a driver get his car unstuck from a ditch late one evening.

Patrick Swords was the other member of our foursome. He was vacationing in the area with his family and had come to the course alone. Patrick was well over six feet, with rounded but not fat features, a dark mustache and a large, friendly face. He spoke in a booming baritone. Patrick Swords was openly and unabashedly in love with every aspect of his life—his wife, his kids, his house, his job, his golf game, his clubs and several other things that he would think of in a minute. This quality might have been annoying except that there was nothing miserly or competitive about his joy. He was on a good ride, and you were more than welcome to join him. He was one of those rare individuals who could in an unqualified way be described as a happy man.

"I love where I live," he would say, and you couldn't help but love it too. "It's out in the country. We have a deck in the back, and I go out there and see nothing but the mountains. No people anywhere. Oh, it's unbelievable. Best place in the world." Or, on his job, as engineer for a company in western Massachusetts that designs aircraft parts, "It's so fun. It's not like working at all. I'm like a kid in a candy shop. I just get to design things."

It was not surprising that Patrick brought the same attitude to golf. He made his own clubs as a hobby and shot in the high seventies or low eighties. Patrick did nothing in a small way, and when he caught a drive right the ball sailed out of sight. For a big man, he had surprising touch. On one par-four with a long carry over water, he wound up in a bunker to the right of the green and hit one of the prettiest bunker shots I had ever seen. The ball lifted out of a cloud of sand and landed three or four feet beyond the pin, then spun sassily back and stopped six inches from the cup.

The threat of rain yielded to a warm, sunny early evening. I kept my sweatshirt on, not wanting to change anything. Despite my fears that the magic slipper would shatter, the carriage turn into a pumpkin and my round go to hell on the back nine, I continued to play well. Hitting the ball solidly involved nothing more than stepping up and swinging. I was certain I had turned a corner that I would never have to turn again.

On the par-three thirteenth hole, I plunked a six-iron over a pond to within twelve feet of the hole. On the green, Patrick approached me with the casual respect of one experienced golfer to another.

"So, what are you, about a twelve handicap?" he asked. I could have kissed him. What could I say? That yesterday at Rockland I would have been ecstatic to break a hundred? That I had been wondering whether this entire trip was a mistake, whether my attempts to play this confounded game were nothing more than a bad joke? I didn't want to spoil the moment. So I just shook my head and said, "I'm kind of inconsistent."

I finished with a good, solid 85 for the round, my spirits soaring. I'd walked thirty-six holes that day, and only the ebbing sunlight prevented me from walking another eighteen. Prodded by Patrick's infectious good nature, we were a jolly foursome by the end, giving each other a hard time in that collegial way usually reserved for longtime friends. The eighteenth hole returns to the clubhouse over a wide point in the river. The sun was beginning to set. We had the course more or less to ourselves. Patrick, unable to control himself, stammered, "This is . . . great. I mean, this is *great*. Can you believe this? We're out here on this beautiful evening, golfing. I just . . . I just, God, I love the United States of America." And then we were all laughing, at everything and nothing all at once.

5

Home Again

There was something different about Sagamore-Hampton Golf Club in Hampton, New Hampshire. At first, I couldn't say just what. But as I gazed out to the busy fairways full of golfers shouldering their bags or pulling them along behind, it dawned on me.

No carts.

"My uncle never believed in carts. It's a walking game. It started that way and he tried to preserve that," Tyler E. Sanborn, the twenty-seven-year-old course manager, explained when I looked him up later in the clubhouse. His uncle was Richard Luff, a Harvard archaeologist who built the course in the early 1960s.

Richard Luff and his descendants belong to a stubborn subset of course owners—individual families as opposed to municipalities or developers. Like small bookstores, family-owned courses are run by people who work insane hours and whose businesses must prosper, without any marketing muscle, through word of mouth and the loyal following of regulars. And, like mom-and-pop bookstores, they offer idiosyncratic taste and personality over finish and polish.

Besides carts, another thing you will never encounter at Sagamore-Hampton are signs warning you they just sprayed. Decades before such ideas became fashionable, Richard Luff declared that Sagamore-Hampton would be an all-natural course, free from pesticides, herbicides and fungicides dumped by the barrelful on other fairways and greens.

"It makes for a lot of extra man-hours, caring for the course," Sanborn said. "We do a lot of pulling. And the fairways still have clover, chickweed, and dandelions. We basically let Mother Nature do her thing here." Such imperfections, if they can be called that, would probably distract touring pros, but Sagamore-Hampton had no greater proportion of weeds than a lot of courses I'd played, and the fairways and greens were in better shape than most.

And, appropriately in a state whose "Live Free or Die" motto is emblazoned on every license plate, Sagamore-Hampton is as stubbornly democratic as a Yankee town council meeting. There are no members here, not even the open-enrollment sort who pay a few hundred dollars up front for a summer's worth of greens fees. Nor does a local golf mafia preside over Wednesday-night tee-time lotteries. It's strictly daily fee, first come, first served. An earlier generation of the Luff family built the Sagamore Spring Golf Club in nearby Lynnfield, Massachusetts, in 1927. Louis Luff, co-founder of that original course, believed memberships create two classes of players. Daily fee, he said in a mission statement when the first course opened, is the only way to ensure that "Goodfellowship exists . . . between the players, and a cordial welcome is extended to all golfers and visitors."

I came across Sagamore-Hampton by chance. The day after my triumph at Cape Arundel found me rolling on a sunlit Saturday morning across the Piscataqua River into Portsmouth, New Hampshire. Portsmouth is an old fishing and manufacturing city of about thirty thousand residents that has successfully revived its brick downtown with lively restaurants and stores. I wanted to golf in each state through which I passed. But Route 1, like I-95, cuts just a fifteen-mile slice off the extreme southern tip of New Hampshire. A few miles out of downtown Portsmouth I already saw signs for Massachusetts. I pulled over at a gas station and asked the attendant for directions to the nearest public course. Route 1 seldom disappoints such inquiries. Sagamore-Hampton was half a mile away.

The swell of cars in the parking lot provided my first real indication that I had left Maine behind and entered the sphere of greater Boston. Maine had lulled me into a sense of entitlement, showing up at courses whenever I chose and more or less walking on. But Sagamore-Hampton was packed. Had I been with a foursome my situation would have been hopeless. But the Single Golfer Rule, facing its first serious test in southern New England, held true. The starter told me I could join a threesome that was set to tee off in a little less than an hour. I drove back to Route 1 to warm up at a driving range I had passed. I bought a bucket of balls and was lucky to find a spot along a busy arc of golfers. Like wildflowers, golfers in southern New England make the most of the brief summer.

Back at the course I hooked up with a pair of attorneys from Boston and a young guy named Chris who worked at the course. He'd been there since 4 A.M. and was getting his free round. Chris was in his early twenties and had a beautiful, fluid swing. On the first hole, a par-four, he pulled out a one-iron (an impressive gesture in its own right) and knocked the ball straight down the fairway, a long, sloping hill, to a blind green below. The two attorneys hit fairly straight shots—not as impressive as Chris's, but passable. My own tee shot whizzed low and left, a puny, ugly shot. It was a bad way to start, in front of three strangers and a dozen milling golfers waiting their turns to tee off, none of whom asked me if I played to a twelve handicap. I fumbled to the cup in seven, a triple bogey. After the magic of Cape Arundel, I was me, again.

Despite the efforts of marshals who patrolled the fairways, the pace of play was glacial. On the second hole, the foursome behind us, already impatient, knocked their tee shots into us while we were waiting to hit our approaches to the green.

"Did you see what those assholes just did?" one of the attorneys said.

With that comment he invoked one of the most durable features of public golf in America, the Asshole Principle. During my travels thus far, and indeed, through the course of the summer, the vast majority of golfers I played with were good people. My partners were young, old, funny, serious, quiet, talkative, but almost without fail we parted as friends. During those same rounds, however, I encountered an astonishingly high percentage of assholes in the groups just in front of or behind my own. This was more than mere coincidence, of course. On public courses, these people are almost by definition assholes. The group behind are the pushy, impatient assholes who don't realize that your group is not the one holding things up. No, that's the fault of those slow, inconsiderate assholes ahead. Establishing the Asshole Principle helps one's own foursome coalesce from a party of strangers into a cohesive unit, us against the world. The Asshole Principle asserts itself only on public links. At private clubs, everybody is painfully decorous in their behavior, mainly because the guy up ahead is probably someone you know, maybe even your boss. When those impudent assholes hit into us, the four of us turned and stared them down like trench-weary doughboys. We then turned our attention to the slow-as-molasses foursome on the green in front of us. Jeez, what is it with *these* assholes? Are they ever going to finish putting?

The front nine at Sagamore-Hampton is laid out on a former dairy farm, and obvious care has been taken not to disrupt the contours of the land. Sagamore-Hampton is the opposite of those resort courses you see superimposed on improbable settings such as the Arizona desert, with patches of brilliant green laid out against brown-black earth and hills. At Sagamore you walk the hills as the cows did. There are some interesting holes, particularly the par-five eighth. You hit over a pond to a landing area at the base of a steep hill sitting in the middle of the fairway. You then hit a blind second shot over the hill into a second valley, then up another steep hill to the green. The attorneys and I hit nice, safe tee shots into the first valley. Chris, the young guy, hit a spectacular drive that cleared the valley and landed somewhere at the top of the first hill. We searched for that ball for what seemed like forever but never found it. Chris wore the look of a man wronged by fate.

It was already late afternoon when we finished the front nine, and the course showed no signs of opening up on the back. I peeled off from my foursome after nine holes so I could talk to Tyler Sanborn, the manager. But as I drove off that evening I was sorry I had bagged out on the wooded back nine, which Sanborn and others told me contained the most interesting holes on the course. I felt like a punk, a quitter. I vowed not to stop another round before finishing, unless compelled to do so by lightning, hurricanes, or other imminent natural disasters. I also vowed to avoid weekend golf in heavily populated areas such as southern New England.

The last bit of New Hampshire along Route 1 does little for the state; mainly it is cheap motels, tattoo parlors, gas stations and the like. I crossed the Merrimack River into Massachusetts at Newburyport on a Monday afternoon, and then rolled into Topsfield. Topsfield is home each autumn to the Topsfield Fair, the nation's oldest town fair, held since 1839. The fairgrounds lay still and fallow in the June sun. Topsfield is a charming country town of stone walls and leafy overhangs, a last semirural outpost before Boston. The New Meadows Golf Club in Topsfield is a short, pleasant, woodsy nine-hole course that was, like Sagamore, family owned. Some of the holes run up along Route 1. I managed to squeeze on just in front of a local tournament and played nine with Joe and Brian, a pair of community college administrators.

None of the par-fours at New Meadows is more than 370 yards, and the lone par-five is just 459 yards. The main challenge is staying out of ponds and the ever-present woods. I played well, mixing pars and bogeys for a forty-three for the nine. The course has some nice touches, such as a hand pump along the par-five seventh, where you pump up your own drinking water from a cold, clear spring.

When I returned to the road, Boston began to rumble in the distance. I passed Danvers, Saugus, Everett and Chelsea, stopping only to work out some kinks with my seven-iron at a roadside driving range. Rush-hour traffic swelled as I crossed the Mystic River Bridge and saw the old Charlestown Navy Yard below, once an area of sailor bars, now spruced up and reinvented as urban living for young commodities brokers. As I crossed the Tobin Bridge in the slow-moving traffic I spotted a sign from the Good Samaritans affixed to the railing, an appeal to would-be jumpers. It read: "Desperate? Depressed? Help's only a phone call away." *Hello, this is Charlie. Can you help me with my shank?*

On the approach to downtown Boston, Route 1 merges with the Southeast Expressway, an artery that cuts through the center of the city. I got off downtown, parked in a garage and walked to the North End. At one point in its history a stronghold of colonial blue bloods (Paul Revere's house still stands), the North End has been transformed by waves of immigration into Boston's most vibrant Italian neighborhood. My destination was the European, a venerable restaurant with gondola paintings on the walls, where weary waiters in dinner jackets with a tomato stain on the lapel served some of the best thin-crust pizza on the planet. I walked past a boarded-up storefront on Hanover Street two or three times before I realized that the boarded-up store was the European. I walked across the street to an Italian confectioners where they made good torrone, an Italian nougat-and-almond candy. It was my wife's favorite. I bought a pound to send to her. I asked the woman in the store what had become of the European. She just shrugged and said, "It closed." I walked under the highway to Quincy Market, the glittering string of shops and restaurants that had transformed Boston's decaying core during the 1970s and started a whole national movement toward gussying up old inner-city warehouses with chrome and ferns and crowds. The place was still going strong. I walked down the long central corridor, taking in the lights and the warm, life-giving food smells. Then I crossed the outdoor plaza and walked over to the Black Rose and ordered a bowl of chowder and a pint of ale. The Black Rose is an old Irish pub where, in my college days, under the influence of Guinness Stout and sad-eyed Irish folksingers, I had cheerfully overlooked my own English ancestry and joined the beery choruses damning those cursed Brits. But it was still early evening now, the performers' platform empty, the bar quiet. I watched pedestrians out the window as I ate.

Then I drove west on the Mass Pike for about eight miles to Newton, the suburb where I'd grown up. I passed huge old wooden homes lining Centre Street and turned right on Commonwealth Avenue, where each spring they run the Boston Marathon. I took a left on a side street and parked my car in front of the familiar white house. My parents were traveling, and the house was empty and echoed with memories. Whenever I think of that house, too large for its tiny yard, raised three feet above street level by a concrete wall, it is in terms of laughter and happy times. The house was a gathering place for my friends and my two sisters' friends. Weekend nights always seemed to begin or end here. Some visitors were invited, many just wandered in from the night to join whatever group of friends, strangers, out-of-town relatives spending a few days had assembled in the living room. Always some boisterous conversation was sure to be brewing. Even long after my sisters and I had moved away, friends would still return, as adults, sometimes with their spouses and children, to see my parents or sit for a while in that living room. I sat in my old bedroom, feeling like a polite stranger among the artifacts of my past life: pennants, old yearbooks, high-school trophies. Something about being here in this empty house amid my forgotten possessions made me long to grab hold of my present life. I called home to Richmond.

My introduction to golf, back in high school, came at Leo J. Martin Memorial Golf Course, a hacker's paradise located just west of Newton, where Newton, Weston and Lexington converge. Before leaving on my trip, I'd phoned my two old golfing buddies, neither of whom I'd seen for more than a decade. Could they make it for a reunion round? Jon Williams was my best friend starting in fourth grade, a friendship tempered by nonstop fights. Willie and I fought over foul shots in gym class, called strikes in Wiffle ball and everything else. We got drunk at fourteen for the first time, on about three beers apiece during the seventh game of the World Series, in 1975, the one the Red Sox lost to the Cincinnati Reds.

We both loved sports, but Willie followed them with a passion and authority that I could never match. Willie lived with his single mother and his four older sisters on the second floor of a two-family house behind the church at the busy corner of Centre Street and Beacon Street. When I think of those long summers I can still hear the voice of Hawk Harrelson on Channel 38, calling the Red Sox games to the accompaniment of a whirring fan in Willie's room. Football, basketball, hockey. It didn't matter. He was the first kid I knew who thought it was cool to watch golf on TV. Even dads didn't think it was cool to watch golf on television back then.

Willie absorbed a sense of style and sophistication from all this viewing that left the rest of us wanting. His baseball socks always stayed up when ours gathered like folds of hound-dog skin around our ankles. His practice swing at the plate was a thing of studied precision. He was the first to use pine tar on his bat; he always wore a batting glove. He spit like an all-star, too, with a casual toss of the head, not bothering to see where the perfectly proportioned gob of saliva landed in the grass. When our interest turned to golf, while I was still trying to figure out which of my father's dusty, too-long clubs were used for what shots, Willie was already snapping on a golf glove, just so, and squatting to line up his putts like a pro.

I found his number by calling my high school's alumni office. He was living in Medford, a few towns over from Newton, working as a distribution manager for a company that made artificial hips. I called him up and identified myself. His voice was deeper than I'd remembered.

"How the hell are you," he said. I'd told him his Boston accent made me homesick. He told me living in Virginia had given me a southern one. Yeah, he'd love to meet for a round at Leo J.

Chris Gilson was a lineman on our high-school football team, a big, gentle kid with an easy laugh. His room was in the basement of a house where he lived with his mom and two younger brothers. I'll never forget the musty smell of that basement, listening to Gilson's interminable drum solos played to the accompaniment of his acid-rock albums. On Saturday nights we'd gather down there, five or six of us, playing poker and smoking cheap, smelly cigars. When I reached Gilson, he was living outside of Washington and working in Baltimore for Catholic Relief Services, heading up their Cuba project. Every few weeks he boarded a DC-6 propeller plane loaded up with food and medicine and rode it down to Havana. After college, he'd spent two years in the Peace Corps in Ecuador. When I phoned him, he said he was planning a trip home to Newton to see his mother and would try to coordinate it with my trip.

Willie and Gilson had been better golfers than I, but none of us was very good. Taking the time to really learn the game would have been uncool. In those days I put most of my energy into football. I was starting quarterback on my high-school team, a key figure in the most glamorous sport. Guys on the golf team toiled in the nerdy nether regions of the high-school social order, alongside the French club and the choral society. Of course, as we would learn much later, high school had it all wrong. How many thousands of aging ex-jocks would give their life savings for one of those maddeningly fluid, lifelong swings born of youth? And where do all those creaky-kneed pro quarterbacks spend every free moment? The golf course.

Leo J. Martin suited us well. You could not feel out of place there. From the sunburnt fairways to the squat brick clubhouse, it was as utilitarian as could be. We golfed through the long summer afternoons when the summer, let alone life itself, seemed as though it would never end. Somehow you scrounged up the greens fee and got someone's mom to drop you off. Later, you drove your own heap out to Leo J., and, if cash was short, you might slip undetected onto the back nine.

Gil and Willie had been to my house so many times they didn't need to ask for directions. Willie was right on time. Maybe five minutes early, looking sharp and ready to go at 7 A.M. Gil was ten minutes late, looking sleepy. Nothing had changed. We loaded our stuff into Gil's rented minivan and tooled through the still-quiet early-morning streets. How fine the old houses looked. Why had we ever left?

We were not the sunburnt youths of fifteen years ago, but grown men now, with jobs and families and responsibilities. We shared pictures of our kids. We were none of us bald or fat or terminally serious, but we were strangers who shared a distant past. Willie was the father of twins, Gil had a daughter and a newborn son. Was it just me or had Leo J. Martin changed as well? In the fresh morning the fairways seemed smoother and greener, the greens less trampled than I remembered. I had hoped that we would find some kids who would remind us of ourselves—in T-shirts and cutoffs, arguing furiously over some rule they knew nothing about. But the course was almost eerily calm. The starter added to our threesome a retired lawyer named Murray, a quiet old guy whose momentous life memory seemed to be the time long ago when he was living in Washington and had been offered an invitation to a presidential inauguration and didn't go. Spurred by our own ceaseless remembrances, Murray told us his story solemnly, ominously. We waited for the punch line, the dramatic twist . . . *Just then the new president and first lady pulled up to my apartment and stopped up unannounced for a drink.* Something . . . But his voice just trailed off in reverie of his missed opportunity to party with history. He left us sometime during the back nine.

The first hole at Leo J. is wide open, short, an easy par-four with little or no trouble to speak of—just 315 yards from the tees to the pin, open, flat and treeless save for a line of trees far to the right lining the driving range. Which is, of course, what makes it such a devilish hole. There's no dogleg to aim for, no brook to concentrate on crossing. The tee box sits out there as obvious as a skyscraper in a cornfield. Teeing off means being watched not only by everybody waiting behind you but also by a gallery of hacks sitting on benches or milling on the blacktop just outside the clubhouse, as well as by anybody and everybody carrying their clubs up from the parking lot. I remember playing Leo J. once with my father, a decent golfer, and watching in slow agony as he took one swing after another, barely skimming the top of the ball. He must have done it four or five times, declining to take a mulligan, walking up to the ball, hitting it, walking another few feet, hitting it again. Each time, his backswing grew more hurried, his setup less assured, making the next mishit only more inevitable. It was a crowded Saturday afternoon, and there were plenty of jokers around. I don't know if they were laughing or if I just imagined it. Finally, he caught one well and the ball gratefully rose out of that cursed turf and sailed in the direction of the green. It was like deliverance.

Today, though, there were only a couple of golfers waiting behind us, and nobody was milling on the blacktop. Gil hit first and drove his ball straight down the fairway. Willie hit a good drive to the right rough. I hit my drive down the middle of the fairway. When I put my second shot on the green, Willie said, "Holy shit, Chuck, you didn't turn into a scratch golfer on us, did you?" I'd always hated that nickname. Now I was glad to hear it again. We started off in fine style, the three of us, with two pars (Willie and I) and a birdie (Gil). Only my game would deteriorate from there.

The holes washed over me like a home movie from long ago, but with everything somehow spruced up. Here was that par-three third hole, the one with an elevated green and a terrible slope in back with scratchy brambles leading to a ball-consuming tangle of woods and vines far below. It was here that I had hit my first great golf shot, at fifteen or sixteen, the shot on which my latent interest in the game probably rested. I was at the bottom of the hill in some horrible rough. It looked like it would take me six shots to push the thing back up the hill. I swung a pitching wedge, and the ball sailed up in the direction of the green. I had no view of the green, let alone the pin. Willie and Gil started to scream, "Go in the hole! Go in the hole! Go! Go!" After what seemed like hours they screamed at once, "Yeeeeeees!"

I had no intention of running up with a Cinderella smile on my face only to find my ball sitting in the sand trap or deep rough and my friends cracking up. So I sauntered to the green with a bored teenage give-a-shit smirk on my face and found the two of them dancing around the pin, still screaming. It took a few moments, but their unhinged glee finally convinced me I had hit a miraculous shot. I experienced one of those rare moments that separates golf from most other sports—I had hit a shot better than I was capable of hitting, a shot Jack Nicklaus would have been lucky to hit. I wanted to do it again. I wanted to become a golfer.

Now, standing on the same green twenty summers later, after sinking a more prosaic putt for a bogey, I reminded Willie and Gil of that moment, assuming they would recall it with a pleasure as great as my own. They nodded blandly and smiled, and I knew they had no idea what I was talking about. So I was left to bask in my own private memory.

The sixth hole brought back lots of memories as well, most of them bad. It was the one hole on a generally improved Leo J. that still looked as it had in the old days. The tee box was hard-packed mud. The hole lay low and hugged a bend in the Charles River, which ran along the left side. The right side of the fairway was dominated by a huge net separating the fairway from the driving range. Even if you did hit a straight drive, the green was well protected in front and fringed in the back by unforgiving woods. I had thrown my clubs here in my youth. Today I swallowed my triple bogey like a man.

That hole was the beginning of a mid-round meltdown that cost me the decent score I had hoped for. I shot 102. Gil shot an 82 and Willie an 83. Later, Gilson pulled out some cigars. Even the cigars had grown up. He ceremoniously produced a fine wood box full of Cohibas from Cuba, a perk from his trips on the DC-6. After holing out on the eighteenth, we had a beer and talked for a while. Willie no longer knew the earned-run averages of every scrub pitcher on the Red Sox roster. Who had the time anymore?

After we said good-bye I drove up to Newton Centre, over to the church at the corner of Beacon and Centre streets, where Willie used to live. I parked on Beacon and walked around to the church parking lot that had served as our street-hockey rink and touch-football field, an asphalt expanse of skinned knees and memories. On the far side of the lot was the big house, painted a different color now. Someone had attached a grotesque-looking fire escape from the second floor, about where Willie's room had been. It jutted out from the house into the center of the back-yard, where it rested on a squat, ugly base about where our pitcher's mound used to be. No doubt this contraption satisfied some new fire code. But it mangled our old Wiffle ball field. The chain-link fence that defined our home runs was rusted now and sagged under its embroidery of honeysuckle hanging heavy and sweet.

6

Our Inalienable Right to Golf

The starter waved his arms like a quarterback imploring the home crowd for quiet. Harried, but determined to maintain his composure, he glanced at the growing list of names, mine included, that he'd scribbled in his notebook.

"I've been here an hour," someone grumbled.

"Be patient, be patient," the starter said. "I'll get to everyone."

I'd driven to the Franklin Park Golf Course in Boston's Dorchester neighborhood early on a weekday morning, figuring I'd walk right on. I wasn't counting on today being Bunker Hill Day, one of those odd holidays they celebrate only in Massachusetts. The hilltop clubhouse at Franklin Park offers a view of most of the front nine, and from where I stood I could see undulating fairways thick with foursomes. Every government worker in Boston, it seemed, was paying respects to our brave colonial ancestors while on the golf course. It would be slow going today. But for once the prospect didn't frustrate me. If you knew anything about the history of Franklin Park, or about Boston's tortured racial dynamics, you couldn't help but be pleasantly astonished at the sight of dozens of golfers, black and white, jockeying for position on the starter's list. Had I shown up at Franklin Park on a similar morning just fifteen years earlier, I'd have walked on, all right, but I would have been fortunate to walk off without being mugged, or worse.

Built in the late nineteenth century, Franklin Park has an impeccable pedigree. The park itself was designed by Frederick Law Olmsted, father of New York's Central Park. Donald Ross, the great Scottish-born golf course architect, laid out the course, which opened in the 1890s, as just the second public course in the United States, after Van Cortlandt in the Bronx. For decades it was considered one of the nation's best public courses.

The decline and near death of the golf course from the 1960s to the 1980s traced the economic decline of Dorchester itself—a familiar tale of white flight and urban neglect. By the 1970s, Dorchester and neighboring Roxbury were known as high-crime areas, places to avoid. Even as a schoolkid growing up in the safety of the suburbs I knew the code of Boston's rigidly defined ethnic neighborhoods. The Italians lived in East Boston and the North End, the Irish in Southie. And while some parts of Dorchester remained white and Irish, the parts around Franklin Park, and virtually all of Roxbury, were black neighborhoods. The rescue of this grand old golf course from the brink of extinction, and its subsequent return to glory, is largely the story of a determined group of black golfers who refused to see the course die. One of the leaders, a man named George Lyons, is now the head pro.

The day I played Franklin Park, I knocked on Lyons's door and introduced myself. He was a serious, softspoken man, busy with lessons that day, and I couldn't tell if he was pleased or irritated by my presence. Nevertheless, within a few minutes he had invited me to join him on a golf-cart tour of the course. As we bumped along the cart paths and fairways, dodging golfers and balls, he told me about himself and the course.

Lyons had first picked up a golf club in the Air Force in Hawaii during the early 1950s.

"I had no money," he said. "I couldn't go to town. I had a friend, Herbert Miner. He'd spend his time hitting golf balls on the grass between the runways of the airstrip. He kept asking me to join him, and one day I did. That was 1954 or 1955. Before long, I was getting pretty good. I knew how to play, I just didn't have any clubs. My first clubs were a set of J. C. Higgins, from Sears."

He liked the self-reliance that golf demanded, the personal integrity. He liked the fact that you could tell a lot about a man by the way he kept his scorecard.

"Golf is a game where you must think on your feet," he told me. "There's no one to assist you. You stand alone. It's just you and the golf course. It's a game you can play all your life. But if you go out there and start cheating, no one will play with you."

When he left the service, Lyons put his Air Force training to work as an electrical engineer for a company in Connecticut that manufactured time clocks. It was the late 1950s. He joined a group of black golfers called the United Golf Association, playing tournaments at public courses in Connecticut, Rhode Island and Massachusetts—Bridgeport, Ponkapaug, Keeny Park. He was good enough to take runner-up in a national tournament. In 1962, when his company transferred him to Boston, Lyons adopted Franklin Park as his home course. But by that time the decline had already begun.

"There weren't enough golfers to support it. It started going down."

By the early seventies, the entire back nine had closed. The ponds were dried up and choked with vegetation, and the greens and fairways lay fallow under several feet of grass and weeds. The front nine remained nominally open, but conditions weren't a whole lot better. Local residents would drive their cars onto the fairways for picnics, or to change their oil, leaving tire tracks, and sometimes the hulk of an old car, behind. They dumped trash among the trees and shrubs fringing the greens and fairways. The old clubhouse had to be condemned. The city had no plans to build a new one.

For the few golfers who still doggedly showed up, the dubious advantage of all this was absurdly low greens fees. As recently as 1981 Boston residents paid $3 on weekdays, $4 on weekends. Nonresidents—not that many bothered to come into Boston to play—forked over $4.50 on weekdays and $6 on weekends. But stories about Franklin Park in those days had less to do with golf and more with crime, random and otherwise. One July afternoon in 1983 a man, beaten, slashed and bleeding, staggered up to the deserted clubhouse from some hidden spot on the course. He was not a golfer. It was a Saturday afternoon in the summer, a time when any golf course should have been teeming with players. And yet, according to a brief account the next day in the *Boston Globe,* it was two young girls walking nearby who spotted him and called the police. The man died before reaching the hospital.

The golf course seemed almost certainly headed for a similar fate.

"Finally, a group of guys, we got together and decided to do something about it," Lyons said simply. Calling themselves the Franklin Park Golf Association, they petitioned the parks commission, city council, state government, anyone who might listen. As a second step, they decided to try direct action. Armed with placards and pickets, the Franklin Park Golfers peaceably assembled in the middle of Circuit Drive, the road that runs around the park. Traffic came to a stop. And so Boston, whose residents had introduced civil disobedience to the New World by dumping tea into the harbor, became the site two centuries later of perhaps the only instance of civil disobedience by citizens demanding their inalienable right to play golf.

At last the city took notice. The parks commissioner, Robert McCoy, provided dozens of enormous granite rocks that were placed strategically around Circuit Drive to prevent cars from entering the course. The mayor, Kevin White, ordered the grass cut.

Emboldened by their success, the Franklin Park Golfers lobbied the state legislature and the governor, Michael Dukakis, for a full-scale restoration. The city and state together put up $1.3 million. The renovations began in 1985 and took four years. Like stripping decades of false siding and shag carpeting away from a fabulous old home, workers discovered a grand course underneath the weeds and brambles and neglect, a course full of personality and grace, shaded by fine old oaks, willows and pines, with mossy pathways and stone bridges crossing lily ponds. Workers resodded the course, dug up and replaced a rotting irrigation system. Among the holes brought lovingly back to life was the par-four twelfth, which holds special significance for golf historians. It was here that a young Bobby Jones came to practice while studying English literature at Harvard during the early 1920s. Jones considered the dastardly uphill twelfth to be the perfect practice hole, so unusual in its contours that he could play it over and over without ever facing the same predicament twice. He would arrive at Franklin Park at off-hours and play just that hole. The twelfth is still known as the "Bobby Jones hole."

Franklin Park held its grand reopening in 1989. The one thing the course needed now was a head pro. The parks commission asked Lyons. He was getting near retirement with the clock company, and he took the job. I asked him what it was like to spend his days on the course that he had helped bring back to life. He searched a moment for the right description, then shrugged. "Words can't describe it."

For the first few years after its reopening, Franklin Park was a hidden gem, known only to a core of golf fanatics, most of them black. My father played there once in the early nineties with a black friend, who afterwards implored him, only half in jest, to go back to Newton and tell everybody how dangerous it was. But it isn't every day that a wonderful golf course blossoms in the heart of a congested city, and once word got out that you could go down to Franklin Park and not get mugged, the draw proved irresistible.

Today, a course that once was all but dead sees 35,000 rounds per year. And the racial mix has shifted to 65 percent white, 35 percent black. Which is why, when I arrived on that weekday morning, expecting an urban golf experience with some black golfers, I wound up playing with three white guys, two of them from the suburbs. One, Noah, was from Newton, the town where I grew up; Rick was from Brookline, one town over, and Rob was a Boston city schoolteacher taking advantage of his Bunker Hill Day holiday.

Despite its city location and the crowds, the course never seems cramped as it meanders over local landmarks known as School Master Hill, the Stone Terrace, and around Scarboro Pond. I could see why the twelfth confounded Bobby Jones. It is not a particularly long hole, just 407 yards uphill from the back tees and 382 from the middle. But the fairway is split lengthwise up the middle by a bony ridge, with downward slopes on either side, like a green carpet draped over the back of a dragon. The hole doglegs to the left, with thick woods on both sides to punish an errant drive. The green sits atop a hill protected by bunkers that you don't see until it is too late. I didn't, at any rate. I triple-bogeyed the hole after stubbing my drive, sending my second shot into the right rough, then finding one of those bunkers. Unlike Bobby Jones, I felt that one time on the twelfth was sufficient.

The prettiest hole is the sixteenth, a short par-four of 347 yards. You hit a medium iron down into a landing area that appears at first to be completely surrounded. At the base of the hill, the trees open to allow a passage over a pond to the green. To get to the green you cross an old stone bridge. We passed a family at the base of the bridge having a picnic. That was the only sign of nongolfers we saw all day on the course. We saw no sign at all of the interlopers who for years had helped run Franklin Park down.

During my tour with Lyons after my round I asked him how he felt about so many golfers returning from the suburbs to play Franklin Park. His voice echoed only pride. "When we first opened, there was talk of people not coming to support the course because of the geographical location. We've found that to be absolutely untrue." The course has also become a magnet for young black golfers from Boston. After Tiger Woods's victory at the Masters in 1997, parents of black kids flooded Lyons's phone, asking how their kids could learn the game. On a wall in the clubhouse are pictures of Woods visiting Franklin Park in 1992, his final year as a junior. Already a rising star, he put on a clinic for some city kids.

"He was on the first tee. He knocked the ball almost to the green," Lyons recalled. "That's three hundred and eighty-seven yards. He was, what, sixteen at the time?"

The Franklin Park Golfers had no intention of creating a model of racial harmony and integration in a city whose national reputation on both counts has taken a beating since school busing during the 1970s. But that's exactly what they did. A city divided by race comes together over golf. Boston politicians like to be seen playing there. On the day I arrived, current Boston Mayor Thomas Menino was just finishing an early-morning round. But all George Lyons wanted was a decent place to golf.

"This course is for golfers," he said. "Any golfers are welcome."

In some large cities Route 1 simply hooks up with a main artery and rides piggyback through town as an expressway or major thoroughfare. In others, it slips into anonymity and hides like a wallflower at the prom. But nothing compares with Providence, Rhode Island, which plays a maddening game of cat and mouse with the legendary road and makes staying on course an exercise in futility. I had approached Providence from the north after passing through a series of Boston suburbs. Shortly before the Rhode Island state line, in Foxboro, Massachusetts, I passed, on the left, the concrete stadium where the New England Patriots play. It's an extraordinarily ugly edifice, still raw and unfinished looking after more than three decades, with all the grace and form of a 1950s Soviet apartment complex. It did not surprise me when, later, the Patriots announced they'd be moving to Hartford.

A few minutes later I was on the outskirts of Providence. Route 1 continues promisingly enough to the north edge of the city, then melts into a sort of tangled oblivion, splintered and lost down one-way side streets in old residential neighborhoods. Every few minutes a sign would appear with that reassuring white shield with the black number 1 in the center, but apparently only as a decoy, for a few moments later I'd come upon a four-way split in the road, with no sign at all. I wound through the narrow downtown streets, past the State House with its gleaming dome. But there was another fork and I guessed wrong. I backtracked. I finally made my way to Cranston, a blue-collar city that borders Providence to the south. At least I was heading in the right direction. At Cranston I stopped at a gas station to ask for directions back to Route 1.

"Where you heading?"

"Route 1 south. I just need to find the road itself. Can you tell me which road is Route 1?"

"If you're going south, just get on the highway. I-95, right up the road, your first right."

"I need Route 1, though," I said.

"Where on Route 1 are you trying to go? What building?"

"Just Route 1. The road. I need to find the road."

She shook her head. I was obviously a fool. She turned back to her work. A man standing nearby stepped in and gave me directions, but these just led me to another entrance to I-95. I had spent the better part of an hour tooling around Providence and Cranston. It was time to golf. I'd have to take the interstate. But just as I was about to enter the highway the Route 1 shield miraculously appeared. I bore to the right instead of the left and was back on Route 1. Cleared of the city, the road became an old, true friend. There was a Donald Ross course in Providence called Triggs Memorial that I had wanted to play, but they were having a tournament that day, so I drove south a few miles to North Kingstown and a municipal course sitting on Narragansett Bay.

The North Kingstown course was located just off Route 1 on Quonset Point, home to Quonset Naval Air Station, one of the largest and most important Navy aircraft testing centers right up through World War II. Next door was another once-mighty military installation, the Quonset Naval Construction Battalion, better known as the CBs, or the "Sea Bees." The Sea Bees, more than any industrialist, politician or financier, were responsible for spreading the image worldwide during World War II of Americans as can-do people. In shattered villages and remote tropical islands, the Sea Bees astonished the natives with their ability to build a bridge in a few hours or lay down a coral runway capable of handling heavy bombers practically overnight. There was nothing the Sea Bees couldn't do with a few bulldozers and some good old American know-how. It was here, at Quonset Point, that the Quonset hut was born.

Sometime around midcentury the admirals from the naval air station got the idea of putting the Sea Bees to work on another crucial project, a golf course. This was no Donald Ross design. The name of the architect, probably some young engineer more accustomed to designing runways than fairways, is lost to history. With a ready supply of highly skilled labor next door, the admirals made some changes to their original course over the years. The fifth hole, a 362-yard par-four with small ponds on the right and the left of the fairway, originally had a stream running across the center of the fairway connecting them. But according to local legend, after one too many admiral lost his ball, the Sea Bees were called in with their bulldozers to fill in the stream.

Shortly after World War II ended, the naval air station had its fate sealed with the decision that Quonset would continue to test only propeller aircraft. The new generation of jets coming off the line after the war would be tested elsewhere. The base hung on until 1973. Today, the only aircraft operating here are those of the Rhode Island Air National Guard, which uses a small corner of runway and hangar space facing out on Narragansett Bay. The rest of the enormous base is an odd mixture of hulking old hangars and buildings rusting away in a gothic gloom, and tender shoots of new industry. The local government is attempting to turn the old base into an industrial park. The Rhode Island Economic Development Corporation has taken over the old Sea Bees headquarters, where a welded metal bumblebee wearing a sailor cap and holding a machine gun, wrench and hammer still guards the front gate. In one hangar some volunteers were keeping the memory of the base alive with an aviation museum. But by far the busiest and most active section of the old base is the golf course, which was conveyed to the town of North Kingstown by the Department of the Interior when the base closed.

Far from being an exclusive enclave for the Navy elite, the course today supports about 58,000 rounds of public golf per year. Even on this midweek morning, the starter moved furiously about trying to keep the backup of golfers moving. I had checked in at the clubhouse, and the man there contacted the starter at the first tee by walkie-talkie. He could fit me on if I went out right now. Could I use the rest room first? Yeah, but you'd better hurry. The Single Golfer Rule in action.

Out at the first tee I joined three college kids, Matt, Nick and Gregg, who had grown up in the area and were enjoying summer break. Matt was a football player at Brown University. He had a natural swing and had obviously played some golf. Nick and Gregg were guys who were more or less picking up the game. From my first shot, which went off in some pine trees to the right, I sensed disaster. I couldn't find my ball, although it should have been lying on pine needles somewhere in the open. Losing a ball on your first shot of the day is a bad deal. For one thing, you identify yourself immediately as a hack to the people you are playing with. Golf is very much a game of first impressions. If a playing partner smacks his first drive cleanly down the center of the fairway, you lodge him somewhere in your mind as a golfer and are willing to grant him any number of flubs thereafter before his game goes down in your estimation. If he tops, misses, slices, hooks or otherwise screws up his first shot, you mark him down as a hack and there is very little he can do to extricate himself. Even three or four pars in a row later will be seen merely as a lucky streak. It's even worse to lose your first ball, thus compelling perfect strangers to help you hunt. In this case, as a consolation, my playing partners started no better.

The front nine at North Kingstown is unremarkable and not especially challenging. The holes are mostly straight and open. It made no matter to me. After double-bogeying the first, I followed suit on the second and third, an easy par-three despite a carry over water. But all that was just a prelude to disaster on the par-five fourth hole, a straight, perfunctory hole that I completely screwed up. I started with a topped drive that skidded off the tee into the left rough after about thirty or forty dismal yards. I shot a 9. My delicate confidence that had been building since Cape Arundel melted away in the hot sun in Rhode Island. Wasn't I learning anything? Hadn't I gotten over this hump? On the sixth hole, a tricky par-four with a diagonal cross over water and through some trees, I couldn't even get the ball to the water. I scored an 8 on that hole and the same on the ninth and finished the side with a 59, the sort of score I felt I had left behind me in my golfing infancy. Matt, Nick and Gregg had to leave after nine and I might have done the same out of sheer disgust, except that after Sagamore-Hampton I had decided not to quit in mid-round.

I continued on alone. On the back nine, at least, the scenery improved. Here the course sweeps out to embrace sparkling Narragansett Bay. Across the bay lies the island of Jamestown and, just beyond Jamestown, Newport. The signature hole is the thirteenth, a downhill par-four. You hit out from a tee at the top of a hill that opens into a broad vista of the bay below. Off to the right huge green transport planes sit on the tarmac still used by the

National Guard. An unassuming-looking grass mound sticks out of the rough just to the right of the fairway. You don't notice anything unusual about this mound unless you happen to hit on the far side of it. From there you can see that the mound is actually a reinforced concrete bunker. A narrow slit on the bunker from the far side leads down a narrow concrete corridor to a locked door and signs to keep out. This mild-looking grassy mound for many years was a munitions dump.

On the twelfth hole I waved to a twosome back on the tee to join me. One of them was tall and lanky, the other shorter and powerfully built. The lanky one hit first, putting it somewhere up around my middling drive, which I had popped up. Then the shorter guy got up and boomed his tee shot way over my head, at least seventy-five yards in front of me.

"Great drive!" I called as he approached in his cart.

He shook his head. "Didn't really hit it solid."

"If that's not solid, I'd hate to see what it looks like when you do hit it solid," I said.

His partner deadpanned, "He never has. I play with him every week and he's never hit it solid."

Robert Petrella and Adam Arzoomanian worked at Marchetti's, a popular Italian restaurant in Cranston. Adam, who hit the great shot, was the manager. The pair had just finished playing nine with the owners of the restaurant, who had to leave. Adam and Robert were like a comedy team, giving each other grief on cue. If Robert, who had picked up the game fairly recently, whiffed on a shot, Adam, an experienced golfer, was sure to say, "There's the swing."

On the sixteenth green, I sorely underhit a putt and cried out, "More, more, more!"

"Jesus Christ," Adam said. "He sounds just like my ex-wife."

Adam and Robert left me with a standing invitation to drop by Marchetti's for some veal. Unfortunately, the restaurant was closed that day (which was why they were out golfing) and I went to bed veal-less.

7

Never Give a Sucker a Stroke a Hole

From North Kingstown Route 1 skirts quaint seaside resort towns, bending with the land around Narragansett Bay, which soon yields to Block Island Sound. There were several courses right around the Connecticut/Rhode Island border. The nearest off Route 1 was in Pawcatuck, just over the state line in Connecticut.

Elmridge Golf Course lies a couple of miles down country roads from Route 1. It is a well-kept, privately owned course with twenty-seven holes (three color-coded nines) that you can mix and match as you please. I started off solo on the red nine. I double-bogeyed the first hole, then put together a string of bogeys and pars for a front nine 43 that went a long way toward erasing thoughts of my horrible score at Kingstown. It's a short, hilly course, with plenty of holes where the best shot off the tee is an iron. For a while, I seemed to have the course to myself. When I finished the "red nine," the closest tee box was for the "white nine," so I started off there, even though management had posted a sign warning of pesticides having been sprayed within the past twenty-four hours. I had seen these signs on other courses. No doubt the Environmental Protection Agency or some other well-meaning bureaucracy demands that golfers be warned after groundskeepers have sprayed. But I never know what I'm supposed to do when I see those signs. Not golf? Am I being told the course is temporarily unsafe? If so, close the place down. Otherwise, I'm good to go, and those signs just put me in a bad mood. They must not have any golfers at the EPA. If they did, they would know that no golfer is going to change his mind about playing because of a sign, not unless the sign is accompanied by physical restraints. A golfer standing on the first tee with an open fairway in front of him, if told that the fairway was sprayed that morning with DDT, the traps filled with quicksand, the ponds laced with e. coli bacteria and the greens sown with Agent Orange, would have one question: "Am I up?"

I forged on, Rachel Carson be damned. I hooked up with a threesome of local guys who were friendly enough but already well into whatever weekly wager made their golf rounds more interesting. I screwed up three or four holes and took 50 on this nine, giving me an eighteen-hole score of 93. Not great, but it beat the hell out of a 109.

From Pawcatuck I followed Route 1 along the coast, crawling with the slow summer traffic through Mystic, New London, Old Saybrook. The names of these towns had a musical quality to me; they brought back train rides I had taken as a child to visit my cousins in Stamford. I remembered the weary song of the conductor's voice, calling out the stops: "Olllllld Saybrook is next, Olllllld Saybrook."

I stopped at a motel in Branford for the night. The next morning I ate a golfer's breakfast of Dunkin' Donuts and coffee and rolled through Bridgeport. Connecticut's large cities are as bleak as the rest of the state is affluent. Route 1 cuts through the heart of Bridgeport as Boston Avenue, past blocks and blocks of vacant, burned-out houses and boarded-up shops. Just as suddenly, the blight of Bridgeport lifted and I was rolling through the town of Fairfield, all winding roads and gracious homes, toward a municipal course called H. Smith Richardson.

The starter was an amiable grouch who relished the thin reed of authority bestowed on him by his position. There was already a crowd around him when I arrived. "Fontineau! Fontineau foursome. Where the hell are you?" he called, rolling his eyes. When the offending parties finally appeared from the pro shop, the starter barked, "Come on, guys, where ya been?!? Fer cryin' out loud!"

The farther south I went, the more rules I encountered. Whereas the Maine courses had beckoned and welcomed, in southern New England courses advertised their barriers. A simple case of supply and demand, I suppose. A large sign next to the first tee at H. Smith Richardson shouted "Rules and Regulations" in large black letters, in case somebody thought they were coming out to the golf course to have fun. "No fivesomes," it warned. "No stopping for lunch," "No loitering on greens," "No spectators allowed."

I paid the cashier in the clubhouse, took my tag out to the waiting area and, during a lull when the starter seemed to be casting about for golfers to inject into the rotation, I flashed my tag for him.

"What, you paid already? You shouldna paid. You don't pay until I call your name!"

"I figured I'd better be ready to jump in."

He shook his head and ran a forefinger down his closely guarded chart. "You shouldna paid. How do you know I can squeeze you in? I may not be able to."

I went back into the clubhouse to buy some tees and some bug spray.

"The starter seems to be having a tough day," I said.

"Yes, well, life is tough," the cashier said reflectively.

After a half hour's wait, the starter grudgingly matched me with Bill Kerrigan, who was seventy-seven years old, and Bill's grandson, Matt Stewart, fourteen. Bill had retired to Marietta, Ohio, to be near his wife's family, after a career in Connecticut, where his grandson still lived. Our fourth was David Tooley, a railroad electrician. Bill Kerrigan impressed me right off because he was walking the course at seventy-seven, without so much as a pull cart. He wore a bright yellow shirt and a straw hat with a yellow bandanna underneath. Bill was a tall man, and his tiny golf bag, just a long cylinder with a strap and room enough for five clubs, looked more like a quiver of arrows. His clubs included a seven-iron, a pitching wedge, a three-wood, a seven-wood, and a putter.

"As soon as I learn to use these ones, I'll start using the rest of 'em," Bill said with a smile.

He had a point. Most nonprofessionals could probably improve their games by jettisoning half their clubs. I once played with a good golfer who ruined his round because he couldn't keep his hands off a funky club called a T-wedge. The T-wedge, for "Trouble wedge," has more loft than a sand wedge, and is designed for getting out of nasty rough or other tight spots. PGA players, of course, know just what to do with these clubs, but for mere mortals such as my friend, the loft and distance were simply too hard to judge. He'd get right close to the green in two and then, instead of knocking a soft pitching wedge or seven-iron to the hole, he'd whip out the T-wedge. After all, he'd bought the damn thing *for just such situations.* It wasn't going to sit in the bag. He'd take a nice, full swing, and the ball would scream over the green or dribble forward two feet. The club cost him eight or nine strokes in one round, but he used it right up through the eighteenth hole.

The lack of clubs didn't hurt Bill Kerrigan's game. Nor did age, fatigue or the hot sun, for that matter. He got his stamina, he said, from walking his course in Marietta with a regular foursome. Nobody was allowed to ride. On the greens, his uncanny consistency approached the sublime. About halfway through the round the rest of us started noticing how many long putts he was sinking. H. Smith Richardson is not a pushover course. One feature that makes it difficult are the fast, contoured greens. If you aren't careful, you can three-putt your way around the course. But Bill rarely putted more than once. I asked him how long he'd been golfing, and he surprised me by saying he hadn't picked up a club until his late forties.

He had worked for a company that manufactured medical equipment. The city where he lived, Norwalk, in 1969 built a public golf course called Oak Hills, a couple of miles from his house. He started playing out of curiosity.

"Because I was starting so late, I knew I'd never be able to hit it as well off the tee and fairway as the guys I was playing with. So I concentrated on the short game. I'd walk over to Oak Hills in the evenings, before dark, and practice on one hole, from around the green. Chip up, one putt in. Chip up, one putt in. Chip up, one putt in. The guys I played with could all outdrive me, and they had beautiful swings. They could never understand how I beat them. I'll tell you what it was. It was chip up, one putt in."

I outdrove Bill on just about every hole, smacked some crisp beauties down the center of the fairway, arced some fantastic eight-irons to within a few feet of the pin. There was no question that my round would have provided the better highlight film. When we tallied the scores, I had shot a 95, thanks mainly to poor putting. Playing with a handful of clubs, Bill had beaten me by three strokes. Chip up, one putt in.

I drove down from Fairfield toward Norwalk on the Post Road (as Route 1 is called in these parts) feeling a little nervous about my next round. It wasn't the course that intimidated me. I'd be playing at Oak Hills, the same municipal course where Bill Kerrigan had taught himself the game. No, it was my partner I was worried about. In his younger days he had played to scratch and won the Norwalk city championship. He was good enough that Bill Kerrigan, who hadn't lived in Norwalk for many years, still recognized the name when I mentioned it. Would I embarrass myself? Would I embarrass him? He was a silent man, difficult to know, a man who took his golf game seriously. He was my father-in-law.

It was just like Tony DiPanni not to ask a single question about my trip when I pulled up to his house and spilled out of my road-grungy car. It seemed to me that Tony might be keenly interested in my project on at least two fronts. First, as a golfer, he might want to know which courses I'd played, whom I'd played with, which courses were great, which poor and why. And then, as the father of my wife, he might want to know just what sort of cockamamie plan I'd cooked up that involved leaving his pregnant daughter and five-year-old granddaughter behind and golfing my way down the East Coast. Lord knows I'd been grilled on the subject by people with a lot less of a personal stake in the matter. But he just greeted me with his usual reserved smile, devoid of encouragement or condemnation, as if I'd dropped by from next door to borrow the latest issue of *Golf Digest*.

Tony DiPanni is a product of that generation of young men who in the forties and fifties served in the military, then returned home to build the greatest, most productive economy in the history of the world. They were the last generation for whom the separate roles of men and women were so clearly defined as to remain unspoken. Among the things these men did not do were change diapers, wash dishes and "share." So you had to take your satisfaction where you could get it with Tony. I'd seen his eyes fill with tears the first time he held his granddaughter. He was uncomfortable with the rituals of gift giving; about the most enthusiasm he could muster around the Christmas tree was a look of strained patience. And yet he was generous to a fault, pressing on me through unexpected gifts my entire first set of golf equipment.

Tony spent most of his career selling cars for a business owned by his brothers-in-law. I don't think he cared much for selling cars, but he worked hard at it and developed a loyal following of customers who came to cherish the fact that they were dealing with an honest man, one who would rather cheat himself than them. In the early years of my marriage, I would scout around for books on military or aviation history, subjects I knew he loved. Accustomed to my own family's effusive displays over even minor gifts, I was insulted by his lack of response when he opened them. It was only later that I realized his way of thanking me was to hole up for the next three days and read every word.

My mother-in-law, Jo-Ann, is a natural counterbalance to my father-in-law, as gregarious as he is silent. Warm and emotional, she gets teary over sentimental movies and can barely contain her excitement over gifts at Christmas. The drive from Richmond to Norwalk for Christmas or Easter is seven hours of eight-lane, white-knuckle hell. But arriving has always been a kind of wonderful deliverance, full of warm hugs and spectacular home-cooked meals that somehow seem to have been timed precisely to our arrival. But it was not to be on this trip of mine. Jo-Ann was out of town with friends when I arrived and would not be home until the next day. Her absence was palpable.

Tony and I drove to a restaurant in Westport called John's Best for bowls of spicy calamari over linguine. As we drove to the restaurant in cordial silence, I offered leading comments, hoping Tony would ask me questions about my trip. I come from a family where silences must be filled, emotions mulled over and explained. But he wasn't biting.

If Tony has a language, and he does, it is golf. When playing golf, he is an eloquent and graceful speechmaker. Even now, approaching seventy, with a bad hip and after triple bypass surgery, his swing has the timeless elegance and precision of Tony Bennett wooing a nightclub audience. When my in-laws visit us in Richmond I take him out to one of the local courses where he proceeds, wearing sneakers and swinging rented clubs on an unfamiliar course, to shoot in the seventies. And now here we were on his home turf, where all his buddies played. Despite my recent passion for golf, he had been cautious about inviting me to play at Oak Hills. We'd played there once, at an off-hour, when I was just picking up the game. I'd played miserably, and the invitations hadn't come pouring in since. I could not take offense. That was Tony. His family was one world, his golf another. But now I had requested, and he obliged.

We drove over to Oak Hills the next morning.

With the concentrated population in southern Connecticut, Norwalk could easily support a half dozen public golf courses. But Oak Hills is it for public golfers. While many of his relatives moved on to private clubs in the area, Tony, the best golfer in the bunch, remains a denizen of the public links. For many years Tony was responsible every fourth week for securing a tee time for his foursome for the following week. This meant getting to the golf course around 2 A.M. Sunday and sleeping in his car until the course staff arrived around five and started taking tee times. With a time for the following week now secured, he'd run home for a couple of hours of sleep or just wait in his car before teeing off for this week's round.

When we arrived at the course, Tony introduced me to Vinnie Grillo, who has been the head pro since the course opened in 1969. In the first year, the course saw 24,000 rounds of golf. Today, 58,000 rounds is customary. Grillo was taking the course through an attempt to become semi-independent from the city of Norwalk, and thus to be able to hang on to its own revenue for course improvements. As one of the few public facilities that actually made money, the course brought in more than $800,000, which it was compelled to turn over to the city in exchange for a budget of $600,000, Grillo explained.

"This is not a private country club. This is not the Taj Mahal. But this course can be self-supporting," Grillo said. "This is the right way to go. This is the only way to go."

As Tony led me around, he showed me the pro shop, the computer where you enter the scores for your handicap, the cart shack that he and another retiree had helped redesign inside. He was at ease here, more at home than I had seen him just about any other place, including his own kitchen filled with relatives. He was greeted with a hearty "Hey, Tony!" and a pat on the shoulder—a familiarity I hadn't seen before.

When Tony stepped away for a moment, Grillo looked at me confidentially and said, in a serious tone, "There's only two words for him: top shelf."

I wanted to golf well here, not just to impress my father-in-law but also to fit in somehow with this intensely golf-oriented crowd. All golf courses have their core of regulars, the cast of characters who are the backbone of the course, give it its personality and flavor. But even on the courses I play regularly near my home I am an outsider. I pay my money, golf, then leave, never penetrating the local golf guild. Now, by proxy, I was for a few minutes at the epicenter. I wanted to be one of the boys. Tony pulled our cart up to the hardtop outside the clubhouse. When he got out of the cart he forgot to engage the brake. The cart inched forward, and probably would have stopped soon, but I decided to reach in with my foot and click the brake pedal. Of course, instead of the brake pedal I stamped heavily down on the accelerator. The cart lurched forward. I had to lunge toward the cart and jam on the brake pedal, which brought it to a screeching stop. I looked up; a dozen or so men had stopped their conversations and were looking my way to see what the commotion was. Who is this guy, Tony? Hey, what can I do, my daughter married him. He didn't say that; I only felt it.

A few minutes later, gratefully, we moved out to the first tee. Tony's brother, Chase, was joining us. Tony is third of four children, the son of a hardworking Italian immigrant. He had grown up in a poor neighborhood tucked away in one of the East Coast's wealthiest enclaves, New Canaan, Connecticut. Chase, two years Tony's senior, discovered golf when he signed up as a caddie at the Country Club of New Canaan.

"I was ten years old when I started," Chase recalled. "I was so small that they couldn't find a shirt small enough to fit me. The shirts said C.C.N.C., for Country Club of New Canaan. I wanted one pretty badly. Then someone said to me, 'You don't want one of those shirts anyway. Don't you know what C.C.N.C. stands for? It stands for 'Can't Caddie, Never Could.' That made me feel better."

Tony joined his brother at the club a couple of years later. Along with the position of caddie came golf privileges during off hours.

"In those days, none of us had money for a complete set of clubs," Tony said. "So, when you played you didn't choose your playing partners because they were your best friends, or because they were the best players. You chose them because of what clubs they had. Maybe you had a putter and a three-iron, and the other guy had a couple of woods. Maybe a third guy had a pitching wedge and a seven. Like that. Eventually, between three or four guys you had pretty close to a complete set of clubs, and you'd go out and play."

By the time Tony was in his early teens, World War II had drawn off all the young men. It left a wide-open niche for younger boys on the caddie roster. By the time he was fourteen years old, Tony held the exalted position of head caddie, which put him in charge of who would carry which bag, matching the best caddies with the best golfers, and the best tippers. The going rate was a quarter for eighteen holes, and perhaps a nickel tip at the end.

"It was a snobby club. Caddies weren't allowed to change clothes in the locker room. You could change your shoes in the pro shop. That was it. I hardly ever played a full eighteen holes there. But the first and second holes ran right past the clubhouse, up and back. I played those two holes over and over again. Up and down, up and down, up and down. When I caddied, if it was for a good golfer, I paid attention to what he was doing, how he swung the club and hit the ball, how he responded to different situations. If he was a bad golfer, I tried to figure out what he was doing wrong. I never had a lesson, but that's how I learned to golf."

Tony kept golfing, interrupted only by a stint in the Army in Europe during the Korean War. He and Chase kept golfing together, forming the basis of a golfing friendship that continues to this day.

Oak Hills had the most elaborate scorecard I had seen for a course, public or private. It was more like a glossy, pocket-sized brochure. Stapled in the center was a conventional cardboard scorecard with the holes and yardage and handicap rating and all the rest. But the glossy brochure around it devoted a page to each hole, with a full-color diagram, detailed yardage markers, and a "Pro's Tip" for that hole. The tip for the first hole, a par-four, said, for example: "Take long iron or three-wood off tee. Favor right side of fairway. Approach, play a little shorter. Trouble on left." I appreciated the advice, although the appropriate advice for me was "If you can't keep it in the fairway, at least try not to lose the damn thing."

On my first shot, I topped the ball about fifty yards down the fairway, but at least the ball was playable. I was able to recover and on my third shot hit a nice eight-iron over some high trees and to the fringe of the green. I chipped on and two-putted for a 6. Chase also shot a 6 after getting into some trouble off the tee, and Tony parred the hole for the eight thousandth time in his golfing life. Chase and Tony had some kind of spare-change bet going and casually included me.

Chase said, "We'll give you a stroke a hole."

"That's a mistake," Tony said.

For Tony, that amounted to showering me with praise. Inwardly I beamed. I parred the second, bogeyed the third, and, on the fourth hole, broke a solemn vow of my journey and took my lone mulligan. The fourth tee box sits atop a high mound. Just to the left and far below is the green for the previous hole. My nearly whiffed tee shot skittered down the side slope near some wooden railroad ties set in place to prevent the soil from eroding. I may have had a shot out of there, but the chorus of "take a mulligan" from Tony and Chase was difficult to resist. They were just trying to be nice, and being a little intimidated by the whole situation, I relented after a couple of weak protests. I regretted it for the rest of the day and added a stroke to my final score. The bad thing about mulligans (aside from the fact that they make you feel cheap) is that they often are useless. I put my rehit off to the right in some scraggly trees and bushes. I hit a nice shot under some branches and came away with six counting my mulligan, but I probably could have scored the same playing it straight up and honest.

From the back tees, I finished nine holes with a 48, ten strokes in back of Tony and five behind Chase, which I considered a not horrible showing. Plus I had hit some impressive shots, including a four-iron on the 195-yard par-three fifth hole, a somewhat daunting hole from an elevated tee over a pond to the green. And though the ball sailed several feet over the green it was among the prettiest shots I had ever hit, and I was thrilled to put the ball over the green from that far out with a four-iron, especially since Tony, at sixty-eight, and Chase, seventy, were using woods.

The tenth hole, a 547-yard par-five, has a bunker on the left side, about 260 yards from the tee. The bunker marks a gentle curve to the left. As we stood on the tee, Chase said wistfully, "There was a time Tony and I used to aim for that bunker from the tee. We'd clear it no problem. But no more. It's just age. The muscles . . ." He held out a forearm to show me the effects of time.

Chase told me about some other brothers from Norwalk who hadn't spoken with each other for twenty years because of an argument over a golf game. They were playing at a private club where one of the brothers had wangled an invitation. The other brother came along. He kept hitting up into a slow group ahead. His brother told him to stop. He continued. They argued and parted that day and didn't speak for twenty years. It wasn't until one of them had a near-fatal heart attack that the other rushed to his hospital bed full of remorse and apologies.

"Stupid," Chase said.

My game improved on the back nine, while Tony's deteriorated. He shot a 44, a miserable score for him. Playing close to my best, I shot the same score. It was the first time I had tied him for a nine. Although he still bested me by ten strokes on the day, I could tell that it was a blow to his ego that we tied that nine holes.

The eighteenth hole is a short par-four of just 341 yards with a sharp dogleg to the right and nasty woods on both sides. A four-iron followed by an eight is plenty of club to get the ball to the green in two, but you have to be straight. Tony put his tee shot off to the left in the woods, on a tree-covered ridge. It was then that he hit his shot of the day. He had been left with a decent lie but with a tree standing between himself and the green. He was somewhere back in the trees when his ball came sailing out at a low trajectory, on a fade that had carried it around the tree. The ball hit just short of the green and rolled on. It was an amazing enough shot to have hit through blind good luck, but to hit it intentionally, with a fade off fallen leaves in the woods, was extraordinary. Chase, after getting a fortuitous bounce off a tree limb, got on the green in two and, like Tony, parred the hole. But neither could match my own finale. I put the ball on in two, with my second shot coming to rest just on the green on the far left side. I had a sloping putt of around forty feet for birdie. I hit the putt solidly and it curved around and plunked into the hole as if rolling down a track. Chase had beat me by nine strokes, with an 83, and Tony had beaten me by ten. But with Chase's stroke-a-hole generosity, I came out on top. Well, I wasn't in a position to throw anything back.

Part Two

The Mid-Atlantic

8

Bronx Cheers

If not for the sporadic sound of gunfire in the distance, you would never have known you were in the Bronx. At least Rob said it was gunfire, and he had grown up in a military family and identified the staccato *pop! pop! pop!* that we heard from our perch on the third tee not just as gunfire but by the type and caliber of weapon. His technical description meant nothing to me, but it certainly sounded authentic.

As he rolled down the fairway, his cart just ahead of mine, he called back, "Small-arms fire is not that unusual in the Bronx."

I had hooked up with Rob and his friend Sam on the first tee at Van Cortlandt Golf Course. Van Cortlandt sits about a mile off Route 1, which passes through the Bronx first as the Boston Post Road, then cuts west past Fordham University at Fordham Road. Finally, it turns due south as Webster Avenue before hooking up with I-95 to cross the George Washington Bridge into New Jersey.

Van Cortlandt, which opened in 1895, is the oldest public golf course in the United States. It sits amid an immense park with a botanical garden, horseback riding, nature trails, all of it seeming too expansive to be a part of New York City. Like

Franklin Park in Boston, the golf course seems to have been laid out as though conservation of space was the last concern on the architect's mind. And that probably was true in 1895, when the Bronx still had its share of farms. The first tee box is a half mile from the clubhouse, and the holes themselves are strung almost casually together. Two of the three par-fives measure over six hundred yards. At Van Cortlandt, where I had expected to be closed in on all sides by tenements and highways and teeming life, I frequently had the sense of being all alone in the wilderness. I had to remind myself that I was in the Bronx.

One unmistakable sign that I was golfing in the city: a $2 fee for parking. A sign over the rambling old clubhouse identified Van Cortlandt as the nation's oldest course. I had called ahead that morning for directions. A woman with a thick New York accent called me "dear" and cheerfully gave them to me. I paid my greens fee in the clubhouse and then started in the direction of the first tee, down a long wooded path with a pond on the left.

A cart attendant named Miguel saw me walking and offered to give me a lift to the first tee. We got about halfway there and the first tee was still nowhere in sight.

"It's a pretty long way," I ventured.

Miguel smiled. "Yes."

"Is it a long walk between holes?"

"Yes."

"Is the eighteenth green anywhere near the clubhouse?"

"No."

"Maybe I'll do a cart, on second thought."

Miguel may have been a good salesman, or perhaps I was having second thoughts about long walks alone in the Bronx, even in these pleasant surroundings. Miguel returned me to the clubhouse, where I rented a cart. This turned out to be a good move, since my playing partners drove a cart.

Rob Kendall and Sam Ellis were a woolly-looking pair sporting a day's growth of beard, taking practice swings on the first tee. They had gotten up at some ungodly hour and driven north from Manhattan and were now, at 11 A.M., embarking on their second round of eighteen holes at Van Cortlandt.

"What brings you to the Bronx?" Sam asked. "Besides golf."

I had been getting a lot of interesting responses to my trip, including numerous whimsical offers to come along as a partner or even a caddie. But none was so cheerfully direct as Rob's when he learned that I was spending the summer golfing my way down the East Coast.

"That's a great idea," he said. "And fuck you while we're at it."

Sam said, "You'll have more people following you than Forrest Gump."

Rob, a native of New York, was a designer in Manhattan who helped clients redo the interiors of old apartments and buildings. Sam, who had grown up in West Virginia but lived in New York for decades, was a music and entertainment producer. He had produced Meat Loaf's Bat Out of Hell tour in the late seventies. "Meat's doing great," he said when I asked. "Just spoke to him on Saturday."

We exchanged the usual disparaging comments about our golf games.

"Sam's a scratch golfer," Rob said. "That's why he uses bug spray."

It was a muggy day, with low full clouds shifting overhead. The air felt warmer than it probably was. The moisture intensified the green of everything. I started off with a double-bogey six on the first hole and a triple-bogey eight on the second, an inauspicious start to what would prove to be one of the best rounds I had played.

On the third hole, a par-three, a teenage boy sat at a card table selling $5 chances at a hole in one that would pay off $1,000. Hit the green and you got a sleeve of new balls. The contest benefited a diabetes charity. Sam treated us all to a shot. Of course, this became a straight $15 donation from Sam to diabetes, because none of us came near the green.

"'Least we tried," Sam said.

The boy behind the table laughed. "Couple of days ago there was a guy out here shot a hole in one. But he didn't buy a ticket! Was he kicking himself." Oddly bolstered by that stranger's misfortune, we marched on.

"Buncha four whores," Rob said after all three of us chalked up bogey fours.

Sam and Rob had been golfing together for several years, public links only, and mainly around the city. "Everybody thinks being a golfer in New York is no good," Rob said. "It isn't true. There are thousands of places. And if you drive a little ways beyond the city, there are thousands more. We played a couple of weekends ago in Pennsylvania, in the middle of nowhere. An hour outside New York we were in open countryside."

In fact, Van Cortlandt is one of thirteen public courses in the five boroughs of New York City, a number at once paltry and impressive. Paltry because it still only amounts to one course for every 1.3 million residents, the same as if the entire state of Maine had a single course. Impressive because anything as space consuming and horizontal as a golf course is a statement of defiance against the teeming vertical city. America's renewed fascination with golf, starting in the late 1980s and gaining steam in the 1990s, had been good for the New York courses. Van Cortlandt is one of several courses whose operation has been taken over by an outfit from Texas called American Golf, which rescued the fairways and greens from years of neglect, cleared out graffiti and debris, and streamlined the tee-time reservations.

The staff at Van Cortlandt was affable in that blustery New York City way. Two groundskeepers, an older, heavy man and a young guy in his early twenties, were working near the tee box of the fourth hole. Their cart was in our path.

"Hey, get outta the way," the older man said to his co-worker. "These golfers don't want to look at you. Me, it's different. I'm *gorgeous*. Say, did you hear about the guy back on the par-three the other day that hit a hole in one and didn't buy a ticket? Ha ha!"

The round proceeded slowly, as I'd expected it would. The main problem seemed to be a foursome of women two groups in front of us who took forever to wander up to their balls, practice their swings, and hit. Directly in front of us were an older couple and what looked like their grown grandson. While we waited to tee off on the sixth hole, Rob took some slow-motion practice swings.

"What a follow-through," Sam said.

"Gimme a break. I'm trying to figure out what I'm doing wrong."

Sam said, "First thing, when the alarm goes off in the morning, stay in bed."

The sixth was a 290-yard par-four, too tempting not to try for the green. I got out my driver and hit a long drive with a little bit of an unintentional fade, so that I missed the green. But the drive had plenty of distance to reach. I chipped on and two-putted for a par. I was swinging easily, enjoying myself, starting to score well. It was about this time that one player from a foursome of young guys behind us rode up.

"Jesus Christ, this is fucking ridiculous," he barked. "It's those Japanese women up there. Holding up the whole damn course. They got nobody in front of 'em. Friggin' Japanese."

"They're not Japanese," Rob said evenly. "They're Korean." When the man rejoined his group, Rob said, "My girlfriend's Japanese."

The guys behind us turned out to be archetypes of the Asshole Principle—loud, rude and obnoxious, yet intolerant of what they perceived to be other people's rudeness. As we waited to tee off on the next hole, a par-three, 215-yarder, the guys behind us zoomed up. One of the carts diverted. "Beer run!" the driver shouted. In the other cart, a tall young man with short blond hair, a blue shirt and a face red with rage hopped out of his cart, stomped around to the back and began slugging his bag like a welterweight. Blue Shirt was a good golfer, very long off the tee. We knew this because every time we got up the fairway he'd hit his drive, not into us exactly, but close enough to let us know he was there. And now he was flailing away at his clubs, apparently after missing a putt on the previous hole. Then the other cart returned and the four of them cracked open some more cold ones.

The threesome ahead waved us onto the green. We readily accepted the offer, if only to put some distance between ourselves and the guys behind us. The beer cart was located at a point just behind the twelfth tee box where about five holes converged, meaning that every few minutes you passed the cart and its temptations. I said something about being surprised you could buy beer out on the course and Rob said, "We have rules on New York courses. You're not allowed to bring bazookas."

"On weekdays," Sam added.

I turned the corner playing well, hitting my three-wood long and straight off the tee. I parred the par-five tenth hole, then on the 150-yard par-three eleventh, the threesome ahead waved us on again. I took a swipe with my eight-iron, and the ball landed about three feet from the cup. A shot like that, with people standing on the green having waved you on, was almost too good to be true.

"Where was that shot on the hole-in-one contest?" Rob demanded.

I sunk my birdie putt, then found myself with the same situation two holes later, the threesome ahead waving us on to another 150-yard par-three. Again I stuck the ball on the green, this time about 10 feet from the pin.

I had hit one of those blissful stretches when I felt I could not miss or even get myself seriously in trouble. Funny how when you're playing poorly it always seems to be your turn to hit. Me again? Oh, God. Today I couldn't wait to hit my next ball. I'd felt the same at Cape Arundel in Maine a couple of weeks earlier, only this time it felt less like an aberration, less like a lucky streak. My game *was* improving. One of the great mysteries of golf is why one club can be your best friend while the next one up or down in order relishes every opportunity to destroy your self-confidence.

For a long time I loved my seven-iron but couldn't hit an eight, loved my three-iron but would avoid at all costs hitting a four. Slowly but surely I was broadening my circle of friends in the bag. Now I was developing a peculiar fondness for my eight, looking forward to being 150 yards out. Getting better at golf is not a linear process. There is no steady trimming of strokes like pounds lost on a diet. It happens in fits and starts, with plenty of discouraging lapses that make you want to give up altogether. But it happens.

The last four holes at Van Cortlandt are so far removed geographically from the rest of the course that they don't even fit on the scorecard map. The fifteenth is a 280-yard par-four, another one of those short fours that begs you to go for the green. The green sits at the top of a steep hill and the hole curves to the right with some trees partially blocking the approach.

"Go for it," Rob advised me. "The way you're hitting it."

"The best shot here is an easy iron to the base of the hill," Sam said.

"Bullshit. Go for the green," Rob said. They were the devil and the angel, one on each shoulder.

"If you go for it and only make it halfway up the hill you've got big trouble," Sam said.

"Come on, go for the green."

I opted for the smart golf shot, a five-iron that landed nicely at the base of the hill. Rob shook his head in disgust.

"Tactical golf motherfuckers."

Maybe so, but I got my par. Things were just going my way. On the sixteenth, yet another reachable par-four, downhill with a great yawning cavity for a fairway, I could not resist the temptation. I took out my driver and hit a screaming slice that by all rights should have been lost in the far woods. Instead, it landed in a narrow inlet between two clumps of trees. I hit a good wedge shot over trees to the green and two-putted for another par.

We hadn't seen much of the foursome behind us for several holes. But they roared up as we prepared to hit off the eighteenth.

Their beery exuberance had boiled off into sullenness. Blue Shirt, the long hitter, stared straight ahead. The eighteenth runs down a steep hill to a fairway hidden from the tee box. Rob, Sam and I hit decent drives and made our way to the bottom of the hill. I was getting ready to hit my second shot when I heard a *thunk* about ten yards to my right and saw a ball roll to a stop. Blue Shirt had obviously decided to tee off without bothering to yell "fore." We couldn't see the tee box and they couldn't see us. I hit up to the edge of the green. I looked around to see Sam standing about where Blue Shirt's ball had landed. I saw Sam, but no ball.

"I gave it a little hockey shot," he explained with a mischievous grin. He pointed back to the base of the hill, covered with nasty, foot-long weeds. Blue Shirt would soon come looking for his perfect tee shot. If he was lucky enough to find his ball, he would find it buried in some weed-choked lie from hell.

"That jerk almost hit you," Sam said. "He had no right to do that."

I finished the round with three pars and two bogeys for a 38 on the back side. It was the first time I had broken 40 for nine holes, and came as encouraging evidence that breaking 80 for eighteen might be in reach. My final score was 85. I drove off happy. Here was a round that could have happened only on a public course, and it's one I will remember all my life. Public golf in its purest form, all the good and bad rolled into one—assholes, profanity, sheer, raucous fun. Rob, Sam and I were laughing like old friends, bound in golf friendship. I might not die for those guys, but I'd sure as hell knock Blue Shirt's ball back into the woods for them. We made some "if you're ever in New York, if you're ever in Richmond" promises, and Sam said something about a brother of his in Florida whom I ought to look up. But it was time to move on.

Route 1 cuts only a tiny tip off the far north end of Manhattan, but I couldn't resist a trip into the city. There are no golf courses, public or private, in Manhattan, but that doesn't mean it's impossible to swing a club. The day after my round at Van Cortlandt, I found myself in Manhattan, bound for Chelsea Piers, home of "the nation's most advanced driving range."

I had parked my car at my sister Jennifer and brother-in-law Erik's house outside New York and taken a commuter train into the city. I spent the morning wandering, taking in the city sights, sounds and smells. Around noon I stopped at the Carnegie Deli near Fifty-fifth Street on Seventh Avenue. I announced myself as a single and was led to a tiny corner table, a third the size of a card table, where another man sat eating a roast beef sandwich. If that wasn't bad enough, two sides of the table were pressed up against walls, so we were forced to sit catty-corner, like newlyweds.

We mumbled embarrassed greetings. He looked away and gnawed at his roast beef. Odd how the Single Golfer Rule does not transfer to restaurants or other public places. Had we been standing on the first tee of some golf course, Roast Beef and I would already have shaken hands, begun establishing the first tenuous strands of friendship. I ordered a sandwich and a Coke and read a newspaper while trying not to invade his space. The Carnegie Deli specializes in sandwiches that are so big that it is not possible to eat them. Mine arrived on rye bread with about four inches of corned beef, topped by another slice of rye and about four more inches of turkey, then about twelve slices of cheese.

"What percentage of your customers finish their sandwiches?" I asked my waiter.

"You'd be surprised," he said in a conspiratorial tone, as though sharing some juicy piece of gossip.

I couldn't even get the thing in my mouth. I settled for cutting off little pieces of meat with my knife and eating them with a fork, in the dainty way my grandmother used to eat a grilled-cheese sandwich. The lunch, including tip, set me back $26. When I'd finished, I walked twenty or thirty blocks down Seventh and hailed a cab and instructed the driver to take me to Chelsea Piers. The cab pulled up a few minutes later in a nondescript part of lower Manhattan, around Twenty-third Street and the Hudson River, dominated by warehouses. The Chelsea Piers were built in 1910 as a berthing place for ocean liners. It was here that the *Titanic* was bound in 1912 on her maiden voyage. A few days after she sank off Newfoundland, survivors landed here aboard the *Carpathia*. By the 1960s the transatlantic liner trade was over and the piers closed down.

Thirty years later, Chelsea Piers reopened as a breathtaking tribute to America's fascination with sports, acre after acre of indoor field houses, gymnasiums, ice rinks, health clubs, spas, soccer fields, along with what is billed as the largest indoor rock-climbing wall in the Northeast. When I visited, they were busy building an equestrian center.

The golf range occupies Pier 59, the farthest one down. The entrance is a full-scale country club facade, made to look like Shinnecock Hills, that is, if Shinnecock Hills were wedged up under a bridge like a troll scene at Disney World. Inside the club-house is a fully stocked pro shop, locker room, bar, everything, in short, to make for a complete golf club. Except, of course, a golf course. Which means the range has to rise to the occasion.

This is the only driving range I have ever seen where you reserve tee times, even become a member. For $1,000 per year, you become a "Masters Member," allowing you to book times up to sixty days in advance and qualifying you for discounts at the pro shop and other perks. Five hundred dollars makes you a "Tour Member," allowing you to book a week in advance. A $200 standard membership lets you book two days in advance. Or, if you really want to blow it all out, you can fork over $2,000 for a "Gold Membership," including membership in the other sports centers around the piers. The driving range seems con-sciously tailored to the crowd that favors restaurants with sepa-rate menus for cigars and single-malt scotches. Looking around, I wondered how Chelsea Piers would fare when the trend winds changed, the single-malt crowd found something else to spend its money on and the range was forced to survive on serious golfers who just wanted a bucket of balls and a place to work on their swing. Still, you had to admire the bravado of the place.

The range occupies the full length and width of a 200-yard-long pier, enclosed in nets more than 100 feet high. In a concept borrowed from the Japanese, tee boxes are stacked like high-rise apartments. After waiting in line for several minutes in the clubhouse (this at 3 P.M. on a weekday afternoon), I plunked down $15 for the smallest-size bucket offered—108 balls. Since I didn't have clubs with me, I paid an extra $4—$2 per club—for a driver and a five-iron. I was not actually handed a bucket of balls, but rather a computerized card. Clutching my card and rented clubs I proceeded to some doors at the back of the clubhouse, which opened onto the range. The first level was full, so I went upstairs to the second, and found an open spot. I took a few practice swings, then inserted my card in a slot on the podiumlike machine at my stall. Instructions were in English and Japanese. The machine lit up, informing me that I had 108 balls to hit and asking me at what level, in millimeters, I wanted the balls teed up. The level could be readjusted between shots, and after a few strokes I settled on around forty millimeters for the driver and eight for the irons.

Each time I hit a ball, the rubber tee descended into the floor, retrieved another ball and popped back up. It was a hot afternoon, and after a few minutes I took a cue from the Wall Streeters around me and stripped down to my T-shirt. The pier had been covered with AstroTurf to give it a grassy feel, and here and there were nylon "greens" sticking out of the surface like half-erected tents. The view was about as nice as you'll ever find at a driving range, a broad sweep out to the Hudson and across to New Jersey, yachts and sailboats, seagulls, Circle Line cruise boats, somebody paragliding.

Even as I hit, an attendant taped a notice on my machine saying the stall was reserved at 4:30 for a man named Ray.

Whether I'd gotten my money's worth out of the day was hard to say. By one measure, I was in New York, loving it, visiting the world-famous Carnegie Deli and hitting golf balls out toward the Hudson River with the whole teeming city rising up around me. Looked at another way, all I'd done was grab a sandwich and hit a bucket of range balls, and it had set me back $50.

The next morning I set out for lower Brooklyn and Dyker Beach Golf Course, wedged between Bay Ridge and Benson-hurst, in the shadows of the Verrazano Bridge, at the borough's southern tip. Dyker Beach was a bit off my path, but I'd heard some colorful things about it. Stephen Goldfinger, a physician in the Boston area who'd grown up playing Dyker Beach during the 1950s, told me, "Back then, Dyker Beach was listed in *Ripley's Believe It or Not* as the world's most crowded golf course. I'd get up at 3 A.M. and take two different buses to get there. I'd arrive at the clubhouse at around 4:30, and there would already be a huge line for a tee time. It was strictly first come, first served. Play was so slow that you'd finish a hole and walk to the next tee box and the guys in front of you would be playing pinochle waiting to tee off. There were some decent golfers out there, but there were an awful lot of hackers. I remember one time a guy in the foursome in front of me pulled a putter out of his bag on the tee and used it to swat the ball up the fairway. Finally, on the next hole I asked him what he was doing. He shrugged and said, 'I'm learning golf one club at a time.'"

Then there was the notorious fifteenth hole, where you had to hit your drive down a hill and to the right.

"If you hit into the right rough you were bound to lose your ball. The rough was short and wide open, but for some reason balls kept getting lost. Golfers would come over the hill and the ball just wouldn't be there. There was a blind man who used to take walks up and down the fairway, carrying a large cane. Nobody ever paid any attention to him. Finally, of course, some-one discovered that the blind man wasn't blind at all and the cane was hollow, and that's where all the lost balls were going."

I'd heard other stories about Dyker Beach, less charming ones. During the 1970s and 1980s the golf course deteriorated.

A book called *America's Worst Golf Courses* showed on its cover a picture of a golfer at Dyker Beach hitting a shot around an obstacle never envisioned by the course architect—the burned-out hulk of a car.

The Hutchinson River Parkway took me through the Bronx to the Whitestone Bridge, where I sat in traffic for forty-five minutes with vacationers bound for Long Island. Then I burst into Queens, rushed past the Flushing Tennis Center, home of the U.S. Open, and LaGuardia Airport. I bore left on the Brooklyn-Queens Expressway in a long swoop that took me south and west into the heart of vast Brooklyn. From the elevated Brooklyn-Queens Expressway, you get an appreciation of the sheer size of Brooklyn. If Manhattan's skyline inspires vertical awe, Brooklyn's impressiveness is purely horizontal, an endless patchwork of brick homes marching to the horizon. I felt the same combination of exhilaration and dread that I'd felt years before on a trip in a Land Rover across the Sahara Desert to visit my sister in the Peace Corps. Then, the feeling had been inspired by the absence of humanity and noise; here, it was the precise opposite, inescapable humanity. I descended from the expressway into a rumble of city sights and sounds, blaring horns, graffiti, white people, black people, Hispanics, Asians, Middle Easterners, ethnic markets, junky auto repair shops, flower stores, bars, Spanish restaurants, razor wire, windows with iron gates.

American Golf Corp., the same company that runs Van Cortlandt in the Bronx, took over Dyker Beach in the early nineties. The entrance is a brick building on the sharp corner of Seventh Avenue and Eighty-sixth Street in Bay Ridge. The course is surrounded by neat brick homes packed closely together in a predominantly white section of the city, stubbornly Irish and Italian.

In the spacious clubhouse I met Richard Bowditch, a professional photographer, a friend of a friend whom I'd called in advance, asking if he'd meet me at Dyker Beach for a round. With a wife and two young children, Richard had moved to Brooklyn from Manhattan for more room and for trees and relatively open spaces. He worked out of his home. On the first tee the starter hooked us up with a man named Pat Macri, who managed a Lexus car dealership on Staten Island, and Pat's son, Jonathan, who was fourteen. Pat had grown up in the neighborhood near the course but had moved to Staten Island thirty years ago.

"Staten Island is like another world," he said. "Unbelievable. My wife's family is all from there. I've been there thirty years, and I know my way around better than any of them. But I'm still *you, from Brooklyn.*" Pat had been playing golf about four or five years and had gotten his son interested in the game about the same time. Jonathan was going to be playing in a free, citywide youth tournament at Dyker Beach in a week or two, and Pat wanted his son to get a feel for the course. Together, Pat and Jonathan had played around the public courses of New York, including the three Staten Island public courses, Van Cortlandt and others.

"You should see this course in the springtime, flowers everywhere. It's absolutely beautiful," Pat said of Dyker.

The course was crowded, but we moved fairly steadily along. The principal geographic feature of Dyker Beach is the Verrazano Bridge, which looms like Oz over the course. On the holes bordering Fourteenth Avenue and the Belt Parkway you get a sense of being in the city. From the fifth, a 450-yard par-five, you can look back off to your left from the fairway and see majestic views of the Verrazano. But on the interior holes you'd swear you were in New England countryside. My favorite stretch was the eleventh through thirteenth holes. The eleventh is a shaded, secluded par-three, 187 yards, in the very center of the course, with a small pond off to the right. The twelfth may be the most interesting hole, a short, 338-yard par-four with a serious dogleg to the left. From the tee box you look straight ahead to a bluff of trees and what appears to be a New England church spire. The spire is actually a clock tower of Poly Prep, a well-known Brooklyn private school, but the effect is of having stumbled on a village green in Vermont. The thirteenth is a par-five fringed on the left by tall grass, hundreds of yards of it, taller than any man, at least fifteen feet high, that whispers to you as you walk past.

The pace was slow, but steady. I was astounded to learn when we finished that the round had taken more than six hours. I had played well, shooting an 87. There were rough spots and dry, burned-out grass on fairways and all the usual ragged-edged stuff you expect from busy municipal golf courses. But the greens were in fine shape, especially for a course 300 to 400 golfers track across each day. Fresh flowers grew around the clubhouse, a guy grilled hamburgers and chicken for sale on the patio, a friendly starter sent golfers off in orderly fashion. It made for pleasant golf, and it was good to see an old city course doing so well. But it wasn't quite the Dyker Beach experience one had somehow expected. Richard seemed a little disappointed that I wasn't getting the full scope.

"I could tell you some stories," he assured me. "We got lucky today because we're hooked up with nice guys and the course isn't too packed. You can get just some real . . . assholes out here."

A minute or two after he spoke, three guys teed off on an adjacent hole. One of them, a huge, shapeless mass of flesh kept in check by red baseball pants and a tight red T-shirt, took a round-house swing and the ball sailed off God knows where.

"FUCK!" he screamed. Then the three of them piled onto the same cart and zoomed off in search of their errant shots. The guy in the red pants stood at the back of the cart, straddling the bags and holding on to either side.

Richard looked at me and smiled, and waved toward them with a sweeping gesture, as if to say *"Voilà!"*

Some friends had offered me a bed for the night in their apartment off Flatbush Avenue, in an ethnically mixed neighborhood about halfway between the gentrified brownstones on the East River and depressed Bedford-Stuyvesant. I'd dropped my car off at their place on my way in. On the way back up to their apartment from Dyker Beach by cab, we passed an apartment house on President Street that a day earlier had made international news when police arrested a pair of Palestinians who'd been storing bombs they were allegedly going to use to blow up a Brooklyn subway station.

My driver was a Pakistani Muslim who shook his head as we passed the site.

"It is unfair," he said. "Now, everybody will think Muslims are bad people."

A night earlier, he told me, a pair of drunken bar crawlers had spilled into his car, spotted the Muslim prayer affixed to his dashboard, and chortled, "You're not going to bomb us, are you?"

He shook his head sadly as he recalled the incident. "You can't judge all Muslim people because some are bad."

As we approached the neighborhood where I was staying, he peered out his window at the many black faces on the streets. He turned warily toward me. Was I sure I had the right address? Yes, I said.

"After dark, don't go outside around here," he said. "Too many black people. All they want to do is steal your money."

That night, my friends Logan and Heather and I had dinner at an Italian restaurant under the Brooklyn Bridge. Then we walked up to the promenade where the brownstones of Brooklyn Heights gaze over the East River to the towering lights of Manhattan. The lights painted wet lines across the water. The promenade was crowded with tourists and strollers and lovers. Manhattan was so close it beckoned like a promise. Somewhere back in the night, Dyker Beach rested and healed before the start of another day of public golf in New York.

9

Did You Steal My Ball?

Just over the George Washington Bridge from Manhattan, Route 1 and I-95 diverge. I-95 rolls on to join the New Jersey Turnpike, running past Newark and Elizabeth and then down the length of the state toward the Delaware Memorial Bridge. Route 1 cuts down east of the Turnpike, hugging closer to the Hudson, through an elongated finger of land, like a larger, less well defined Manhattan, through Ridgefield, North Bergen, Union City and Jersey City.

If Manhattan across the river is the glittering deck of an ocean liner, New Jersey, this part of it anyway, is the engine room, its intricate mechanisms splayed open for the public to see. Huge oil cylinders squat amid untold miles of pipe, coiled like intestines, with blue flames dancing here and there like birthday candles. In this part of New Jersey everything seems to be in motion at once—container ships, freight railroads, highways all converge. Jets approaching Newark International Airport seem close enough to touch. At Jersey City, Route 1 becomes the Pulaski Skyway, a long, elevated highway and bridge over the Hackensack River to Newark. Maps of New Jersey had shown a public golf course, Lincoln Park, butting right up against the skyway, a golf course in the shadow of Route 1, so to speak.

Lincoln Park proved to be a pitch-and-putt course across the street from a high-rise housing project. The course sits on a small, featureless parcel of scrub land hemmed in by two busy roads and a muddy spit of the Hackensack River. I found myself there on a hot, humid morning, playing golf with the mayor of Jersey City, Bret Schundler. A couple of other groups played in the distance, but business was slow. A young man in blue jeans with pasty skin and a shock of bright orange hair played through.

Bret is the only mayor of any city whom I can say I know personally, even though we hadn't spoken to one another in more than a decade. We went to college together, lived in the same house. Lately I'd seen profiles of him in the *New York Times* and *Reader's Digest,* describing his transition from Wall Street whiz to against-all-odds white Republican mayor of Jersey City, New Jersey's second-largest city and one of its poorest and most ethnically diverse. I'd remembered him as being politically liberal in college. Somewhere on the way to making a small fortune on Wall Street, he'd taken a turn to the right. Then suddenly he'd left finance for politics and gotten himself elected mayor, not of some cozy Republican stronghold, but of Jersey City, which hadn't had a Republican mayor in seventy-five years. Bret had won by preaching a steady line of education, crime reduction, fiscal responsibility and an end to rampant corruption in city government. His initial victory came in a special election to fill out the term of a mayor jailed for corruption. The local Democratic machine tried to pass that victory off as a fluke, but Bret dug in and won a second election several months later, carrying 68 percent of the vote, the largest margin for a mayoral race in the city's history. He carried 40 percent of the black vote and 60 percent of the Hispanic vote. By the time of my trip, he'd been reelected to a second full term. Now, national Republicans had marked him as a rising star.

When I saw Lincoln Park on the map, I called Bret's office to see if he'd play a round with me. I knew he'd remember me but was uncertain how he'd react—what effect a dozen years and his budding national celebrity would have on the tenuous ties of college friendship. His assistants on the telephone seemed terminally busy in that Greater New York way. "Mayor Schundler's office . . . You say you're an old friend of his? Hold on . . . . I'm sorry, Mayor Schundler is tied up in a meeting right now." I left my number.

A few minutes later, my phone rang.

"This is Mayor Schundler's office. I have the mayor on the line."

Bret and I exchanged pleasantries for a moment or two. His voice came at me canned from his speaker phone. Then he asked me what I was up to and when I planned to be in Jersey City. His next question was, "Do you have a place to stay?"

He asked me to meet him the next Friday night at Liberty State Park on the Hudson River. I arrived on a clear, soft summer evening. From Liberty State Park you can catch a ferry to the Statue of Liberty or Ellis Island. The story of Jersey City has always been an immigrant's story. Only now the newcomers are Asian and Hispanic rather than German and Irish. The park has a youth baseball complex, and on this night, the city was kicking off a baseball tournament for the Sandy Koufax league, drawing teams of teenagers from California, Tennessee and Puerto Rico. I arrived early and wandered around the complex. Jersey City's reputation had long run toward poverty, hopelessness and crime. But the scene that greeted me at the ball field was wonderfully hopeful and wholesome. Groups of black, white, Asian and Hispanic kids wandered about, helping set up stands and concessions. They sold programs to the evening's festivities. A girl sold Italian ices from a cart; not the rock-hard, prefrozen cannonballs you get at the grocery store but freshly made and scooped from ice-cream drums in lemon-lime, rainbow, vanilla, chocolate or raspberry, $1 for a large scoop. I bought myself a vanilla and climbed the bleachers. A tape of native son Bruce Springsteen filled the air with "My Hometown." I sat licking my Italian ice, watching the last rays of sun splash off the towers of banks and brokerage firms of lower Manhattan, just across the river. The sky behind the World Trade Center was pink. Between two stands of trees you could make out the Statue of Liberty with her arm raised toward the heavens.

The mayor arrived with his entourage. I recognized him immediately, a bit older, a bit thicker around the middle but unmistakable. A buzz followed his every move. He spotted me in the stands and waved me down.

Bret coached our house tackle football team in college. House football was a sort of loosely organized extracurricular sport for which they handed out full sets of pads and basically let a bunch of former high-school players go at each other; I can still see him presiding over our ragtag practices, a stoic grin on his face as he tried to pull order from chaos. Even then he was driven to lead. He'd laugh and joke with the guys, but he always seemed some-what aloof from the revelry, as if partaking and analyzing at the same time, as if his moral center, controlled by some internal cen-trifugal force, never allowed him to get too out of control. He'd talked then about becoming a minister. It didn't surprise me at all that he'd become a crusading politician.

"I didn't like him at first," one tough-looking, tough-talking, lifelong Jersey City resident said as we stood on the baseball dia-mond at Liberty State Park. "I said, he's got to be lying because nobody's this sincere. But he is. One of the first things he did was get new, clean uniforms for all the kids playing baseball. He said, you wear a new uniform you start to feel good about yourself. Jersey City is a tough town politically. They'll eat you up. But the mayor's doing all right."

It was nearly midnight when the opening ceremonies, includ-ing a softball game and a pizza party afterward in a crowded little parks-and-recreation building, finally disbanded. Bret had spent the evening shaking hands, schmoozing. In the parking lot, he said something to a man in a brown suit with slicked-back hair who had been hanging around Bret all evening. The man nodded, got into his car, and drove off.

"Who is that guy?" I asked.

"Security," Bret said simply. "Most people would never bother you. But you never know when some lunatic . . ."

We eased out of the Cochrane Stadium parking lot and onto the nearly deserted streets of Jersey City. We wound through the downtown, stopped at a plaza overlooking the Hudson, and walked out to the edge of the river. Here was the same view of Manhattan, in reverse, that I had just recently seen from Brooklyn. It's a toss-up which side has the better view, but you couldn't help but see why from either side New York is the source of incalculable dreams.

We left Jersey City and drove over to neighboring Hoboken. We turned on to a boulevard of bars and trendy restaurants, still lively at this hour, with sculpted neon signs and ferns in the windows. Young professionals, many of whom commuted into New York each weekday morning, roamed the streets. The buildings looked freshly scrubbed, and the street reminded me of Georgetown in Washington, or Newbury Street in Boston.

"They brought themselves back essentially by displacing the poor," Bret said. "We weren't going to do that in Jersey City. It's the most ethnically diverse city in the country." Bret's own grandparents, German immigrants by way of the Caribbean, had landed in Jersey City, before moving out to greener acres in Westfield. We made our way back to the 130-year-old, three-story brownstone house Bret shares with his wife and daughter, who were away visiting relatives. We sat out back on a small patio and garden, talking and reminiscing. I asked him how far he planned to go with politics, whether he had designs on the governorship, the senate, the presidency. He demurred, already versed in the automatic, tactful evasions of the skilled politician.

The next morning Bret had set aside time for a round with me at Lincoln Park, between meetings at City Hall and an afternoon commitment to speak to a local school group. I followed him and his driver/bodyguard, in their Chevrolet sedan, out to Lincoln Park. Bret had retrieved some old, dust-covered, mismatched clubs from his basement, real-wood woods and old bladed irons that looked like they'd last seen action during the Eisenhower administration. Somewhat incongruously, he also had a brand-new golf glove from the Old Course at St. Andrews and a ball with that fabled course's insignia, from a trip he'd taken there a few years earlier.

I remarked on his woods.

"They're not making them from wood anymore?" he said innocently.

"No, they've already gone through steel and now they're into titanium," I said.

He shrugged.

Lincoln Park is basically a pitch-and-putt course, with each hole around eighty yards. Some men at the driving range recognized Bret as we walked from the clubhouse to the first tee. "Congratulations," one of them said. "I voted for you." Bret gestured to the nearby housing project. During his campaign, Bret told me, he'd gone door to door through that project, winning over skeptical voters. He carried the project.

The tee boxes were patches of AstroTurf and the course was flat. You had to look carefully at your scorecard to make sure you were hitting at the correct hole. As it turned out, we misjudged anyway and played our tee shots out to the second green, then had to make our way back to the first. Bret hadn't played golf in a while. On one shot he caught the ball well with a seven-iron, way too much club for this dinky course. The ball sailed straight and landed about 100 yards past our own hole, up against a fence. It passed under the nose of a man playing a different hole. As Bret jogged over sheepishly to retrieve his ball the man, apparently not recognizing him as the mayor, mocked his long shot. "What, Wheaties this morning?"

I'd brought my whole set of clubs out of the trunk and now felt ridiculous lugging the bag around when all I needed was the sand wedge and a putter. Bret had taken off his suit jacket but had on his suit pants, loafers, blue dress shirt, and a gold-patterned tie tucked in between two front shirt buttons. We must have made an odd-looking pair. After a while, we didn't even keep score. There didn't seem to be much point. Mainly, Bret told me about the changes under way for Jersey City, plans for the future. His voice full of excitement, he described a plan to build an eighteen-hole golf course, fine enough to attract tournaments but always open to the public. The course would be built at Caven Point, an area just off Liberty State Park. Bret hoped Tom Kite would design it. We sank our putts on the final hole and walked over to the parking lot, where Bret's driver waited patiently to whisk him off to his speech at the school. As I drove away I carried a poignant image of my friend, the eternal believer, standing on that dilapidated patch of scrub grass, speaking with such conviction and hope about Jersey City. A traveler cruising along the Pulaski Skyway might look down on this city and involuntarily shudder at the rusting industrial yards and dank buildings, then check his gas gauge, just to make sure he wasn't going to run out around here. But Bret looked around and saw only possibility. I thought suddenly of George Lyons, the old pro who had driven me around Franklin Park in Boston on his golf cart. It occurred to me now that this Route 1 journey was not, as I had foreseen, an exercise in nostalgia, down a road whose time had come and gone. Everywhere I went there were signs of renewal, rebirth, signs of America reinventing itself.

"Anybody tells you that black people don't golf, tell them to go to Weequahic."

That's what Pat Macri, the Staten Island car dealer whom I'd played with in Brooklyn, told me when I mentioned Weequahic Park in Newark. He called it a gem of a course, tight and hilly, with fine, old trees. He was one of the few people I'd spoken with who had even heard of Weequahic. It wasn't listed in the *Golf Digest* guide, and when I mentioned it in passing a few days earlier to the editor of a different golf travel magazine in New York, I'd gotten only a glassy-eyed stare. And yet, there it was, on my road map of New Jersey, nestled in the shadows of Newark International Airport, just off Route 1, and listed as a public course.

Just beyond the airport I got off at Haynes Avenue and followed Haynes over a short bridge. This led me into a residential neighborhood fronted by what appeared to be a large park. I curved around the park for about a quarter mile until I came to an entrance marked Weequahic Park, with signs for the golf course. The park road led around a small lake to the clubhouse.

It was a few minutes after noon. I paid $22 to walk, but it would have been $11 with an Essex County resident card. The starter, a young man sitting on a cart next to the first tee, told me I could hit right off.

"There's a guy who teed off just a few minutes ago. You should catch him with no problem."

As often is the case with these courses deep in urban America, Weequahic (pronounced Wee-QUAY-ic) is surprising in its abundance of greenery. I played alone for the first three holes but on the fourth tee caught up with the man in front of me.

"I'm just learning the game," he warned me. "Here, put your bag on my cart." Richard was forty-eight years old, divorced and lived in East Orange, just north of Newark. He had a teenage son living in Maryland. Richard was an attorney for an insurance company but was about to leave that job for . . . he wasn't sure yet. He was also an ordained minister.

Richard Johnson had spent the first few years of his life right here in Weequahic Park. During World War II the park had housed barracks for soldiers, and after the war the government had converted them to apartments for veterans and their families.

"We lived right over there by the lake," he said, pointing. "I remember there was also a horse-racing park here, right over there in that field, the area next to the road you drove in on. The golf course was there then too." But Richard Johnson had not golfed until just a few months before today. He'd served in the Marines, then attended Virginia Union University, a mostly black college in Richmond. After that he'd gone to divinity school, and also the University of Pittsburgh and finally had returned to New Jersey and his job as an insurance lawyer.

"I had a friend who kept bugging me to golf. 'Come on, try it!' he said. But I didn't see the attraction. Then one day I said okay and came out. That was it. I'm planning to take some lessons and really work on my game. I've been practicing my short game. My goal is to be a scratch golfer within two years."

"Think you can do that?" I asked.

"No. But that's my goal."

On the fourth hole, the first we played together, Richard hit one of the strangest shots I had ever seen. He'd stuck his first shot off into the right rough behind some low trees and shrubs. His second shot, an iron, sailed about thirty yards and smacked into one of the low scrub pines. Two balls, not one, shot out of the tree.

"Patent that shot and you'll never have to buy another ball," I said.

Weequahic is a hilly course lined, like most of these old city courses I'd been playing, with monstrous, mature oaks and pines. Holes five and six, a short par-three followed by a 477-yard par-four, run along the outer edges of the course. The fifth borders the park where Richard said the horse track once was. As we teed off, we could see lines of cars parked with people sitting on them or next to them, sunning themselves. A man was stomping the chain-link fence separating the field from the course, as if trying to put a hole in it. The sixth hole runs along a city street. As we teed off, we could see and hear some sort of drama unfolding. We hit our drives to the screech of sirens and the peal of tires from police cars that descended on the street from four or five directions at once. The commotion brought out the neighbors, and soon the street was filled with people, many of them small children, laughing and gawking. Just as suddenly as they had arrived, the police disappeared, and we never did learn what had caused the commotion.

Richard Johnson, a soft-spoken, serious, thoughtful man, seemed intensely devoted to learning this game. With his athletic build, it was only a matter of time before his swing became fluid. But you felt for him when he hit a poor shot, because he seemed to throw all his concentration into each stroke and was disappointed when it didn't go as planned. He was almost painfully aware of the courtesies of the game. We congratulated each other when we hit well, commiserated on our bad shots. Within two or three holes we were no longer strangers but friends. We'd fallen into that limited but warm camaraderie, the public golf friendship. As we sank our putts on the seventh green, a large man with a menacing scowl, playing an adjacent hole, approached us.

"You pick up a Maxfli with writing on it?" Not, did you see a Maxfli with writing on it, as most golfers would say, but, did you *pick up* a Maxfli with writing on it. The subtle shift in wording, instead of requesting help finding a lost ball, implied an accusation and, given the man's demeanor, a threat.

"No, sorry," I said.

"Haven't seen it," Richard said.

The man stared at us for a moment, then shook his head slowly and sauntered off. Richard and I looked at each other.

We had just teed off on the eighth when the man appeared again.

"I *asked* you if you picked up a *Maxfli* with *writing* on it," he said slowly.

Richard said just as slowly and evenly, "And we *said* no."

The standoff lasted a couple of seconds. Then the man turned away again, and walked off. Richard shook his head. "Some people are such jerks."

Holes twelve and fourteen at Weequahic form a V. For both holes you hit off tee boxes that are attached like Siamese twins, shooting off at different angles. The thirteenth hole runs in the opposite direction, straight into the crux of the V. The result is that approaching the thirteenth green you have to worry about slices from the twelfth tee and hooks from the fourteenth. And then, to get from the thirteenth green to the fourteenth tee box, you must pass a sort of gauntlet between the two holes, protected by a narrow corridor of chain-link fence.

Although Richard had played Weequahic several times before, the arrangement was still somewhat confusing, and my own abortive attempts at directing didn't help. A group of golfers in front of us watched with amusement as we circled the tee boxes for the twelfth and fourteenth, trying to figure out where, precisely, we were supposed to hit.

Finally, one of them cackled, "What are youse guys, *lost?*"

"Oh no," we lied.

We made our way down the twelfth and up the thirteenth without incident, and came to the fourteenth tee box. You couldn't hit from the fourteenth if there were golfers hitting from the twelfth, and vice versa, so we waited while a group of golfers, three black and one white, hit off the twelfth. The black men were older, slightly past middle age, but they marched up to the tee box casually, comfortably, laughing and teasing each other. One after another they lined up their tee shots, swung easily, and smacked the ball a mile. They looked as though they were born playing Weequahic.

"Man, those guys can hit the ball," Richard said as they headed up their fairway. Then he added, "You've got to be careful out here. There's some good players. They'll get you going on a bet. They start off playing bad for a few holes, then they want to double the bet. And all of a sudden you see how they really play."

At the end of the round Richard and I cooled off with a drink in the modest clubhouse and made plans to play a round in Richmond sometime. He'd spent so much time there he considered it a second home, he said. I followed Richard back out to Route 1 and we saluted each other. Within a few minutes, though, I took a wrong turn and spent forty-five minutes tooling around Elizabeth, New Jersey, searching for a way back to the highway. Anybody who thinks America is not a melting pot needs to drive around Elizabeth for an hour or so. I passed the Express Driving Academy. A sign offered written driving tests in English, German, Portuguese, Spanish, French, Italian, Korean and Chinese.

10

O Youth!

I am not one of those who believe in the decline of American youth. However if I *were* inclined to such beliefs, I would produce as Exhibit "A" the two teenagers I hooked up with in Princeton, New Jersey.

This was the Princeton Country Club on a Monday morning. From the name of the course, I had half expected to find the ghost of F. Scott Fitzgerald haunting the veranda in a soiled dinner jacket. But the Princeton Country Club, just a block off Route 1, several miles from the university, has no pretensions whatsoever. Built as a private course during the 1950s as part of a middle-income housing development, it was taken over a few years later by Mercer County, which has operated it ever since as a municipal course. The clubhouse is a large, yellowish building of indistinct architecture, and the course—short, ragged around the edges and very crowded—provides good, basic golf.

I made a halfhearted attempt to golf there on a Sunday morning, but when I arrived about six foursomes were stacked up waiting to tee off. As one group grabbed their bags and started up the first fairway, a fat guy smoking a pipe called out, "Have a nice seven-hour round!" I returned to my hotel to write and to organize my ever-growing and ever-more-disorganized stack of notes, brochures and scorecards.

Monday morning was better, but not much. A starter at the first tee barked out names from a waiting list. When I heard mine, I hurried over from the practice green and introduced myself to Jeff and Dan, the teenagers, and to Bob, like me, a single golfer.

Bob and I walked. Jeff and Dan shared a cart. It was Jeff's first time golfing. But Dan had golfed before, or so he said.

The round started pleasantly enough, though Jeff predictably had trouble even making contact with the ball and Dan, despite his claims of experience, wasn't much better. But after a couple of holes Bob and I wanted to stomp them. It wasn't their poor play. After all, it's no shame to stink at golf, and only a jerk with a short memory gets mad playing with beginners. What infuriated us was their absolute lack of curiosity about the game, their willful indifference to its courtesies. It wasn't that they couldn't do it right; they didn't give a damn.

"So, what brought you guys out here?" I asked finally.

Dan said nothing.

Jeff said, "Dunno. You know? Seems interesting, I guess."

Our foursome soon dissolved into two twosomes playing the same holes, as the laconic teens wheeled off into their own world and Bob and I walked the fairways together. Bob was a good golfer, thirty-one years old. He was the fourth generation to run his family's importing company.

"It must be great keeping a family tradition going," I said.

Bob laughed. "You ever work for your father?"

Bob had been married for about four years and had a six-month-old son at home. Between work and family he tried to get in a round of golf whenever he could.

"How does your wife feel about your golfing?" I asked. As if I had a right to ask anybody that question.

"She's cool about it," he said. Then he added, "'Course, what she doesn't know won't hurt her." It turned out that I was bearing witness to Bob's wife-proof, clandestine golfing system. The system was based on a portable phone and a tube of sunblock, forty factor. The phone, which he kept in his bag, was for handling any unexpected calls from business or home. Since his business required him to be on the road throughout much of the day, there was nothing suspicious in being reachable only on the portable phone. The sunblock, meanwhile, prevented even a hint of a tan from darkening his features and blowing his cover. Devious, perhaps, but it helped Bob maintain a ten handicap.

"Still, I don't get out here as often as I'd like," he said.

We finished the front nine, both playing pretty well. Bob knew the course and was a good guide to its turns. We struggled for the first few holes but settled down, ending the nine with a 42 for Bob and a 44 for me. Bob begged off before the back nine, citing his one o'clock appointment. As luck would have it, Jeff and Dan were free to continue. I thought at first they were quitting. They slipped off without a word toward the clubhouse from the ninth green. I double-timed it to the tenth tee, hit my drive, and practically ran up the fairway. When I reached the green, I looked back and saw a cart heading my way.

"I thought you guys left," I said when the cart jerked to a stop next to me.

"Got something to eat," Jeff mumbled.

Slow foursomes were stacked up ahead like 737s at LaGuardia. There was nothing to do but continue on together. Little things started to annoy me. Jeff and Dan kept using the same putter, forgetting to bring two to the green. At the tee box, Jeff, honors be damned, kept jumping up and hitting first, then leaving his tee sticking out of the tee box.

I picked it up three or four holes running, then said, through clenched teeth, "Take your tee next time."

On the next hole, a foursome of old guys was clearing off the tee box when we arrived. They were slowing us up a bit, losing steam. The oldest was about seventy-five years old. He wore khakis, a plain white T-shirt and the sort of wide-billed cap that

Ernest Hemingway wore when fishing for marlin aboard the *Pilar*. I'd seen him strike good, clean shots all afternoon. This time he hit a weak shot, grabbed his pull cart and started slowly up the fairway.

"Are you losing it?" his friend asked him.

"A little," he said, then added gamely, "I'm all right."

I watched the old trooper walk away. I turned and saw Jeff and Dan reclining with their feet kicked up on the crossbar of the cart.

"Let me ask you something," I said. "What made you guys decide to rent a cart on a beautiful day like today?"

"A cart is so much easier," Jeff said.

"Doesn't it make you feel guilty at all to see an old guy like that walking? Look around. Everybody else on the course is walking. Here you are, seventeen years old, riding a cart."

"I'm not seventeen years old," Dan deadpanned. "I'm sixteen. That gives me a year. I'll feel guilty when I'm seventeen."

Jeff snickered.

Oh, God, I thought. For in that moment I saw myself as Jeff and Dan must have seen me. A sour old man—Christ, he must be thirty-five, if not older—one of these serious dudes with a house and a yard and some awful job and tax forms to fill out and a medicine cabinet full of weird ointment, who probably hasn't smoked a joint in a hundred years, and now he's getting himself all worked up over some stupid game. Then I thought, What have I done? I have lectured teenagers on the virtues of sunshine and exercise. And here on this trip of mine, this—what?—elaborate protest against the approach of middle age? The casual sneers of Jeff and Dan had blown my pretense wide open. They looked at me now with detached curiosity, as if I was a specimen from Planet Lame-o. For surely now I was *one of those people,* part of that other, grown-up world that bored kids to death with the importance of fresh air and staying in school and eating your vegetables and stuff. Standing before these young jokers I felt a pang of regret and longing for something indefinable that was gone forever.

About this time I realized I was having a decent round. On the fifteenth hole, a 290-yard par-four, I missed driving the green by about twenty yards. On the next hole, a 150-yard par-three, I sailed an eight-iron to within five inches of the cup. It was not a good shot, it was a perfect shot. It hung in the air for a day, arcing like a Greg Louganis swan dive, then dropped lightly to the green and bounced to the pin as if commanded by some scientific law. And all I could think of was that I had wasted a perfect shot—maybe the best of my life—on Jeff and Dan. I thought suddenly of the people I would have liked to have shared that moment with. My dad. My father-in-law. My brothers-in-law. It would have been fine even to be serenely alone. I could feel Jeff and Dan behind me, slouched on their cart, gazing indifferently, not saying a word.

On the seventeenth fairway, a par-five, Dan was 180 yards from the pin, lying fourteen. Bored from missing shot after shot, he suddenly took a two-step hop toward the ball with a round-house swing like a jai alai player. It was a spectacular shot. The ball sailed straight toward the green, bounced just short, rolled across it to the back fringe. Unfortunately, this all happened as the foursome ahead of us was putting.

"Oh, wow, man," Dan said happily.

"Wow," said Jeff. "Great shot."

The guys on the green turned around and stared at us.

Having already established myself as the disapproving old pain in the ass, I saw no reason to stop now.

"What you need to do," I said, "is get in your cart and drive up there, and apologize to those guys."

Ignoring my suggestion, Dan said, "You mean I hit it all the way to the green? Cool."

"How'd you hit that," Jeff asked. "Two steps or three?"

"Two," Dan explained.

Jeff tried to repeat Dan's magic, with two hops and a round-house, but his ball took off sideways for some trees.

I parred the seventeenth, bogeyed the eighteenth and finished the round with an 87. By the time we finished, Jeff, Dan and I settled into a sort of cold war. They rolled off in their cart without a word. I packed my bag into my trunk, grabbed a bottle of water from my cooler, changed my shoes. A score that would have left me ecstatic a few weeks earlier barely moved me. I was ready for the next course, ready to move on.

The next morning was clear and bright. I stopped at a course a few miles south of Princeton, in Trenton, the capital. It was a pleasant-looking course but there was already a major backup at the first tee, with a tournament about to start, so I got back on the road. Soon I crossed the Delaware River and saw off to the right Trenton's oddly pugnacious motto affixed in large letters to a railroad bridge: "Trenton Makes, the World Takes." Once over the river I was in Pennsylvania, a half hour north of Philadelphia. Unlike in some cities, Route 1 remains a distinct and important thoroughfare through Philadelphia, blessedly easy to follow. It turns into Roosevelt Boulevard through north Philadelphia, leading past miles of aging industry and vast brick middle-class neighborhoods. I plunged into the city with the late commuting stragglers. Just before reaching downtown, the road skirts to the west, crossing the Schuylkill River. Here Route 1 becomes City Line Avenue, and in a few minutes I saw, to my left, the seventh fairway of Cobb's Creek Golf Club.

One of the joys of this journey was discovering grand old turn-of-the-century courses in the hearts of major cities, courses that somehow have survived the decades and the odds. Though somewhat dog-eared, they retain the charm of an earlier era, with enormous trees, unhurried layouts, and gimmick-free honesty. Cobb's Creek, which has been a municipal course for all its eighty-odd years, sits in a gritty, working-class neighborhood on Philadelphia's West Side. It was designed by Hugh Wilson, who four years earlier had designed the famed East Course at Merion, just three miles away amid the old money of suburban Delaware County. Merion has hosted four U.S. Opens, most recently in 1981, and is a solid A-list entry among the nation's most hallowed and exclusive private courses. With this blood-line connection to fame and fortune, Cobb's Creek rolls along as the poor relation; threadbare, needy, bitter and proud. While Merion's pristine fairways whisper memories of Hogan, Palmer and Nicklaus, it is Cobb's Creek's fate to open its arms to everybody else: good golfers and bad, young, old, divot takers, club throwers, oath hurlers, untold thousands of Philadelphia's best and worst, not to mention odd, lost, wandering hackers such as me.

I've often thought that, once a year, touring pros should play a tournament on a well-worn municipal course. No effort would be made to spruce the course up before they arrived. In my tournament, called the Greater Heartbreak Open, golfers would have to meet not the invented challenges of some famous course architect—lightning greens, bottleneck fairways and so forth—but the incidental challenges that face golfers every day on the public links. At the Greater Heartbreak Open, Fred Couples would hit a perfect drive only to find his ball resting in the middle of the fairway on a slab of dried mud. Nick Faldo would knock an eight-iron into a greenside bunker only to discover, instead of that uniform sugar bowl of fluffy sand, an ever-changing landscape: packed hard one day, heavy and wet the next. Greg Norman would have to overcome his frustration as he tried to jam his tee into a grassless tee box. Players would be prevented from repairing their ball marks on the greens, and spectators, under penalty of eviction from the tournament, would be discouraged from locating lost balls. The pros might hate it, but it would be fun to watch.

I parked my car and walked through a clubhouse jammed with youngsters watching a video on golf course etiquette. The kids were part of a city-run instruction program. As a testament to the influence of Tiger Woods, whose twelve-stroke Masters victory was still just a couple of months old, most of the eager young faces were black.

I paid my greens fee in the clubhouse and walked across Lansdowne Avenue to the first tee. There was no starter, so I introduced myself to the only other walker I spotted, a man dragging a pull cart, and asked if he'd like to hook up. He introduced himself as Frank Marcellino, eighty-one years old. Two elderly Korean men, who spent much of the round speaking to each other in their native tongue, completed our foursome.

The first four holes at Cobb's Creek are tight, short and curious—two short par-fours and two par-threes that snake around the eponymous creek. Locals call these the "finesse holes." They are fine holes but seem a poor introduction to the course. It's disconcerting to be greeted with tight placement holes right from the start. They trick you into believing you are in for a short, shady round of target golf when in fact Cobb's Creek is a long, backbreaking walk in the sun.

As Frank Marcellino, my new partner, explained, Hugh Wilson never intended these as the opening holes. Under the original design they were holes three through six. The original first and second were two straightforward holes on the same side of the street as the clubhouse.

"Course managers didn't like players finishing up on the other side of the road from the clubhouse. So they converted the first and second holes to seventeen and eighteen," he said.

It's a testament to Wilson's wonderful design that I could sense on this, my first round at Cobb's Creek, that something was amiss. The original finishing hole was a dramatic par-four that dropped down a steep hill before kicking left. That hole is now the sixteenth, so the comparatively mundane seventeenth and eighteenth play almost as an afterthought. Under its current layout Cobb's Creek is like a great old movie colorized and edited for television.

Frank, a native of Philadelphia, had golfed Cobb's Creek for nearly forty years.

"I've shot two holes-in-one in my life," he said as we approached the par-three second hole. "They were both on this hole, one hundred fifty-nine yards. The first one was in 1971, I used a seven-iron. The next time was eighteen years later, in 1989. I needed a five. It shows you how much I lost. I used to be a twelve handicap, but a good twelve handicap, you know? Lots of rounds in the seventies. I was nice and loose. Now, I can't seem to follow through all the way. Sometimes I can, sometimes I can't. It's age. There's nothing I can do about it."

As we waited for the group in front of us to clear off the green, eight or ten youngsters from the neighborhood ambled past us along the cart path. The youngest was probably four years old; the oldest couldn't have been more than eight. We told them to watch out for flying golf balls, but they barely acknowledged us. By the time we were ready to tee off, the kids had congregated by the creek near the green. I hit a high eight-iron that landed on the fringe, just short and to the left of the green. We watched in stunned silence as one of the older boys, a cigarette dangling from his mouth, walked casually to the edge of the green, picked up my ball, and started walking away. The twosome behind us, who had by now pulled up and were waiting in their cart, were the first to cry out.

"Hey, get away from that ball!" they screamed. Suddenly, every golfer within eyesight of the green started screaming. This was a crime not just against me, but against all golfers. The boy holding my ball sauntered a few more steps, just to show us how unimpressed he was by our rage, then tossed my ball over his shoulder, back toward the green, without looking to see where it landed. As the youngsters wandered off, we looked at each other incredulously. A course employee passed by on a cart. We flagged him down and explained what had happened. He gave a sympathetic shrug.

"They're out here all the time," he said. "No way to keep 'em off." Then he zoomed away. When we arrived on the green my anger was mitigated by the fact that the young vandal had improved my lie.

The third hole uses a bend in the creek in an ingenious way. You have to hit left over the creek with your tee shot, then right over the same creek to reach the green. I bogeyed that one and parred the fourth, feeling pretty good about my chances for a nice round. It seemed to me that Cobb's Creek, legendary designer or no, was a pretty tame little course. Then I triple-bogeyed a long but straightforward par-three and double-bogeyed the next two holes, and my troubles began in earnest.

The par-four ninth is the only truly bad hole on the course, and once again this is not the fault of the designer. Under pressure from the neighbors, Frank said, the course had relocated the tee box in order to make it impossible for an errant shot to fly into the backyards of some row houses running along the left side of the fairway. Unfortunately, under the current configuration, the better your tee shot, the more chance you had of catching the trees along the right.

"This used to be a beautiful driving hole," Frank said wistfully.

By now I had logged a depressing stretch of 6s and 7s that shattered my hopes for a sub-90 round and left me hoping I could break 100. The holes in the midsection of the course ran up and down long hills, switching back on one another, accordion style. On the twelfth hole, a monster par-five of better than 600 yards, seven or eight golfers from other foursomes milled about our fairway, looking for lost balls.

But Cobb's Creek has an undeniable majesty, and Frank was the sort of playing partner you hope for but too seldom find. He knew the course better than a Scottish caddy knows his and generously shared his knowledge.

"Now, this hole has a terrible down slope if you hit left, so try to keep it right if you can," he would say. "The best shot you can hit is one that goes toward those two big trees. There are bunkers on both sides of the green but you can't see the one on the right until you get up on it."

My swing had deteriorated to the point that any shot that landed near the fairway constituted a moral victory. Still, Frank's gentle insistence on relaying the minute strategy of each hole kept me in the game and made me feel like a player. Even when I was at my worst, halfway through the round, he bolstered me with undeserved but cheering compliments. "The way you hit the ball you shouldn't have any trouble clearing that valley," he'd say. "Strong as you are, you won't need more than an eight-iron."

A retired mechanical engineer, Frank would have made a wonderful teacher, or an even better father. He had been married for fifty-six years, he told me. Although he and his wife had no children, they had plenty of nieces, nephews and godchildren to dote on. Though quick to point out Cobb's Creek's flaws, the grassless tee boxes, baked fairways and the rest, he was immensely proud of his home course and more than a little disdainful of his friends who played private clubs.

"I have a couple of friends who golf at Llanerch," he said, referring to a private club a couple of miles west of Cobb's Creek on Route 1. "I used to golf with them sometimes when they'd invite me over to their club. One day they couldn't play over there for some reason. I said, 'Hey, why don't you come over to Cobb's Creek.' Well, these guys usually shot anywhere from ninety-one to ninety-eight on their home course, never higher, never lower. They figured they'd come over to the *public* course and shoot about eighty. Neither one of 'em broke one ten."

After my dreadful mid-round stretch, I settled down and finished fairly strong, with bogeys and pars on the last five holes, for a 98. The middle stretch had killed me. Combining the first four holes with the last five would have given me a 39 for nine holes. Such are the mathematical gyrations we'll undertake in the service of self-delusion.

I shook hands with the Korean men, then stood and talked with Frank for a while in the parking lot. He told me to give him a call the next time I passed that way.

He said, "You always have a golf partner in Philadelphia."

A 700-mile Road Check: When I first set out on my trip I felt something I can only describe as *otherness*, as if I were sitting on the hood of the car looking in at myself and saying, with a mixture of glee and guilt, How did he manage to pull this one off? And how the hell is he going to justify it? An endless strip of tar and nothing but golf and cheeseburgers lay before me then. By now, the newness of the road had worn off. I had hardened into a Route 1 soldier. The golf never got old, but finding a room and a place to eat could. My body had begun to adapt itself to this new life. The skin on my right thumb, where the thumb meets the grip, had split painfully and then healed over with a roughness suited to everyday golf. Calluses developed on the palms of both hands, just below the pinkies. First thing each morning, a dull ache in the muscle behind my left shoulder, the one stretched tight by a thousand backswings, greeted me like a friend. My equipment looked as though it was years, not weeks, old. Screws had popped loose on my cheap golf bag. Now, when I tried to use the automatic stand, sometimes the bag stayed upright, other times it groaned and sagged to the ground with its legs splayed out in front, like a fat, old hound dog. Slathering myself in sunscreen had become a sort of daily ritual, a thirty-factor baptism. Now, everything I owned had the faint, unctuous aroma of coconuts. For my whole life the smell of sunscreen had made me think of the sea. No more. Now the smell reminds me of golf.

All adults living with spouses and children entertain at least benign fantasies of escape—the sort of fantasies that get you through another lawn-mowing exercise, another greasy pan in the sink, another crying child at 2 A.M. Here I was living that fantasy, and yet so many thoughts called me home. I envisioned my yard and saw not the weeds but the white picket fence and the trellis covered with roses. I could not imagine my daughter misbehaving, I could think only of our nightly bedtime stories and how she looked dressed up for school. I could not imagine ever having argued with Barbara, could not recall any of the frustrations that even happily married people endure. Instead I envisioned only tender moments. I saw her at home, carrying our second child. I found myself playing back images in my mind of how we met, our early dates, our wedding. At night, trying to fall asleep in another strange bed, I longed to hold her in my arms. I've heard guys say that golf is better than sex. It's safe to say those guys never took a road trip like mine. After a few weeks on the road you can become sexually stirred by a shapely plant. Motels, aware of the commercial potential of Road Loneliness, try to lure you with in-room screenings of soft-porn movies, for eight or nine dollars. They tease you with three minutes of sweaty "previews" before the picture dissolves into squeals and squiggly lines. It was weeks before I worked up the nerve to actually watch one of these movies. Despite the pledges of discretion on the order form, I could not get over an image of some smirking desk attendant handing me my room bill the next morning: Room: $69; Long Distance Phone: $7; Breakfast, $8; *Naughty Nubile Nurses*, $8.95. Finally, somewhere in Georgia, a hotel included a video of my choice with the room fee. I watched a few minutes of two people bumping pelvises and pretending to like it when I realized what I should have known all along—the suggestiveness of the squiggly lines was more erotic than the unscrambled picture. As for the other temptations of the road, it would have been too easy to fall into a pattern of whiling away the nights with a few brews. Much as I love the stuff, I needed my nights for organizing and sleeping, and I needed my mornings, unclouded, for golf. Early on I set a maximum of two beers with dinner to slake a golf thirst, and I maintained that more or less faithfully throughout the journey.

11

No Fear

As I passed through the suburbs south of Philadelphia, I came across the headquarters of the Franklin Mint, the outfit that advertises in *Parade* magazine for replicas of famous cars and dinner plates with pictures of nativity scenes or Elvis. I saw a sign for the Franklin Mint Museum. Curiosity forced me to pull over. A museum devoted to imitations? The Franklin Mint headquarters is actually a series of modern buildings (called a "campus" no doubt) and manicured grounds. The air smelled of freshly cut grass. The biggest attraction in the museum was Jacqueline Kennedy Onassis's favorite fake pearl necklace, the one that she wore in countless famous photographs. The Franklin Mint had bought it at Sotheby's recent auction of Kennedy memorabilia. The mint was planning to sell reproductions of the necklace, which is to say, *imitation* imitation pearls. In the gift shop you could buy a toy fire truck, a plate with Frank Sinatra's face on it, or, for five easy installments of $39, an official tri-level *Star Trek* chess set.

It is tempting to think of the Northeast Corridor from Boston to Washington as an unbroken chain of cities, suburbs and industrial wastelands. I was surprised when, just a few miles south of Philadelphia, Route 1 became a country road, winding past fields, farmlands and Revolutionary battlefields. The corn stood tall in the fields. Every so often I'd pass a roadside stand selling fresh local produce. I passed through the Brandywine Valley, where Washington wintered and massed his forces for the famous crossing of the Delaware River in 1776. I had planned to make it to the small town of Oxford, where there was a new links-style golf course called Wyncote, just off Route 1. Twenty or thirty miles from Oxford, though, I spotted a sign reading Loch Nairn Golf Course and The Farm House Restaurant. I pulled off at the exit. I wound along country lanes, past cornfields tall enough to hide a baseball team. Loch Nairn was a lovely little course. The Scottish name, the peaceful setting and the fact that I had stumbled upon it by accident made me think of *Brigadoon*. The restaurant, set in an old stone farmhouse with a stone foundation and a smart white-and-yellow awning around back, was run by the same family that owned the golf course. The golf course was almost empty when I started off. So I played alone. That was okay with me. I'd been playing an endless stretch of crowded, sun-baked city courses from Boston to Philadelphia. A solitary round in the country suited me fine. As if to oblige me, the day had broken fair and about ten degrees cooler than the day before.

The biggest problem I had with Loch Nairn was judging distances. It's a tight little course, and on the front nine I overclubbed a lot of holes. The first hole is a short par-four, just 300 yards tee to green. The best shot is a mid-iron into a basin landing area, followed by another iron across a stream to an elevated green protected by several bunkers. The second hole drops down an embankment, and you have to watch out for a pond on the right with a little island of cattails in the middle of it. Another tee shot where anything more than an iron could kill you. I found out the hard way when I hit my three-wood straight and long and wound up behind some trees beyond where the hole kicked right. I was paying a heavy price for my ignorance on this trip;

you need three or four rounds on any course before you can begin to understand its idiosyncrasies or adequately judge the appropriate club in any given situation.

The fifth was the only hole that annoyed me. It is another 300-yard par-four but turns left at such a sharp angle that anything more than a pitching wedge off the tee is too much club. Again, I paid dearly for this knowledge. I pulled out my seven-iron and tried to cut a corner off the turn. But the trees were too high. I caught a branch and dropped into the thick stand of pines. From here, my only real option was to play through the trees to the hole. I slapped the ball through, right up to the tee of an adjoining hole, then put the ball on the green and two-putted for a bogey. The only things missing from that hole were a windmill and a fiberglass bear. I finished the front nine with a 48.

Between nines, I left my clubs with the starter and walked over to the Farm House Restaurant for lunch. The Farm House was filled with a luncheon crowd of well-dressed, elderly women, who sat on the patio under the yellow-and-white awning. I sat in the cozy bar—dark wood, heavy ceiling beams, a central bartender's station that reminded me of *Cheers*. A great place to while away a dark winter's night with three or four feet of snow piled up outside and a hot rum drink in hand. But it was summer, and I had holes to go before I slept. I made do with a couple of hot dogs and a Coke.

I had learned by the end of the first nine to adjust my game to Loch Nairn's size and scope, leaving my big clubs in my bag and swatting my way around this placid little course mainly with irons. I liked the back nine even more than the front. At last, a couple of long par-fours. It was nice to take a wood out of the bag now and then. I saw muskrats and egrets and lots of geese and ducks, and every time I walked past a pond there was a furious *clop clop clop* of frogs leaping into the water to avoid me. The ponds were clear enough to support a generous supply of bass.

I played the back in 42 and finished with a 90—a score I'd begun thinking of as my mental break-even point. Anything below counted as a success, anything above a disappointment. As I made my way around a course, I would keep score in my head, allowing myself a base allotment of five strokes per hole (or, ninety for the round) regardless of the par of the individual hole. A score of 3 on one hole, for example, would put me two strokes ahead of schedule. If I could average 5s the rest of the way, I'd finish with 88. But a 7 on the next hole would bring me back to the pace for an even 90. This method provided a useful way of holding myself accountable to a standard, without measuring myself against true par for the course—an exercise in futility for someone at my level. It also allowed me to compete against myself, creating a competitive tension even when playing alone. At Loch Nairn, for example, my 48 on the front nine put me three strokes in the hole. I had to mount a comeback on the back nine to finish with 90.

I left those rolling hills and cornfields regretfully. Loch Nairn was uncrowded, scenic and, best of all, I'd had no idea it was there. I rolled on toward Oxford and Wyncote Golf Club, the course I had originally intended to play.

Like Loch Nairn, Wyncote lay right along Route 1, amid rolling farmland. But the similarities ended there. In fact, it would be difficult to imagine two more different golf courses than the tight, wooded Loch Nairn and long, barren Wyncote. Wyncote, just four years old when I played it, is a high-ticket, fancy public course designed to look like something in the British Isles. The clubhouse sits atop a windswept hill overlooking the course, treeless as a moonscape. I paid $49 to walk. Had I arrived on a weekend, the fee would have been $75, a mandatory cart included.

The course was in magnificent shape, with a sort of wonderful spongy turf on the fairways. Long pockets of deep rough, spilling over with wildflowers, ran down the fairways. Not only were these areas of rough out of bounds; you weren't even allowed to look for your ball. They were posted as "environmentally protected wetlands." I started off alone, then played through a group of guys who were smoking big cigars. Wyncote was part and parcel of that peculiar ethos of the late 1990s that said you could smoke cigars but not cigarettes; drink single-malt scotch but not vodka or Budweiser; and convert an entire American hillside into an approximation of the British moors, so long as you didn't step on a daisy.

Having never played a treeless, British-style course before, I fell into the trap of thinking I was in for an easy round. I felt an initial rush of freedom, like finding myself suddenly on a road without stop signs or traffic lights. But of course the lack of trees, like a lack of lights or stop signs, presents its own hazards. For one thing, trees can help contain bad shots as well as punish them. At Wyncote there are no fortunate deflections. You must stay on the fairway. Slices and hooks inevitably roll until they find some sort of bad trouble—hellish rough, moguls, traps. Small ponds, without the customary fringe of trees or bushes, become black holes sucking in any small white objects that drift into their vicinity.

After playing through the cigar-chomping foursome, I hooked up on the third hole with a couple of guys who worked for a company that made office furniture. Joe worked at the midwestern headquarters in Wisconsin, Tony for a branch office near Philadelphia. They had started on the back nine because of a tournament earlier in the day and were winding down their round when I joined them.

The fourth hole is a 350-yard par-four bordered on the right by a road and an immense cornfield. All three of us sliced our drives far into the unforgiving corn. But then Tony and Joe straightened out their second tee shots, and I put mine even farther into the corn. I'd walked the eighteen at Loch Nairn and eaten nothing besides the two hot dogs. Hunger and fatigue were taking their toll. I managed to eke out a quadruple-bogey 8. I triple-bogeyed the next hole, a par-three.

I settled down on the last four holes of the front nine, managing a couple of pars, a bogey and a double, including a par on the ninth, a tough uphill par-five that required hitting past a series of moonscape mounds. The immaculate greens were slick and unforgiving. Two-putting was a real accomplishment.

Tony and Joe left me after the ninth. I had now walked twenty-seven holes and felt the weight of the bag on my shoulder. If there is such a thing as too much golf (and I'm not saying there is, mind you) then I was knocking on that door. It took effort just to bend down and yank that bag off the ground. I waved good-bye to Tony and Joe and set off on my own to the tenth hole, a mirror image of the first. The two holes run down opposite sides of the same environmental area. The shared green looks like a cell in end-stage mitosis, two globs connected by a strand.

After the twelfth hole the course opens into a lovely walk along an area of converted pastures, far from the clubhouse. It was now after seven o'clock, and most of the golfers had disappeared. A fresh wind kicked up and blew without resistance across the mounds. I'd pushed myself too hard today. I wanted to keep my ball in play, not so much for my score, but to avoid climbing any more of those mounds. Clouds drifted in, turning the pre-dusk sky from blue to a deep, haunting purple. Cows on a nearby hillside were my only company. On the sixteenth hole I stopped to pick up a ball lying like an omen in plain sight in the middle of the fairway. Someone had written in black Magic Marker the words: NO FEAR. I climbed the uphill eighteenth fairway leaning into a strong headwind, my bag pushing me back like a sail. I thought the wind might blow me over. I holed out the last putt, thankful to finish, and turned back to look at the moonscape behind me. Next to the clubhouse, on a barren hill, a group of golfers, probably the pro and his staff, stood on the range driving balls into the purple gale.

My great mood from earlier in the day had darkened with the sky. The town of Oxford looked to be little more than a quaint collection of white houses with a tiny downtown, so I pushed on toward the Maryland line. Unlike I-95 a few miles south, Route 1 crosses the Susquehanna River in dramatic fashion. The bridge forms the dam for a hydroelectric plant. Off to the right side sits a placid lake; to the left, a vertigo-inducing drop of more than one hundred feet to the river below. As I crossed the dam I noticed a doe and fawn by the side of the road, staring at me. They darted into the woods as I passed. Around Bel Air the rural countryside slowly yields to the stirrings of city life. I pressed on to the city limits of Baltimore, looking for a motel. Without luck. I hopped out onto I-695, which skirted the city. I kept looking for an exit with that familiar cluster of blinking lights announcing motels and restaurants. But all of Baltimore seemed to be without a place to stay. After about a dozen false starts, I pulled off the highway at last and checked into a threadbare hotel, part of a once-proud chain that had gone to seed. My room smelled like 1978, the torn bedspread was the color of mustard left on a plate overnight, the bed sagged, the toilet sported a complimentary pubic hair. The whole thing set me back more than $100. I phoned home and began to whine to Barbara about my exhausting day. I was a minute or so into a Charlie-centric diatribe about the lousy Baltimore motel scene and my bone-wearying round at Wyncote and my hungry belly when I noticed that Barbara's responses were clipped and precise. I realized a minute too late that unloading like this was a bad idea. That maybe a pregnant woman holding down the fort by herself while caring for a five-year-old daughter doesn't really want to hear all about your tough day on the links, at least not first thing. I tried feebly to reverse course, to ask her about her day, to tell her I was only 150 miles from home and would be there soon. But I'd already steered this conversation toward an iceberg and there was nothing to do but wait for the ship to go down. I hung up after a few minutes of strained conversation, feeling low. Unfair as this may be, I had come to rely on Barbara's cheerful voice on the phone. The thing of it was, there *were* tough days on the road, when the irritation of finding another hotel and dealing with the endless stop-and-go of Route 1 and finding dinner and so forth frayed my nerves. The fact that this whole thing was my idea, that I'd gotten exactly what I asked for, didn't help. I showered and made my way downstairs. The hotel restaurant was still open—barely—but it looked like the sort of place where the special of the day is fettuccine à la salmonella. So I sank into a Naugahyde chair in the lounge and washed down a few cardboard chicken fingers with a cold Budweiser and watched a bored cocktail waitress fend off advances from a bored salesman.

But then, of course, there was always the next morning. I slept soundly, woke early, and joined the early rush-hour traffic on I-695, which led me back to Route 1. Thousands of frowning drivers, each of them staring straight ahead, fighting one another to get to some office, reminded me to enjoy what I had while I had it. That other, more serious world lay ready and waiting to reclaim me soon enough.

Route 1, called Bel Air Road through North Baltimore, winds past block after block of modest brick bungalows and crab restaurants. I came to the crest of a hill and saw, to my right, a sunburned fairway. Clifton Park Golf Course is a genial, unpretentious city course, bounded on all sides by Baltimore row houses. I walked into a squat clubhouse where half the old men of North Baltimore seemed to be milling about the snack shop, laughing out loud and telling lies. They hacked and snorted and cleared phlegm from their throats. One man sounded like he was having seizures.

"That sounds pretty bad," said the woman behind the cash register.

"I just ate some toast. It happens every time," the man said when he came up for air.

"Every time you eat? Or every time you eat toast."

"How's that?"

"You cough every time you eat anything? Or every time you eat toast?"

"Toast."

"Oh. I was going to say. That could be a problem if it happened every time you eat anything."

"No. Just toast. It's like it gets stuck somewhere. I don't know what it is."

"Oh, yeah," injected a man in a pink shirt, standing in line to pay his greens fee. "That's your streptocilliac . . ." The word, begun with such confidence, trailed off on the last syllable as the man realized he had no idea what he was talking about and everybody was looking at him. He changed the subject quickly, calling across the room to a buddy, "Hey, Bobby, you got four bucks? Bobby, come here and loan me four bucks."

"Jeez," said Bobby, ambling over and producing his wallet. "Don't you ever have anything good to say?"

I paid the cashier $9 to walk and left the old guys to their talk.

"There's a twosome just started a few minutes ago," the starter told me. "You'll have no problems catching them." The first hole was a straight par-five more than five hundred yards uphill. I pushed my tee shot right and struggled up the hill, then three-putted for a disappointing eight. What a way to start. After the long uphill climb on the first hole, the second yielded wonderful views east to the harbor and south to downtown. On the second hole I introduced myself to Paul Adriani and Joseph Czajkowski. Paul, seventy-seven, and Joe, seventy-three, were Baltimore natives and had been golfing together for about forty years.

Joe pronounced his last name just like Tchaikovsky, the composer. His eyes glimmered. "The only difference between me and the musician," he said, "is my fifth movement was because I didn't pay the rent." Joe had retired from his job in the graphics department of a Baltimore television station.

A widower twice over, he'd lost his second wife just five years earlier. Golfing is his therapy, he explained—a chance to get out in the air, be with friends. When not golfing he sings in a seniors' choir that has traveled to New York and Las Vegas to perform at retirement homes.

Paul had been a photographer for the Maryland State Police, filming crime scenes and lab evidence. In the days of vaudeville he'd played piano at a theater in East Baltimore. Joe and Paul hit the ball solidly and straight. I was hitting well. They were appreciative of my shots and made me feel like Superman every time I hit anything approaching a decent shot. On the par-four fifth hole, from about 175 yards out, I stuck a six-iron pin high with my second shot.

"Wow. Nice shot," Joe said. "What club did you use?"

"Six," I said.

"*Six? Jeez,* I thought you were going to say three. Wow, you sure hit that one." When we convened on the green, Joe said to Paul, "Did you hear what he used on his second shot? *A six-iron.* A hundred and seventy-five yards!" Paul whistled.

Joe proudly swung a new set of Big Bertha irons and woods, given to him by his son, a certified public accountant who had started his own company.

"Last winter, he took me to Arizona on a golf vacation," Joe said. "Guess how much it cost for a round of golf at one of those resort courses out there? A hundred and eighty bucks. One round of golf. Let alone the hotel."

Clifton Park is a standard, playable, somewhat unremarkable course, but it has one amenity that I have not seen anywhere else—a roving water supply. Staff members roam the course in carts with large coolers affixed to the back filled with ice-cold water. On summer days they are the most popular fellows on the course. You can flag them down whenever you get thirsty, and they sometimes just appear out of nowhere, as if sensing you need a drink.

Spurred by Joe and Paul's praise, I began to take big swings at the ball. On the tenth hole, a 157-yard par-three with a dramatic downhill slope to the green, I hit an eight-iron pin high about thirty feet from the hole. I had put together a long string of pars and while this was not a ball-busting course, I couldn't help but feel good about my play. Even with the triple bogey to start things off, I finished the round comfortably in the 80s, where I now felt that I belonged. I was beginning to understand what those books and tapes and Golf Channel experts meant when they talked about the repeating swing, the swing that moves around the body like a tetherball on a swing. The hip turn, the knee flex, the foot position, the wrist snap, the shoulder turn, all were beginning to come together in a single swing. After all these rounds in the sun, something was beginning to click for me. I was nibbling around the edges of a real golf swing, beginning to understand *why* one contorts one's body in so many ways to achieve it. They no longer felt like contortions. I experienced a mental *yes!* when I swung properly.

Baltimore, that old, industrial city of bricks, long in the shadow of Washington, has transformed itself in recent years into a hot town, a city with a buzz. Camden Yards, the home of the Orioles, draws elegiac praise from baseball fans. When I passed through, the city was building a second stadium, this one for its new pro football team, which Baltimore swiped from Cleveland. The Inner Harbor, a slender basin of water jutting off the Patapsco River, fringed with a first-rate aquarium, hotels, restaurants and nightclubs, draws huge crowds of tourists. But Route 1 is not a part of this success. Though it runs through the heart of the city, Route 1, as in so many cities, serves the parts of Baltimore not shown on tourist maps, neighborhoods kept in the city's closet. The road curls around Clifton Park and faces due west along North Avenue, a long boulevard of hard times ignored by Baltimore's (and the nation's) economic revival. On this hot evening tenants of rundown row houses sat on their stoops to escape the heat. Children played on the sidewalks in front of boarded-up homes. Litter marred the sidewalks. A drunk harassed cars stopped at a stoplight; in the ten minutes it took me in stop-and-go traffic to travel North Avenue I had to pull over twice to make way for police cars screaming by with blue lights flashing. From

North Avenue, I turned south on Monroe Street, at which point Route 1 dwindles to little more than a narrow side street. Businesses tend toward pawnshops and check-cashing services. I crept down Monroe Street, then took a right onto Wilkens in the southwest corner of the city, on into the suburbs, and soon was rolling on toward Washington.

12

Home Again (Again)

After staying the night with my sister Alison and her family in Silver Spring, Maryland, I left the house around daybreak. Even in the pale light of 6:30 A.M. traffic was already beginning to swell around Washington. Route 1 slices across the outer loop of the Beltway that surrounds the city and passes College Park and the University of Maryland. Then it becomes Rhode Island Avenue on approach to the city. I have driven in Washington scores of times but have never lost a gnawing sense that at any moment I am about to become hopelessly lost. The District was originally laid out by a Frenchman named Pierre L'Enfant, in a grid of streets overlaid by diagonal avenues and traffic circles. It looks pretty on a map but makes driving around Washington hell. The diagonal lines and circles disrupt any order imposed by the grid. Streets stop suddenly, only to begin again under the same name several blocks later. Major highways are marked by fleeting signs; the road system is filled with obscure and poorly marked loops that represent the only way to get onto some major thoroughfare. Even a detailed map is only of marginal use. There is no better indication of a city's personality than its traffic, and here in this shrine to bureaucracy the road system represents nothing so much as the traffic equivalent of a federal tax form. You can be going along fine, thinking you have things under control, only to realize by some unforeseen change in direction that you have no idea where you are or how to get out. All the other cars seem to know where they're headed. But then, these are the people who wrote the tax forms.

From Rhode Island, Route 1 south cuts almost without warning down Ninth Street, which I followed to Maine Avenue. My destination was Hains Point, a flat, horn-shaped piece of land in the Potomac River. At the broad, northern end of this horn sits the Jefferson Memorial; at the narrower end is East Potomac Golf Course, one of three public courses within the District and the one most central to downtown. My drive had been fairly smooth until I approached the turnoff for Hains Point. Then, predictably, things got hairy. I had to make two loops around a small pond called the Little Basin in order to get on the poorly marked exit leading to Hains Point. I cursed as I pulled into the parking lot.

A private company operates East Potomac under contract from the U.S. Department of the Interior, which owns the land. The complex includes a pair of nine-hole courses, a miniature golf course, and a double-decker driving range. East Potomac, referred to by locals simply as Hains Point, is as effective a symbol of democracy as the Washington Monument. There are no advance tee times, just first come, first served. And though the course itself is flat and unremarkable, the surroundings make Hains Point irreplaceable. You can overlook the crabgrass in the fairways, the casual ditches, the weedy tee boxes. Here you have the feeling of being in the center of everything. To the southeast, across the river, is Washington National Airport. I know from my days covering transportation that pilots hate National Airport because its single, short runway demands a tricky approach over the river, involving a sharp bank just before landing. Conventional wisdom says that if National were not so convenient to the capital and the members of Congress who control its fortunes, it would have been closed years ago. If you don't mind jet engines roaring through your backswing, it's exhilarating to watch planes veer so close they seem to be headed for a landing somewhere in the vicinity of the fifteenth fairway. Forget the hush-hush etiquette of the pro circuit—here's a test for the Greater Heartbreak Open: *Ernie Els needs this putt to stay in contention for the $400,000 first prize, Jim. Let's see if he can withstand the pressure being placed on him by Davis Love III . . . not to mention that 737 about to land in his back pocket!* As it turns out, there is an almost mystical relationship between airports and public golf courses. From Weequahic Park in New Jersey to the Pompano Beach Golf Course in Florida, any number of courses on my trip sidled up snugly against runways. Show me a place where planes take off and land and I'll find you a golf course open to anyone with a few bucks and a bag of mismatched clubs. A prosaic explanation for this relationship, of course, might be the mutual need for cheap, open acreage. But I like to think there's something more at work here, something in the restless American spirit that makes us take to the skies and the fairways by the millions, in the fervent belief that whatever it is we're looking for may be had by moving forward, moving on.

To the north from Hains Point you can see the spires of the Smithsonian Institution. But the most spectacular sight of all is reserved for the holes that stretch back toward the clubhouse. From that vantage point the immense pointed tower of the Washington Monument splits the sky. "Hit toward the monuments in our nation's capital" the scorecard cheerfully challenges. And amid all this: wildlife. I was coming up the second fairway when I turned around and saw a red fox darting across the grass.

As I said, the planes veer off just in time to land at National Airport, but if they had to they could probably land on one of the fairways without doing major damage. Or even going out of bounds. The fairways are hard and burnt dry in summer, but as a consolation you have to try hard to lose a ball. It's not a short course, with four par-fives as well as several par-fours of well over 400 yards. But it is almost devoid of trouble. One of the guys I played with, Koji, a pilot for All Nippon Airlines, said that of all the courses he'd played on layovers around the world, East Potomac ranked as his favorite.

"This my home course," he said with a laugh, in halting English. Koji was from Osaka. "Japanese courses, out of bounds here, out of bounds there. Here, no out of bounds. You hit over here, safe. You hit over there, safe."

I hooked up with Koji and another single after playing the first couple of holes by myself. Michelle Harrington was from D.C., born and raised in southeast Washington. He'd raised two kids in the District. They were eighteen and twenty. Now, he said, it was time to pick golf up again. He carried old, bladed clubs. He had a beautiful swing. He was out here for a quick nine before heading to work, in the admissions office at the University of Maryland.

"Mainly, I love to walk," he said. "Carts make me tired. All that hopping on, hopping off, bouncing all over the course. I'd rather walk."

As we hit, a helicopter bearing what appeared to be the presidential seal cruised past us overhead.

"I don't think he golfs here," I said.

"Naw," Michelle said. "Too expensive."

It was still early morning, just after 8 A.M., but already the air felt like a wool blanket sopped with tar. The afternoon promised thunderstorms, which could only come as a blessed relief. Michelle begged off after nine. Koji and I slogged on as a twosome. In the sticky heat Koji began to get a little sloppy. Sweat soaked through his Guinness Stout T-shirt. He began to mishit and curse himself in Japanese. He attempted to guide me around the course, but this may have done more harm than good, particularly when I asked him if I should aim for the "willow tree" and he thought I said "little tree" and nodded. The fairways at East Potomac were in rough shape, but the greens were remarkably smooth. On such a wide-open course I should, I felt, have hit my best round yet. Instead, I bumbled my way to a 91, sorely depressed. Blowing pars on a flat course without serious hazards was a blow to my ego. I could not cite the treacherous hills, the dense woods, the sinister traps; no, East Potomac confronted me with my own shortcomings and handed them back to me on a silver tray. I kept missing the fairway, then chipping up and two- or three-putting. I thought of seventy-seven-year-old Bill Kerrigan back on that course in Connecticut. Chip up, one putt in.

Across the Fourteenth Street Bridge, Route 1 cuts left through a monstrosity of northern Virginia high-rises known as Crystal City, then runs down a few miles in from the Potomac River toward central Virginia. Interstate 95 does most of the heavy lifting for north-south long-distance traffic, relegating Route 1 to status as a local road, a mishmash of stop and go, shopping centers, fast food, donut shops, lube shops and places to rotate your tires. The planners who laid out a pattern of growth for northern Virginia did not anticipate the postwar bureaucracy boom that would convert Washington from a sleepy southern town into a metropolis of four million people within a few decades. The effect on northern Virginia has been catastrophic. When highway planners laid out the design for Interstate 495, the fabled Beltway ("inside the Beltway" being that reference point used by people who consider themselves plugged in to the power structure) they did so believing that all significant development of greater Washington would take place well within the boundaries of the highway. But I-495 just made it possible for ugly, ungainly suburban mini-cities to spring up almost overnight. Washington commuters pushed ever farther into Virginia looking for affordable housing, with the result that northern Virginia now has some of the worst commuter traffic in the country.

Lorton, Virginia, my next stop, had once been a country town far south of D.C.'s sprawl, but by now was engulfed. I turned off Route 1 onto Mason's Neck, a boot-shaped spit of land containing Gunston Hall, the ancestral home of George Mason. Mason was one of the extraordinary band of colonial Virginia planters, born to quasi-aristocracy, who laid the intellectual foundation for the world's most open and democratic society. Mason wrote the Virginia Bill of Rights and was the loudest and most insistent advocate of a national Bill of Rights being attached to the Constitution. Mason's Neck also contains a regional park and, at its southern tip, a national wildlife refuge. At the entrance to the neck sits Pohick Bay Golf Course, a public course run by the Northern Virginia Park Authority. The clubhouse is a converted eighteenth-century brick plantation house. The course itself meanders up and down steep hills of the old plantation.

After walking a couple of holes by myself, I hooked up with another single, Jeff, and two guys golfing together, Sam and Joe. Hauling my bag up and down the hills in the heat had me puffing by the third hole, sucking in moist air by the gallon. When Jeff offered me a seat on his cart, I took it.

Pohick Bay, in addition to being hilly, features tight, wood-lined fairways. I parred the first hole, a downhill par-four dogleg to the right, and took that as a good omen. Even better was the second hole, where I rescued myself from deep trouble. It's a 157-yard par-three with tee box and green sitting on hilltops, separated by a deep valley—the sort of hole where you want so badly to put the ball on the green that you almost never do. I didn't. I topped the ball, sending it to the bottom of the hill. It struggled about a third of the way up and came to rest under a branch. I was setting myself up for a double or triple bogey. But I grabbed my pitching wedge and knocked the ball up the hill. My view was blocked by leaves in my face, but I found the ball on the green about twelve feet from the hole. I two-putted for a bogey. I struggled to a lost-ball triple bogey on the next hole, but that was my only awful hole of the day. The par-four fourth, rated toughest on the course, requires hitting over a valley to a fairway that turns sharply to the right. I smacked a nice drive. My second plunked into a sand trap to the right of the green, but I rescued my par with a good sand shot that rolled to within two feet of the cup.

"Uh oh," Sam said. "Looks like we've got a player here."

Sam was a jovial goof, cheerfully profane, a guy whose favorite word for any occasion was *fuck*. "Fuck you!" he screamed at the ball. "Fuck! Motherfucker! You Fuckin' suck!" He was a tolerable partner for one round, but just barely. By the fifteenth or sixteenth hole I wished he'd disappear. He'd lift his ball out of the woods and place it on the fairway without subtracting a stroke, then announce on the green that he was putting for par. A funny thing about golf is that it causes some guys to cheat even when nobody's competing, even when all four players are keeping their own scores. What did we care how Sam scored? He could mark down a string of eagles for all it affected us. This wasn't tennis, where a cheater automatically costs you points. But Sam insisted on making us party to his self-deception, as though proclaiming fake scores loudly enough would make them real. Sam would talk during your backswing and had a penchant for unfunny misogynist jokes. He made so many lewd comments about his own wife that you could only surmise he was as meek as a lamb on the home front. He also seemed to take other people's good play as a personal insult. I ran a string of pars, and with each hole his jovial comments became more strained, until finally, unable to contain himself, he demanded, "How long have you been golfing?" When I told him I'd been picking it up in fits and starts over several years, he said triumphantly, "I've been playing for *one year*." As if any of us cared. Beneath that big, blustery, jokester exterior beat the heart of a three-year-old. Every time he hit a poor shot, he'd explain to us just what went wrong. (His answer never touched on the most plausible explanation: He sucked at golf.) I heard a story once about a man who played a round with a guy just like Sam. The next day the man ordered a dozen balls delivered to the guy, each with this message stenciled in bold black letters: NOBODY CARES.

Joe, Sam's friend, was by contrast a quiet, introspective guy, a soldier stationed at one of northern Virginia's military installations. Joe was a nice guy with decent form who was wrestling with a debilitating "grip and rip" complex. He couldn't stop himself from overswinging at the ball. He'd take a nice, easy practice swing, then step up to the ball, clutching his club as though playing tug-of-war with it. The club face came back with a jerk, then descended with a furious chop. The ball never did the same thing twice. It sliced or hooked or popped up. Joe had taken active steps to improve the situation: He'd bought new clubs.

"I had graphites," he explained. "But I couldn't get any control. I swung so hard the shafts were bending. Then I went to all-steel shafts. I basically had no choice." Of course, he might have tried easing up on his swing. But he couldn't seem to get past that mental block. On one hole toward the end of the round, when despair or fatigue had dulled his overconcentration, he did in fact take a nice, easy swing, as smooth as one of his practice swings. The shot, his best of the day, soared long and straight. He was so pleased that the next time he approached the ball he decided to really give it a ride, cranked his backswing, and powered the ball off into the pines.

Pohick Bay was a much harder course than East Potomac had been the day before. In addition to the tight, winding fairways, the sharply angled greens are about as challenging as you'll find on a public course. For instance, I double-bogeyed a par-three hole after placing my tee shot nicely on the green. Four putts to get the ball in the hole from about fifteen feet away. And yet I played much better here than I had the day before, as if the woods, hills and tough greens imposed discipline on my game. The par-five thirteenth is the sort of hole that could kill your round if you let it. It runs straight for about 250 tree-lined yards, then kicks right with a shot over a large pond. I nailed my drive to the left side of the fairway, then stuck a five-wood to about twenty yards right of the green. I chipped on and two-putted for my par. I felt I was getting stronger as the day progressed. The fifteenth hole is a par-three listed at 164 yards, with a large, inviting green. I felt so powerful that I plucked an eight-iron from my bag and stuck the ball on the green, about twenty feet beyond the pin. I also parred the eighteenth hole and pulled a 41 on the back nine, an 86 for the round. As I packed my stuff into my trunk, Sam wheeled up to me in his cart.

"I shot a ninety-eight," he said, as if I'd been waiting for his score. "Anytime I break a hundred I'm happy."

The road through Virginia is marked with Civil War historical markers, describing this battle or that troop movement. Fredericksburg, about forty miles south of Washington, is a historic town that in 1862 was the site of perhaps the most lopsided and costly Union defeat of the war. On December 13, Union troops crossed an open field and attacked Robert E. Lee's Confederate forces, arrayed behind a stone wall and atop a steep hill known as Marye's Heights. The result was predictably disastrous; in a few hours of battle more than eight thousand Union soldiers lay dead. I entered town along the Jefferson Davis Highway, as Route 1 is named through Virginia, for the erstwhile president of the Confederacy.

The course I would play, Lee's Hill, is part of a new housing development just south of the city. Many of the new residents are Washington commuters. Fredericksburg is being pulled inexorably into the sphere of Washington; even from forty miles away it shows signs of becoming a commuter town. Lee's Hill lies near the spot of the Confederates' southern flank on that day in 1862. In the clubhouse is the mounted remnant of a musket found when the course was being built. Markers at various holes point out where Lee and Longstreet wintered with their forces just a few hundred yards away. Some of the holes are lined with former Confederate trenches. Lee's Hill makes the most of this Civil War association. The emblem on the scorecard shows a cannon sitting on a green. The tees range from "cannon" for the pro to "pistol" for women. But these days the sharp reports of *Bang! Bang! Bang!* ringing through the woods are not from musket fire but from carpenters' hammers driving nails into another new fairway home. The course, as hinted by its description as a "golfer's club," has upscale aspirations to go with its $39 weekday greens fee, mandatory cart included.

John, Al and I started off from the rifle tees, the moderates. Lee's Hill, built in the early 1990s, had been rough around the edges for the first few years, John told me, but had markedly improved this year.

John, in his fifties, had taken early retirement from the Navy. A native of California, he'd lived all over the country and settled with his wife and son in Fredericksburg. He was what I'd call a sleight-of-hand player. By which I mean no dishonesty or conscious deception on his part but simply that he did not look like a golfer—not until you compared his scorecard with your own. To begin with, he had a quick, short, jerky motion, with all the fluidity of a rooster picking corn off the floor of a coop. No follow-through at all. The swing was poor in every way except one: it worked. The ball did not travel far, but it went straight just about every time.

"I know I have an ugly swing," he told me simply. "I know it. Everybody tells me. I don't care." He just kept plodding along, putting the ball on the fairway, chipping up, putting in. I outdrove him on almost every shot. He scored a 39 on the front side to my 45.

Ed, a pharmacist, was a nice guy with a decent swing who had somehow convinced himself that the only club he was capable of hitting off the tee was a one-iron.

"Best purchase I ever made," he said. Now, most average golfers would just as soon use a hockey stick, or a garden hoe, as a one-iron. Most don't even keep the club in their bags, figuring a zero-loft club is best left in the hands of a pro. But Ed, despairing over his seemingly incurable slice, had bought a one-iron as a last resort and found that he could hit it straight most of the time, and even get some loft out of the club. If you needed any proof that golf is a game of psychology, Ed was it.

Al was a large, powerful man who had recently retired from a job with a satellite communications company. Al said his goal in retirement was to play all eighty-odd courses at Myrtle Beach in South Carolina. He was already halfway there.

I picked up speed on the back nine, putting together a string of pars and birdies. I badly flubbed the last two holes, double-bogeying an easy par-three and triple-bogeying a par-five, but still managed to squeak home with an 89.

After my round, I wound through the streets of Fredericks-burg to the battlefield, run by the National Park Service. I stood on Marye's Heights, from which the Confederates had mowed down so many Union soldiers that they cheered the bluecoats on for their bravery as they fired. Marye's Heights is now a cemetery for those fallen Union soldiers. Most of the graves are unmarked; they rest now in the same impersonality with which they died in blue waves. Every family has at least one ancestral hero and mine has a certain Lieutenant Col. A. J. Warner, my great-great-grand-father, who would have been among the dead buried in the hill-top cemetery if not for a minié ball he'd taken in the hip a few months earlier in the cornfield at Antietam. As he lay recuperat-ing in a hospital, virtually his entire regiment, including his own replacement, had been wiped out here.

On my way out of town I stopped at Carl's, a venerable ice-cream stand that has been serving the same custard-style soft ice cream, cranked out of its old-fashioned Elektro-Freeze ice-cream makers, for forty years. Armed with a jumbo chocolate cone, I pushed on toward Barbara and Natalie, forty-five minutes away in Richmond, the warm, mothering arms of home.

For several days I rested my clubs and my muscles and wallowed in the small joys of domestic life and the large joys of being with Barbara and Natalie. Natalie, tanned and happy, hugged me as if I'd been away for years. After my procession of motel rooms, fast food, and unfamiliar towns, such routines as taking Natalie to the grocery store, chatting with neighbors, eating with my family and sleeping in my own bed next to my wife seemed like indescribable luxuries. Of course, this sense of freshness had come at the expense of Barbara, who had been holding down a double burden on the home front. And soon I'd be heading out again. But any guilt I felt was self-imposed. I wondered if I'd have so much equanimity were the situations reversed. Barbara was lovely and growing larger, and now in the stillness of the night I could reach over and feel the newest member of our family kicking away.

As I drove around Richmond on weekday mornings, along shady residential streets lined with fine old brick homes, or through the busy financial district downtown, I felt disembodied, as if the other me were out there somewhere in a jacket and tie, chasing down another story for the *Times-Dispatch*. I ended my brief golf hiatus by hitting a few buckets of balls at a driving range run by the city parks department on School Street, just off Chamberlayne Avenue, behind the city dump. Chamberlayne is the name given to Route 1 as it runs through the northern suburbs and into downtown Richmond. It's one of two historic boulevards approaching the city, the other being Monument Avenue, which approaches from the west.

Monument, with its grand statues of Confederate leaders (and, paradoxically, the great tennis star Arthur Ashe, a Richmond native), remains a gracious, brick-paved thoroughfare of large houses and gas streetlights. Chamberlayne has fared less well. The old mansions today are interspersed with cheap motels, apartments and industrial buildings. The driving range was built on landfill from the dump. But this range is the sort of gem that a golfer discovers and holds on to. Drawing an equal mix of black and white golfers, the range is clean, bright and run by a friendly staff. It has both artificial and grass tee boxes, plus a putting green and a chipping green with a sand trap. A high, grass-covered berm separates the dump from the range and keeps aromas from drifting over. The first time I visited, the man behind the counter took down a large bucket, then fished out two or three more handfuls of balls from a bin and piled them on top of my bucket. I noticed that all the balls were sparkling. When I remarked on this, the man said, "Nothing worse than hitting a dirty ball." I've been going back ever since.

Limbered up, I was ready to head back out to the fairways. Belmont Golf Course, just north of the city line in Richmond, was the natural choice for my homecoming round, since the first hole dead-ends at Route 1. More than a few cars over the years, waiting for a green light at the intersection of Route 1 and Hilliard Road, have driven home with dented roofs, courtesy of some hopped-up hacker overshooting the green on his second shot of the day.

The thought of Belmont made me a little nervous. I'd suffered some major meltdowns here. Once, when I was just learning, I'd foolishly signed up for a company tournament held at Belmont and had made myself an object of pity among my co-workers by barely breaking 130. Later, playing with my father-in-law, I carried my first serious hopes of breaking 100 all the way to the seventeenth hole, where I got hung up in some landscaping near the green and flubbed my way over the century mark with an 8. Some courses just have your number.

Belmont has an impressive lineage for a municipal golf course. It was designed as a private country club in 1916 by A. W. Tillinghast (designer of Winged Foot and Baltusrol), then redesigned in 1940 by Donald Ross. In 1949 Sam Snead won the PGA championship here. After the country club pulled up stakes and moved west of Richmond, Belmont went public. Untold thousands of public rounds had stripped Belmont of much of its luster. Treading those sun-baked fairways on a midsummer day, you find it difficult to detect vestiges of the championship course that once challenged the finest players in the world. Except, that is, on two holes, two dastardly par-fours, the first and the fifth.

The first hole at Belmont may not be the toughest opening hole in golf, but it scares the hell out of most golfers in Richmond. It stretches nearly 400 yards from the white tees, but length isn't the half of it. A project to widen Hilliard Road, which runs down the right side of the fairway, pinched an already narrow fairway into a treacherous needle of grass. Moguls and thick bushes start a few feet to the right of the tee and run the length of the hole. Even a moderate slice finds the road. A line of trees guards the other side of the fairway, so you can't play safely to the left. The green lies down an incline, hemmed in on the front by a ball-eating brook and on the back by Route 1. It's the sort of hole that gives even good golfers pause. For a hacker, it's an invitation to ruin your day before the day has even started. I always consider myself lucky to come away with a 6.

But now, with my new, improved golf game, I would tame this beast. How difficult had that first hole really been? Had it just *seemed* hard? I was eager to return, to torment my tormentor. I arrived early and hooked up with three men, Jack Brayley, Ray Petitjean and Charlie Brumm. They were in their seventies and eighties. Ray and Charlie had been golfing together at Belmont for more than twenty years. Jack, the youngest of the threesome at seventy-four, had recently started playing with them. They hit from the front tees. I used the intermediates, which put me in the position of shooting first on every hole.

I lined up my first ball of the morning, trying not to notice that cursed row of shrubs on the right, or the road behind it. Slow down that backswing, I told myself, turn those shoulders and hips. I had a tendency to slice, and one of the things that caused it was when I neglected to turn my shoulders with the swing. In that case my swing became all arm and, reaching down to scoop the ball, as opposed to swinging my whole body, I inevitably came at the ball from the outside in and the result was a bad slice. So I turned my shoulders and hips and, of course, sliced anyway, a bad fade that flew so purposely toward the American Legion hall across Hilliard Road that it might have been late for a meeting. I won't describe all the ugly details of that hole, but I will say that on my way to a quintuple-bogey 9 I lost every ounce of self-confidence.

The second hole, a short par-four, went scarcely better. Shell-shocked by the first hole, I caught my drive on the heel of the club. The ball squirted to the left and climbed through a chain-link barrier and onto the fringe of the green of the third hole. My playing partners waited patiently to move up to the forward tees to hit, in a silence so thorough it might have been painted on with a brush. I wandered blankly over to my ball. I put my second shot, a six-iron, over a tree and back onto the fairway but shanked my third shot, an easy approach to the green. I took an 8 on that easy hole, meaning that after two holes I was already nine strokes over par. I thought about calling it a morning. Who would know? I could run down to a driving range, work out the kinks, and return that afternoon. One thing I'd learned, though, was that giving up on a round of golf was the surest way to screw up your next round, to carry all your troubles with you like a bad smell. Better to stay and take the beating, and work it out.

The third hole, a very short par-four, just over 250 yards, with a gentle dogleg to the left, started no better. It was hard to resist going for the green, and few golfers did. I hit a decent drive that, unfortunately, faded right and came to a stop about thirty yards to the right of the green, with my approach blocked by a large tree with low branches. My only option was to scoot the ball under the branches, trying to avoid the tree and also a silver electrical box sticking out of the ground. My little quarter-swing six-iron clanked off the electrical box with a humiliating metallic sound and ricocheted to just in front of the tee box for the next hole. As Ray, Jack and Charlie put their balls onto the green, I had to wait patiently for the group in front to tee off before hitting my next shot. Hitting off hard-pan ground, over a trap, I hit a soft sand wedge that bounced onto the green and rolled to within inches of the cup. It was a hell of a way to save a par, but it started me on a long, slow, satisfying turnaround. I also parred the par-three fourth hole, in a more conventional way. Then came the dreaded fifth hole. The fifth is technically a par-four, but most people play it as a five and call themselves lucky to escape with a six. The hole measures 460 yards from the intermediate tees. You must hit a perfect drive to have any hope reaching the green in two. But even a perfect drive leaves you with a second shot of more than 200 yards to a small, sloping, uphill green protected by a bunker and trees. Luck intervened on my behalf. I hit a screaming low hook that disappeared over some hedges and appeared headed for the clubhouse parking lot. But we found my ball between two trees with an open shot at the fairway. I double-bogeyed the hole and was pleased. From there I went on a sort of tear. I parred three of the four remaining holes to finish the front nine with a 47, respectable considering my debacle on the first two holes.

The best part of the round was playing with Jack, Ray and Charlie. They warmed up to me once I stopped playing like a dope. After the first few holes, when I began to hit long, clean shots off the tee, we got along famously. Ray seemed relieved.

"At first I thought you were going to shoot a one-fifty," he said.

Charlie, who was eighty-four, still hit the ball long off the tee and pulled off two birdies in a row. On the thirteenth hole, a downhill par-three that is probably the most fun hole on the course, Charlie stuck his tee shot to the back edge of the green, using something called an eleven-wood. "I can even use this club out of the sand," he said proudly. Left with a long putt over an impossible sloping bump in the green, Charlie watched his putt crest the bump and roll with perfect speed straight into the cup for a birdie. On the next hole, a par-four, 324 yards from the gold tees, he hit to the fringe of the green in two. Then he sank his chip for a second straight birdie.

On the next couple of holes, short par-fours, I used irons to stay in play off the tee. Charlie, using his driver and hitting from the golds, put his drive ten yards beyond mine. As he passed my ball he yelled out, "Hey, short-knocker, there's your ball!" I parred five of the nine holes on the back for a 39, and finished the round at 87, the sweetest 87 of my life.

Part Three

The South

13

Mind If I Play Through?

Route 1, called Chamberlayne Avenue through Richmond, crosses the James River and becomes Jeff Davis Highway once again. It rolls through the heart of South Richmond, past barbecue restaurants, cheap motels and tobacco factories. When the breeze blows up from the south, the entire city is saturated with the sweet smell of cut tobacco. Philip Morris's manufacturing headquarters here makes 150 billion cigarettes a year and employs 8,000 workers, more than any other private business in Richmond.

About twenty miles south of Richmond lies Petersburg, an industrial town of brick buildings that had been the site of crucial battles in the Civil War. The city had fallen on hard times in the twentieth century and never fully recovered. I made my way to Lee Park, a sunburned public course across the street from Petersburg High School. Even the most basic public courses often have some signature claim that could make them difficult to play. At Lee Park, it was postage stamp–sized greens that made the course much harder than it looked. I couldn't uncork my game at all on this solitary round on a sweltering day. I shot a 90 and felt, as at East Potomac, that I should have done much better.

At Petersburg Route 1 and I-95 diverge, not to meet again until Jacksonville, Florida. I-95 follows an easterly path down the coast; Route 1 pushes inland, picking up a new dancing partner, Interstate 85, which runs a parallel course all the way to Raleigh. These are the loneliest stretches of all on Route 1, rural areas with an interstate not far away. Here the old highway seems to have lost its reason for being. Hollowed-out husks of roadside motels molder in the sun like beetle shells, giving mute testimony to the fact that unless you live on a nearby farm, you have no business on this road at all.

Just north of the North Carolina state line, Route 1 crosses a river connecting two large manmade bodies of water, Kerr Lake and Lake Gaston. The bridge was closed for repairs, so I took a detour down some winding country road that I figured would lead to someplace or other. It was such a beautiful day, I didn't care. It was about eighty-five degrees and sunny, and I had the road and the world to myself. I picked up a radio station from Raleigh. The disc jockey informed me that the sky was Carolina blue. I made my way around the lakes, found the familiar shield for Route 1 South and hooked up again with Route 1 south into North Carolina.

I hadn't passed any courses since Petersburg, or even any signs for courses. I was just beginning to despair when I came to the town of Wake Forest. Wake Forest had once had been a small town and home to the university of the same name. But the university had long since packed up and moved to Winston-Salem, and the town was gradually being absorbed into that budding metropolis of the New South, Raleigh-Durham and Chapel Hill. Housing developments with fake English names sprouted like tobacco in the hot red soil. About three on a Friday afternoon I passed a sign for the Wake Forest Golf Club, public welcome. I stopped, turned around in the parking lot of a Burger King and hurried back. The man in the pro shop took my $20 and waved me down to the first tee.

I stood on the tee box staring at the sign for several moments. Was I reading this correctly? Could there be some mistake? No, that's what it said: "Hole No. 1, par-five, 711 yards." *Seven hundred and eleven yards.* How far is that? You could travel seven football fields and still be a first down short. And it looked even farther than that. The flag on the green, a mere white speck, danced merrily in the haze like an unattainable dream. "World's longest par-five," a sign proclaimed. "The most famous golf hole in the Triangle." That obscene distance applies only to those foolish enough to play the back tees. I moved up to the intermediate blues, where the distance was a still ominous 625 yards. And they were not easy yards. The hole requires hitting into a valley, with a second shot that must stop short of a brook. The third shot (assuming you are still playing the hole in regulation at this point) requires hitting uphill to a sloping green protected by front bunkers. I scored an 8 and felt lucky. It irritates me when courses start off with their big guns blazing. It makes me wonder what insecurities they are hiding. They remind me of people you meet at cocktail parties who, before you raise a drink to your lips, let you know where they went to college, how many degrees they have and a half dozen other indispensable facts you never asked about.

Brand-new houses and others still under construction lined the fairways. They were built in the Victorian style, with tall windows, patios, gazebos, arched gables, picket fences and all sorts of other features to make you think you were living in a charming, century-old village. The backyards kissed right up on the fairways. I'm sure this is a terrific selling point for real estate agents— "Imagine walking out your back door right onto the fourth fairway!" But on the courses I've played, homes-on-the-fairway wind up being a nuisance to both the homeowner and the golfer. Homeowners sour on having dozens of trespassers wandering their property looking for lost balls. For golfers, houses mean narrow fairways and illogical out-of-bounds markers that make trespassers of otherwise upstanding citizens. Also, there's no place to pee.

About midway through the first nine I caught up with a two-some, a man and a woman, who were gunning for the Guinness record for slowest round of golf. Of all the slow combinations in golf, couples are the slowest, particularly if the woman is just learning. This, by the way, is seldom the woman's fault. More often than not the man has anointed himself resident pro. This particular fellow wouldn't let his girlfriend (she had to be his girl-friend; no wife would have put up with this) take so much as a swing without giving her a scientific swing appraisal and detailed analysis. He had an inexhaustible fund of knowledge on every conceivable aspect of the game—except, of course, on the part of the game that dictates that you keep it moving along.

The woman preceded each swing with an elaborate breathing exercise like a kung fu ritual, followed by three or four practice swings, a duff, and a lecture from the man. The group behind me was growing impatient and starting to hit up into me. Enough was enough. On the fifth hole I shot to the green as they were walking off, putted fast and rushed to the sixth tee, a par-three, where the man and the woman stood at their cart discussing the intricacies of club selection.

"Mind if I play through?" I asked as I walked to the tee box. The woman, the first to hear me, looked at her boyfriend as if to ask "Is that *done*?"

The man looked at me as if I'd questioned his manhood in front of his babe.

"Go ahead if you want," he said sullenly. "But we've got a slow foursome in front of us, and we've been playing on their butt all day."

At that the three of us looked ahead. The nearest foursome was a hole and a half ahead.

"See?" the man said sheepishly. "They just teed off a little while ago."

I shrugged and said if things got slow they could hook up with me. I never saw them again.

At the start of the tenth hole, a member of the foursome ahead dropped out, and the three remaining players waved me up to join them. Adam, whose friend had left, offered me the vacant seat on his cart. I took it. In his early thirties, Adam was a Californian who had moved to Raleigh three years earlier to work for a sporting goods company. He'd always thought golf was a colossal waste of time, until one day, bored, he dropped by a driving range.

"That was it," he said. "I think what I love about golf is that each course is different. You play basketball, and every court has the same dimensions. You play football, and the field's the same. But golf, you never know what you're going to get. Each course has its own personality; each has its own obstacles, no two courses are exactly alike. No two shots are exactly alike. Every challenge is new. It's like life."

Within a few months he'd worked his way into the nineties, stayed there for a while, then started breaking regularly into the eighties, in part with the help of a mysterious stranger.

"I was out hitting some balls one day at a range near here and a little old guy, about eighty years old, started watching me. He was frail and thin and all by himself, and I almost felt bad for him. Then he said, 'I'm no golf pro and maybe you don't want my advice anyway. But if it was me, I'd show another knuckle or two.'"

Adam shifted his left hand over the club a notch or two to demonstrate the change in his grip. "I tried it and it worked, and it's made a huge difference ever since. I gave the guy my name and number and said I'd love to play a round with him sometime. But I never heard from him. I've been back to that same range looking for him, but I've never seen him again. It's like he appeared out of nowhere and then just disappeared. I think of that old man as my golf angel."

My own golf angel was a little hard to find as well. The Wake Forest Golf Club, with narrow turns, closely protected greens and plenty of other hazards, is difficult enough to play for the first time. But now I hit a stretch of bad luck. I use that term cautiously. Golfers as a rule recognize only two phenomena—bad luck and skill. I'd played too much golf this summer, seen too many wicked slices carom off heaven-sent tree limbs and drop back onto the fairway, to kid myself on that score. It all evened out in the end. But today happened to be my day for strange bounces and bad lies.

Whit and Rick, a couple of Raleigh natives who completed our foursome, took to calling me "bad-luck Charlie." On the eleventh hole I hit a long, straight four-iron down the middle of the fairway and watched it dribble into a creek whose distance I had misjudged. I took a drop, then hit a nice approach that landed just short of the green, kicked right on a stone or fallen branch and came to rest directly behind a tree. There was nothing to do but laugh and shrug it off. We were among the last players on the course when we finally holed out on the eighteenth. It was after 8 P.M., the sun was starting to sink. In addition to bad luck my play had been sloppy. I barely missed an excursion into triple digits.

I had not slept well in motels. I couldn't blame the strange smells or the unfamiliar configuration of the furniture, or even my ever-present homesickness. It was that damn television set six feet from my bed, saying "Turn me on, turn me on." I don't understand how people can sleep with televisions in their bedrooms at home. How can you sleep knowing that some station is showing reruns of *The Andy Griffith Show* or an all-night *Star Trek* marathon a few feet from your bed? Despite my plans and my best intentions to turn in early in my motel rooms, rise at dawn and hit the road, inevitably some noisy neighbor would bang into his room at 1 or 2 A.M., jolting me awake, and a few minutes later, unable to sleep, I'd find myself watching James Brolin ham it up as the bomb-toting lunatic in *Skyjacked*. So when the front desk would buzz me at six o'clock the following morning, as I requested, I'd replace the receiver and go back to sleep, only to reawaken at eight-thirty or nine cursing myself for the lost sunlight.

That's why, despite my plans to rise at daybreak, I pulled into Cheviot Hills in Raleigh, a course Adam had recommended to me the day before, shortly after nine. It was another beautiful, clear, dry morning and the gravel parking lot had already swelled with cars. The wood clubhouse, cloaked in shade trees, looked like a gracious country home. Seven or eight carts lined up to tee off. I hit a bucket of balls at the driving range, then walked back up to the clubhouse to watch golfers start their rounds. I like watching other golfers tee off on the first hole. I get the same peculiar thrill as watching a line of jets take off at the airport.

I hadn't decided yet whether to fight the crowds or move on down the road to another course. Then I was drawn into golfing the way only a single golfer can be. On a morning when a four-some wouldn't have had a prayer of getting on without a tee time, I was literally drafted by the starter.

"Hey, where's the rest of your group?" he called to two young guys standing on the tee box.

"They haven't showed up," came the answer.

The starter turned to me.

"You golfing?"

"I haven't decided," I said.

"This fellow's joining you," the starter called to the tee box. He shepherded me into the clubhouse where I paid the greens fee. Then I hurried out to the tee box. In the meantime, a third member of the party had arrived, but the fourth was a no-show. I shook hands with Paul, Kevin and Tim. They were young guys, in their twenties, born and raised around Raleigh. They all worked as troubleshooters for a company that manufactured telephone equipment. As they rolled off in their carts they warned me that the course was long and hilly and I was crazy to walk. But the course that day was enforcing a path-only rule for the carts. And whatever slim claim carts have on efficiency is erased on such days. The path-only rule means that golfers must park their carts on the side of the fairway and walk to the ball. When they hit to the far rough, they wind up doing more walking than if they had simply carried their clubs in the first place. Then, to avoid having to return to the cart for the correct club, you wind up carrying half your irons out to your ball anyway.

Cheviot Hills had baked brown in this summer of little rain, but otherwise it seemed a well-kept course. Its primary distinctions are grass bunkers, rather than sand, surrounding many greens. These are wild tangles of feathery stuff—you can lose your ball three feet from the green.

Paul, Kevin and Tim had been friends for years and gave one another a hard time as if by script.

Paul: "I was reading in a magazine the other day that . . ."

Tim: "I didn't know you could read."

Paul: "Hell, yeah. Didn't I tell you I was hooked on phonics?"

Tim: "Knew you were hooked on something."

Paul, a polite, softspoken kid, probably had the best swing among the four of us. On the back nine he started to melt down, and it was hard to watch. I had never seen such a complete and sudden reversal. He went from a good, solid 45 on the front nine to 63 on the back. Suddenly every shot he hit was topped, sliced, shanked. Paul grew quieter and quieter, trying mightily to maintain his composure. The rest of us offered sympathetic utterances and hoped it wasn't catching.

14

At Least He Can Afford to Play Here

Because the state tree of North Carolina is the billboard, I had plenty of advance warning that I was approaching Pinehurst, "The Golf Capital of the World." I was still about forty miles away when signs popped up for some of the lesser Pinehurst-area resorts, offering time shares and condo deals. Before long, courses themselves materialized by the side of the road. I was tempted to stop and play each one. But I'd already played that morning in Raleigh and decided to get closer to the heart of things.

Pinehurst technically refers only to the planned resort community of that name, with its New England–style homes, quaint downtown, and a resort and country club with a luxury hotel and eight championship courses, including the world-famous Pinehurst No. 2. But the resort's renown has spawned dozens of other courses, communities and resorts in the area. Today, people refer casually to the entire area—home to more than forty golf courses in a twenty-six-mile radius—as Pinehurst.

If most cities and towns owe their existence to some geographical imperative—the fall line of a river, the end of the plains and the start of the mountains, a snug harbor along a windswept shore—Pinehurst joins Las Vegas and Palm Beach as part of that peculiarly American phenomenon, the invented town. Before a soda-fountain magnate from Massachusetts named James Walker Tufts in the 1890s got the idea for a resort halfway between New England and Florida, the area that is now Pinehurst amounted to six thousand acres of scrubby, all-but-useless pine barrens tucked away in a remote corner of south central North Carolina. Whatever natural beauty the area did possess had been ravaged by lumber companies. Disappointed by the lack of good accommodations in the middle South during a journey to Florida for his health, Tufts scouted the Carolinas for likely locations. Eventually, he paid $1 per acre for the land and instructed his architects to create Xanadu in the pine barrens. Workers healed the ravaged landscape with 250,000 tree seedlings, shrubs and flowers. The completed village, which opened in 1895, contained inns, hotels and cottages, all done in a New England style. Even the name was imported from New England—"Pinehurst" had been runner-up in a contest to name a real estate development on Martha's Vineyard. Tufts liked the way it sounded. Although Pinehurst has since been transformed into a refuge for the well-heeled, at the time of its opening the resort fancied itself more a place for the righteous than the rich. You could get a cabin for $3 per week but in order to stay there you were required to present a certificate from your minister and physician affirming your moral worth.

Pinehurst was not initially conceived as a golf resort. The first golfers were hotel guests standing in a meadow taking potshots in the direction of the resort's dairy cows. When a dairy employee complained to Tufts that these duffers were spooking the cows, Tufts built a nine-hole course and clubhouse. The course opened in 1898. He added a back nine the next year. That course, now called Pinehurst No. 1, was designed by Donald Ross and was the first of what are now eight Pinehurst courses, the most of any single resort in the world. Ross in 1907 designed another course, the now-legendary No. 2, which has hosted a Ryder

Cup, a PGA Championship, and dozens of other professional tournaments.

In the end, of course, golf not only defined Pinehurst but also saved it. In the age of air travel, when fliers no longer require a way station on the road to Florida, Pinehurst flourishes where other turn-of-the-century hotels failed, by attracting ever-larger numbers of golfers to these sandy hills. Today it is impossible to think of Pinehurst without thinking of golf.

Route 1 doesn't lead into Pinehurst proper. The highway becomes the main drag of Pinehurst's sister town, Southern Pines, which lacks the faux New England charm but does offer all those necessities of modern life—Wal-marts, supermarkets, strip malls, fast food and cheap motels—that aren't available in the village of Pinehurst. Southern Pines is where golfers on a budget stay when they say they are going to Pinehurst on vacation; and it is where Pinehurst residents go when they need something other than an $8 jar of gift-shop chutney or a $90 golf shirt.

I checked into a motel on the strip in Southern Pines and went to a golf store a few blocks up the road to get myself a map. My plan was to play a couple of the peripheral courses first and save a round on one of the famous Pinehurst eight for last. It was already early evening; too late to play today. I asked the man in the golf shop where I should start the next day.

He considered for a moment. "For your money, Hyland Hills is not a bad course."

I had passed Hyland Hills on my way in. It was right on Route 1. I remembered the sign out front: "The Beauty's Here. The Beast Is in Your Bag."

A couple standing behind me snorted.

"Hyland Hills is Mickey Mouse," the woman said.

"A cow pasture," the man said.

"Well, I just meant that for the money it wasn't a bad course," the shopkeeper said sheepishly.

The retired couple wore matching his-and-hers golf attire. They lived in the area and had played just about every course. As they checked off their favorites and described the attributes of each, it occurred to me that in Pinehurst it is not sufficient merely to be a good golf course. Like restaurants in Manhattan, courses in Pinehurst compete for the attention of a critical and spoiled clientele. Being good is merely the first step; courses that fail to move beyond that plateau in some significant way are scorned. So courses gussy themselves up with gimmicks. One, called the Pit, winds through an old granite quarry with so many traps and hazards that you are supposed to consider your round successful if you don't lose every ball in your bag. At another, called Talamore, you can have a llama haul your bags for $100.

Bumper sticker on a car in Pinehurst: I'D RATHER BE DRIVING A TITLEIST.

I flopped into bed early that night, but my plans for a good night's sleep and early rise were dashed at 2 A.M. by a raucous party that spilled out of somebody's room. Motel tip: Never take a room near the ice machine on a Saturday night. By the time the party quieted down, Lloyd Bridges was motoring across my television in a forty-year-old episode of *Sea Hunt*.

Late the next morning I drove over to Mid Pines Inn and Golf Club, halfway between Southern Pines and Pinehurst—a course that everybody seemed to recommend. It was another Donald Ross course. Ross, a Scotsman, designed something like six hundred courses during his life, most of them in the United States. Unfortunately, Mid Pines was closed that morning for a junior tournament. I stood near the first tee amid a small knot of spectators as foursomes of fifteen-year-old boys teed off. They were slender and athletic-looking, with tousled blond hair. They carried Ping clubs and wore Foot Joy shoes, and had the loose, natural swings of country club boys. Their dads, wearing golf shirts and shorts and tasseled loafers with no socks, watched nervously.

There were a lot of other courses within a five- or ten-minute drive—so many, in fact, that I felt immobilized by the choices. I clung to the idea of golfing at Mid Pines. I drove around, had some lunch, and by the time I returned, the tournament was winding down. A few last competitors were finishing up on the back nine, but the front was wide open. In the wet, thick heat of the mid-afternoon I found that I had the course to myself. The greens fee was $48 whether you walked or rode, but they had no prohibition against walking. I left the cart at the clubhouse and took off with my bag on my shoulder.

From the first hole to the last, Mid Pines is a wonderful course. Golf courses, like people, can be harsh or soft, stingy or generous. Some are cruel and take a peculiar delight in punishing you when you least expect it; others are cowardly and let you walk all over them until, despite your low score, you feel cheapened by the experience. Courses can be cheerful or taciturn, showy, pretentious, modest, devious or plain. Occasionally, rarely, you come across a course bearing some transcendent quality that gives it a certain stamp of greatness. Mid Pines is this; it is the most honest golf course I have ever played. It is challenging but devoid of tricks. If you hit the ball squarely, you will never arrive at your ball to discover some hidden dogleg or rogue tree blocking your approach to the green. The course rewards good shots, punishes bad ones. This may sound axiomatic, but in the world of golf course design, it isn't. Like a good father, Mid Pines wants you to do well but disciplines you when you fail.

The first hole is a classic opener, a long, downhill par-four, straight and inviting, leading to a slightly elevated green. I hit a good drive down the middle and walked confidently down that long first hill with the weight of my bag pressing snugly against my shoulder, feeling somehow cool despite the heat and humidity of the late afternoon. I bogeyed the first hole, then messed up the second hole, a par-three, with a triple. Then I parred the third and the fourth. The third is a tricky dogleg to the right, with a drive that has to carry a wide pond. But my par on the fourth was especially satisfying. I hit my drive left, to the far side of some tall pine trees, leaving me with a blind 110-yard wedge to the green. I hit a nice, soft ball that vaulted the feathery tops of the pines. When I reached the green I found the ball about eight feet from the cup.

To play Pinehurst-area courses with any consistency you must learn to navigate their most treacherous feature—the beds of needles forming the rough. Getting out of this rough looks easy. After all, the high, thick branches of the ubiquitous pines provide plenty of headroom and discourage undergrowth. I rarely lost a ball. But hitting a ball off pine needles, like standup comedy, is a lot harder than it appears. My club wouldn't bite into a pine bed the way it would into dirt or grass; if the club came down too low, the face bounced and twisted on impact, sending the ball off at hideous angles. A pine bed is slippery as ice. As for finding a foothold, you might as well play hockey in loafers. As my hips turned, my feet inevitably did the same. Spikes were useless. After several failed experiments I came upon a method that served me reasonably well—a quarter-swing punch with a five-iron. At least it got me back out on the fairway.

The air remained heavy but cooled a bit as evening came on. As I walked up the fifteenth fairway, a par-five, I passed a large white house, done in a sort of late-twentieth-century interpretation of a Georgian mansion, with floor-to-ceiling windows opening toward the course like an invitation. Voices, laughter and music drifted down from the balcony, as light and sweet as bits of meringue floating on the air. A party. The merry sounds threw my own solitude into relief. I suddenly felt acutely homesick. I wondered what these people were talking about. I wanted to approach and be greeted like an old friend, with a wave and a cold drink. I wanted to share their secrets and laugh with them into the night. But Mid Pines, more than just a course name, might have described my stage in the journey. I was but a little more than halfway done. I walked on amid the aching loveliness of an empty fairway at dusk, wedded to the smell of freshly cut grass.

I chalked up mostly pars and bogeys but doubled all three of the par-fives. Those sevens hurt, but I saved my most disheartening screw-up for the last hole, a straightforward par-four of about four hundred yards, with a slight dogleg to the left. The only trouble was some trees to the left, and I found them. Then I hit another tree trying to extricate myself. I quadruple-bogeyed the hole and wound up with a 95. The fine old trees nodded sadly at me. I felt that I had let Mid Pines down.

I drove back to my motel, showered, changed and went out to find some dinner. Chain restaurants, oddly consoling for a stranger in a strange land, dotted the Southern Pines landscape. I pulled in to the parking lot of an Outback Steakhouse, specializing in Australian food, whatever that was. Everywhere I went on my trip I'd passed an Outback Steakhouse, always packed with cars. Cuisine from Down Under had somehow established itself as indispensable to every city on the East Coast. The decor was Early Boomerang. Everything on the menu came "from the barbie." When I asked my waitress why there was no dressing on my salad, she informed me happily that the dressing was "down under"—buried beneath the greens. "You're in Australia now!" she said, calling me "mate" in a voice that was more Down South than Down Under. Oh, well, the beer was cold and the steak was delicious.

The next morning I rolled out to the much-derided Hyland Hills. One woman in a gift shop had even warned me solemnly not to go there because it was where the black folks golfed. Taking me confidentially into her insular world of racism, she leaned toward me and uttered something about chicken bones in the tee-side garbage bins. My beat-up old car practically drove itself there, as if seeking its own level, after the procession of Lexuses and BMWs and Mercedeses in the parking lots of other courses I had checked out. Nary a chicken bone to be seen, and hardly any golfers, either, black or white. It was a Monday morning. The weekend getaway crowd had gotten away. I paid $19 to walk and made my way out to the first tee. The resort homes fringing Hyland Hills were more modest than those at other courses in the Pinehurst area, the clubhouse more prosaic. But Hyland Hills was a fine course, well maintained, with interesting holes, especially on the back nine. It was no Mid Pines or Whispering Pines, let alone Pinehurst No. 2, but it suffered only in comparison to these great neighbors. In most cities, Hyland Hills would have been the cream of the local public courses.

I began with an indifferent string of bogeys, with a double bogey thrown in here and there. But I put together five pars on holes eight through twelve. I was gaining consistency with my strokes, narrowing the margins of my errors, learning to extricate myself from trouble. On the eighth hole, three maintenance workers were patching up some soggy turf in the right rough. It was a short par-four, just 342 yards. I hit an iron off the tee that landed in the rough, almost at the feet of the workers. Now I could be certain of a critical audience. Course workers can get under your skin merely by standing politely while you hit. Something in their forced silence says, Okay, pal, you're playing and I'm busting my ass. Let's see what you've got. From a muddy lie in the rough, surrounded by the workmen, I hit my best shot of the morning, a towering eight-iron that plunked down about eight feet from the pin.

"Nice shot, son," one of the workers said. I nodded casually.

My par streak ended on the thirteenth with a triple bogey on a par-five, where triple bogeys hurt the most. But still I broke 90 on a fairly challenging course. I thought of what the woman in the golf shop had said about Hyland Hills being Mickey Mouse. There is a certain school of golfers that feels unless a golf course breaks your back, you haven't gotten your money's worth. More power to them. As for me, if a nice course with interesting holes that enable you to put together a string of pars now and then conjures up images of Disney characters, then slap a tail on me and call me Goofy.

I saved the Pinehurst resort itself for my last day in the area. The hallowed No. 2, with a going rate of $200 for the round, wasn't open to the public during my stay, so I had to make do with No. 6, a newer course but one that various golf guides rated nearly as high. I took one of the connector roads from Route 1 to

Pinehurst and wound through the village, past gracious Cape Cod homes, and a quaint cluster of gift shops and restaurants forming the downtown.

Among the prominent features on the serpentine driveway leading to the main clubhouse is an immaculate lawn bowling green with boundaries marked off in crisp, neat lines and a white gazebo so delicate and sugary it seemed to have been plucked off a wedding cake. The lawn bowling area was in little demand today; same for the croquet lawn next to it. But they served their purpose: I knew I was entering a place ritzy enough to maintain a bowling green and a croquet lawn. Five of Pinehurst's eight courses spread around the clubhouse in every direction like a fantastic blossom of golf. No. 6, though, sat a couple of miles away in an area of large new homes. I phoned ahead and got a tee time, which turned out to be completely unnecessary. The combination of hot weather, weekday afternoon, and, perhaps, the high greens fee made No. 6 all but deserted. I played the entire round and encountered only one other group: a jolly foursome of British businessmen who ushered me through. The No. 6 was a taste of elegance to which I was unaccustomed. I pulled up to the parking lot and was heading around to the back of my car to retrieve my clubs when an attendant wheeled up from nowhere on a golf cart, whisked my clubs out of my trunk and placed them on the back of the cart. I wished suddenly that my trunk was neater; that I had a more expensive golf bag, a more expensive set of clubs, a better pair of golf shoes, a fancier car, a better golf swing, a platinum card, some land in the country; I wanted to move naturally among such attentions with the breezy confidence of money, the self-assurance that this was the way things were supposed to be. Instead, I slipped into the sort of idiotic genuflections of someone unused to being fawned over. Thanks for taking my bag! Hey, thanks a lot!

I knew when I walked into the empty clubhouse that I would be playing this round alone. I handed over my credit card with trembling fingers. It was easier than if I had been forced to count out $160 by tens or twenties, but elementary math problems kept leaping to mind, chinking like a cash register. The first hole, that bumbling double bogey? *Chink chink.* Nine bucks. Since I was playing alone on an empty course I'd probably finish in three hours, maximum. Three hours, 180 minutes. *Chink chink.* Ninety cents a minute.

A couple of years earlier at Christmas my father had given me a dozen golf balls, with my name printed on them, that had sat untouched in my closet ever since. For one thing, I had a hard time bringing myself to use new balls at all. Cracking open a new sleeve, running my hands over the virgin dimples, then taking a swing and watching the ball sail into the woods—it was almost too much to bear. Better to play with X-outs or used balls. Used balls came from the woods, and it was natural for them to return there.

For another thing, the name imprint bothered me. I like finding balls with unusual insignias and always take special notice of them. They are like clues to some perpetual mystery. I like to imagine who hit the balls from the Acme Insurance Underwriters or the General Motors Acceptance Corp., or what somebody with a ball from a golf club in Texas is doing on a public course in Richmond. They are like little messages in a bottle. Once, in Richmond, I came across a ball bearing the markings of the Old Course at St. Andrews. Such are the mysteries of golf. But to have your own name splattered across the face of the ball; why leave such damning evidence of your own ineptitude lying around?

So these "Charlie Slack" balls had sat in my closet for a long time. I used them now, figuring that if some old acquaintance were to stumble across a shiny Titleist bearing my name, he might say, "The bastard still can't hit the ball straight, but he must be doing pretty well for himself to afford Pinehurst."

The course is undeniably great. The soft, uniformly springy turf embraced my tees like a lover. The Bermuda fairways, even well into a hot summer that had seen little rain, were so lush and green that each divot I took sent a pang of guilt through me. The bent grass greens were fast and tricky. My motorized cart moved with such quiet confidence that it seemed to be powered by the breath of God. I played the round faster than I wanted, regretting each passing hole. I felt I should consecrate every moment, have something bronzed, my tees, maybe. But I couldn't think of anything to do but slap another ball up the fairway.

I played wildly and inconsistently, careening back and forth between looking like a real golfer, living up to the standards of the course, and someone who needed a few more rounds at the local pitch and putt. I played through the British businessmen on the thirteenth hole, a long but wonderfully fun par-three with a steep drop down to a generous green. As they waited on the fringes, I nonchalantly swung my four-iron, and my only problem was I hit it too well and the ball landed on the back of the green with the pin in front.

But it was the par-five tenth hole that made my day, my week, that validated every penny I spent on Pinehurst No. 6. The tenth hole is rated the second-toughest hole on the course but in my opinion is easily the most difficult; it's the sort of hole with enough trouble to reduce you to tears if you get on its wrong side. Even if you hit a good drive down the narrow fairway, as I did, you face a tortuous second shot. About 190 yards further up, the fairway narrows to a pinched neck no more than twenty yards wide, with water on both sides. The slender, sloping green is elevated and protected on three sides by trees, and on the fourth by a bunker. On my second shot I briefly considered trying for the green, or, at least, for the swatch of fairway just beyond the narrow neck. But I thought better of it and instead hit a seven-iron that landed short of the neck and in the rough just to the left of the fairway. My third shot was one for the ages. I had about 175 yards, uphill, over water, from thick rough, to a green guarded like a fortress. I took a full swing with a five-iron. The ball flew up the hill with a hint of draw to it. It bounced once and came to rest pin high on the green about twenty feet from the hole. The green had a back-to-front slope, so I played about an eight-inch break. The ball rolled in a long, confident arc, straight into the cup for a birdie. That was the hole that would bring me back tomorrow and the next day and for many days after that. It erased the feeble futility of all those other bad holes, the lackluster triple bogeys on five and eighteen, the disastrous 9 on the fifteenth, the humbling 99 I shot, none of that mattered as I drove off after my round, remembering the sweetness of that perfect hole.

That night I stopped in for a beer at the Pinecrest Inn, a rustic old Pinehurst institution that for a time was part-owned by Donald Ross, whose statue gazes perpetually over the eighteenth hole of the No. 2 course. The bar was packed with golfers talking loudly about how they'd played that afternoon. Many had played in a tournament that had prevented me from getting on the No. 2 course. A man from Ohio, clutching a scotch and water, wheeled up to me and began talking about his round that day at Talamore, the club with the llama caddies.

"Didn't use 'em," he said. "They're a hundred bucks each and you have to take two. They have to go out in pairs or they get lonely. Plus, I don't think they had them out at all in this heat."

The man looked up at the television, where two professional women's basketball teams were playing each other. The networks had promoted the league heavily through the summer, but nobody in this overwhelmingly male crowd paid much attention.

"Who the hell wants to watch women play basketball?" the man from Ohio muttered. Then he said to the bartender, "Hey, can't you find the Indians game or something?"

I struck up a conversation with a young guy named Chris, maybe twenty-five years old. He was an assistant golf pro for one of the resort courses in Myrtle Beach. He was a serious young fellow, married for four months, who seemed to be carrying the weight of the world on his youthful shoulders. He'd played golf in high school and college and was now trying to fashion a career as a club pro. I asked him how good a golfer he was.

"Pros aren't permitted to have handicaps," he said, "but if I had one I'd be a one or a two."

He'd played Pinehurst No. 2 that afternoon with his boss. According to Chris, the boss had come out of college as a top prospect for the professional tour. But things hadn't worked out. He was biding his time as a club pro, trying to rediscover the magic.

"The guy is an unbelievable golfer," Chris said. "He's got everything. Power, accuracy, touch. But he had some personal problems. Messed up his head. He lost it. Now he's trying to get it back. It's the toughest thing in the world to watch. Today we went out and he totally fell apart. He shot in the low eighties. He's upstairs now. Too depressed to come down."

I finished my beer, said good-bye to Chris and wandered out into the night. As I walked to my car, the muffled, happy voices of the golfers in the bar subsided, replaced by a whisper of breeze through pine branches hanging over the parking lot. I thought about Chris's friend, the luckless pro, alone in his room. I imagined him lying on his bed in his sweaty golf clothes, staring blankly up at some hairline crack in the ceiling, too depressed to shower and join his friends in the bar. He'd be pondering grips or shoulder turns or putting yips, trying desperately to figure out just how and where he lost what once had seemed as sweet and natural as making love. Or maybe he wasn't analyzing the specifics; perhaps he was running yellowed newspaper clippings of high school and college glories through his mind like a tortured newsreel of his own unfulfilled potential. Then suddenly I wondered what it would be like to play the way he had played that afternoon, to shoot in the low 80s off the pro tees at Pinehurst No. 2. If a wizard offered me five hours to experience one of this guy's *bad* rounds, in exchange for my car, I would have handed over my keys without thinking twice. And yet today had brought him nothing but misery. One night, long after I completed my trip, I spoke with an old friend by phone in that low, commiserating tone that men reserve for deaths in the family or their golf games. My friend had been playing just ten months but was compensating for his late start with impressive intensity: regular visits to the driving range after work, golf package vacations, subscriptions to golf magazines. Back when he had been a once-a-year hacker he could laugh off a terrible round. Now, his slow progress was starting to eat away at his psyche. He'd shot a 98 once, but every other round left him stranded on the parched, barren plains of the low 100s.

"Don't worry," I said. "It'll happen. Your score will improve in spurts. One day you'll start shooting in the mid-nineties, just like that."

"That's all I want," he said, a bit too eagerly. "If I can get in the nineties, I'll be able to go out and relax, have fun. I want to be a nineties golfer. If I can get into the nineties, I'll be a happy man."

Just then that depressed pro at the Pinecrest Inn popped into my mind, shooting in the low 80s and needing to get back to par or below. And me, with this crazy trip, at the root of which was some notion that if I could shave ten strokes off my game, get into the 80s, I might attain some clarity that had eluded me. A sweet and sinister game, golf. The better you get, the better you want to be. You set a goal and then, when you get there, you discover that fulfillment is still just beyond the next fairway. Maybe we're destined to remain ten strokes away from happiness. Maybe there's some consolation in that knowledge, at least.

15

God Didn't Like the Pin Placement

The road from Pinehurst gives up golf reluctantly. On the outskirts heading south toward Rockingham, I passed several more golf communities completed or under construction, each promising links-blessed retirement for snowbound couples from Minneapolis or Cleveland. Eventually, though, I was back in the rural South, and in a few more miles tooled past a huge NASCAR track looming over Rockingham, a quiet town of tidy brick homes.

I crossed into South Carolina over pine-studded hills. About a half hour later I was delivered into a historic town of 6,000 residents called Cheraw, which dubbed itself the Prettiest Town in Dixie. That may not be far from the truth. William Tecumseh Sherman, who laid a path of destruction from Tennessee to the Atlantic coast in the waning days of the Civil War, camped here with his troops while waiting for the swollen waters of the Pee Dee River to subside. Sherman took a liking to the town and spared it from burning, which is why you can drive past the 1790 mansion on McIver Street, where the general stayed, or St. David's Church, built the same year, along with block after block of fine, large early- and mid-nineteenth-century homes. The 213-acre historic district in Cheraw would put to shame those in many larger cities.

Just beyond the town lies Cheraw State Park, which features, in addition to the usual state park activities of boating, swimming and camping, a brand-new golf course. Unfortunately, they were aerating the back nine when I arrived, so my visit was limited to a quick nine on the front in the muggy morning heat. It's an attractive course, with a spacious, new clubhouse and several holes overlooking a large lake. As nice as the course is, I have to admit the aeration gave me a convenient excuse for knocking off early. The heat was growing oppressive: still mid-morning and the temperature already hovered around ninety-five degrees, with the humidity registering around the level of a Roman steam bath. Shades of things to come as I rolled deeper into Dixie. The daily weather forecast, high nineties, with a 30 percent chance of afternoon thunderstorms, might as well have been set on autopilot.

South of Cheraw, Route 1 crests an immense range of sandy hills separating the highland Piedmont region of western South Carolina from the coastal Low Country to the east. Millions of years ago these hills were coastal dunes washed by the shores of a prehistoric ocean. Over the ages the ocean slowly receded, leaving uncovered the broad, fertile plains of the lowlands. Today, these Sand Hills, or Midlands, rest some seventy-five miles from the sea. But the terrain—dry, sandy soil and pine trees—remains so reminiscent of the shore that I kept expecting to see seagulls and an ocean vista just beyond the next rise. Around the town of Patrick ("Home of the Pine Straw Festival") the road slices deep into the piney shadows of a 46,000-acre reserve called the Sand Hills State Forest. I stopped at the McCloud Peach Orchard and bought a huge basket of peaches for $4. From there, a series of small towns: McBee, Bethune ("Home of the Chicken Strut"), Camden, Lugoff. Bumper sticker on a pickup: WANTED: GOOD WOMAN WHO CAN CLEAN AND COOK FISH, SEW, DIG WORMS, AND OWNS BOAT AND MOTOR. SEND PHOTO OF BOAT AND MOTOR.

Before long I was heading into the suburbs of Columbia, the capital. And the whole world was hot and wet, at least my whole world. I stopped at a course called Northwoods Golf Club. The name came, apparently, from the fact that the course was in the northern part of the city, but on this day that frost-invoking name seemed like an odd joke, because the heat was almost unbearable. I walked the course alone.

Northwoods has the look of a resort course even though it's not affiliated with any resort. Opened in 1992, it is a very pretty course to look at, but seems if anything to have been overdesigned. Northwoods has all kinds of swales and bumps and turns in unexpected places, with the result that you can be seriously punished even for hitting good, straight shots, especially if you are playing the course for the first time, as I was. After the wonderful honesty of a course such as Mid Pines, Northwoods struck me as a little sly, a little too pleased to pile on the whippings. Of course, part of my misery owed itself to the weather. The ball traveled like a tired swimmer through the clammy air. The fairways were spongy and the ball plugged instead of rolling. Holes fourteen through seventeen circle a small lake. The fifteenth requires a tee shot over a corner of the water, but even a perfect shot leaves you with a blind second shot to a green protected by mounds so high that you can't see the top of the pin. I walked from my ball to the green to get a line, then retraced my steps and put a wedge exactly where I had intended, only to discover that I had landed about fifteen yards right of the green. At least I missed the hidden bunkers. The next hole, the sixteenth, has a dastardly feature called a "waste bunker" that resembles a poorly maintained sand trap with rock-hard sand and weeds growing out of it. The waste bunker runs the entire length of the right side of the fairway. My reasonably well struck drive, which I expected to find in the near rough, instead found its way into this sea of crap. Try as I might, I couldn't extricate my ball.

Sometimes, when you get on the wrong side of a golf course, you are simply doomed. It was like making the wrong comment to a judge or traffic cop. Northwoods is a very pretty course; maybe I would have liked it better in the spring or fall. I'd certainly caught it at the wrong time of year. I excavated enough plugged balls from the waterlogged turf to earn an advanced degree in archaeology. By the end, though, I couldn't really blame the course for my troubles. I let the course get to me and began shanking and slicing and calling up all the nightmare habits from my pretrip days. I thought I had stashed these missteps away in some attic of bad memories, but here they were, fresh and mean as ever. I hobbled home with a score of 105, so depressed that I wondered if I was having a bad dream. A few hours earlier I would have told you with perfect confidence that I was no longer capable of shooting such a score.

I continued on Route 1 into downtown Columbia. For travelers arriving from the north, Route 1 is not the gateway to Columbia that probably gets recommended too often by Chamber of Commerce types. Columbia is a beautiful, proud old city. But Route 1 winds through the northern suburbs as Two Notch Road, a beleaguered strip of cheap motels offering rooms by the day, the week, the month. The road improves greatly upon reaching the charming old downtown, cutting east as Gervais Street. A couple of blocks over on the right is the mammoth University of South Carolina. Gervais Street feeds through an area of renovated buildings housing trendy restaurants with names like Mais Oui. I continued across a stately bridge over the Congaree River into West Columbia and started looking around for a motel.

I nursed my wounds in a Holiday Inn near the airport. I leafed through the phone book for the name of an old friend from college, Lamar, now a lawyer in Columbia. Though we hadn't spoken in ages, his voice was all friendliness. I'd be passing through Columbia again in a couple of weeks on my way home for a break to see my family. We made plans to meet up then. Lamar invited me to come to his house for dinner and the night, meet his family. I gratefully accepted. For tonight, though, I lay quietly in the air conditioning as an early-evening storm broke, bringing hard rain and some relief from the heat. The thunder was so loud it shook the room. After a while I crept through the rain and traffic to a place called Maurice's Piggy Park, where I ordered a barbecue pork plate. Maurice's is a Columbia institution, with pictures of Confederate generals on the wall, along with a picture of Maurice in his white suit, and bottles of pepper juice on the tables. The barbecue came with a tangy mustard-based yellow sauce, served on top like spaghetti sauce.

The next morning I awoke with an intense, self-destructive desire to return to the scene of yesterday's crimes, to have another go at Northwoods. I hadn't intended to play any courses twice, but I was so upset at having been used and abused that I wanted another crack. Perhaps fortunately, they were having a tournament that morning, so on my way out of town I headed instead to a course near the airport, not far from my motel room, called Indian River Golf Club. I was one of the first golfers there at a little before eight-thirty. A threesome warmed up on the driving range.

"Don't matter to me," one said when I asked if I could join them. "You can play with us, play through, whatever."

Dew still covered the fairways, and our footprints were the first to make their mark. Yesterday's disaster was forgotten.

My playing partners were Ralph, Tim and Hal. Tim and Hal were production workers at a local tire factory. Ralph was their supervisor.

"We work in hell," Tim said simply.

The thought of spending days making tires out of molten rubber, in this heat, made me cringe.

"I hope the plant's air-conditioned," I said.

"It's air-conditioned when management's around," Hal cracked.

Indian River is a newish course, built in 1992, its hills lined with homesites, the air filled with the crack of carpenters' hammers. I bogeyed the first hole, a dogleg left, after a good drive and a second shot that just overshot the green. The second hole is a downhill par-three of a little over 150 yards that requires hitting over an impenetrable, chest-high tangle of wildflowers and weeds. I stuck my first shot into the middle of that crap but rescued myself with a second tee shot that landed a few feet from the hole and enabled me to escape with a double-bogey five. On the third, a par-five, I mishit my first shot into some woods on the right, where it found an unplayable lie. I had to drop in the rough but hit a decent shot that left me lying about 130 yards from the hole. I then hit a nine-iron that stuck a foot from the hole and saved a par.

As we approached the fourth green, we noticed something odd about the flag stick. It was bent over, snapped like a toothpick. At first we thought it was the work of some errant putter with a bad temper. But when we reached the green we could see a telltale circle of scorched grass around the hole, with angry, jagged streaks of brown radiating outward. The pole was snapped and scorched, zapped by lightning during the previous evening's storm.

"Guess God didn't like the pin placement," Tim said.

Shift work had enabled these guys to golf together for years. They were all good, consistent, powerful golfers and were even better at giving each other a hard time. They were betting fifty cents a hole straight up, plus another fifty cents for closest to the pin on par-threes and another fifty cents for closest third shot to the pin on par-fives. Nobody seemed to be cleaning up. Perhaps it was part of their friendship that they took turns getting hot and cold.

Hal left a putt short. Ralph said, "Aw, what's the matter, sweetie? Get caught up in your skirt?"

On the next hole, Ralph sliced a ball into the woods. Hal gave a long, appreciative whistle. "That there's an AMF ball. *Adios,* motherfucker." Then Hal struck his own drive down the middle, a beautiful, long shot. "Did you see my ball look down and wave hello to yours as it passed over? Wasn't that nice?"

"So, what brings you to Columbia?" one of them asked inevitably.

When I told them about my trip, Tim said, "You're not married, I take it."

"Well, actually . . ." It came out that I had a wife and a child and another one on the way.

Tim considered this information carefully, shook his head, and said, "Good woman. Gooooooooood woman." Then he said, "Need a caddie?"

"Why not?" I said.

"If I told my wife I was going to travel down the East Coast going to all the public golf courses, she'd say, 'Have a nice trip. Don't forget to take everything you own with you.'" Tim paused for a moment, then said, "You sure you're really taking this trip? You sure this ain't just some dream you're having? Maybe you're dreaming all this and we're just part of your dream."

Comments to remember when the road gets old and I start feeling sorry for myself.

Hal said, "You ought to stay in South Carolina until the Hooters Invitational in Myrtle Beach. They got them Hooter girls in them itty-bitty T-shirts running around selling you cold beer."

He said cold beer in that southern way, as a single word without the "d" and with the emphasis on the first syllable, so it came out "COLEbeer." I had learned to call it that while living in Chattanooga, Tennessee, in my first reporting job after college. It's a great term but one that, like "y'all," doesn't necessarily travel well. I exasperated a bartender on a trip back home to Boston from Tennessee. I kept ordering COLEbeers until the bartender, a wiry man with a heavy Boston accent and a voice like a pack of unfiltered Camels, snapped, "It's *cold,* already. What do you think I'm gonna do, urinate in it?"

Hal had the remnants of a bottle of tequila in his golf bag. He unzipped the bag and gingerly pulled out just the neck of the bottle, as if handling radioactive materials. The bottle had been sitting there for weeks, since the last trip to Myrtle Beach. Just the sight of it gave him a hangover.

"That ain't never coming out again," Hal said, shaking his head at some memory of debauchery. "I'm scared to touch it."

When I left, Tim said, "Don't forget to put us in the book. Tell 'em you played with three rednecks in Columbia, South Carolina."

South of Columbia, Route 1, called the Augusta Highway, rolls through miles of farmland interrupted occasionally by neat, attractive little crossroads towns such as Leesville and Batesburg. In Leesville, a town of shady streets and old Victorian homes with generous porches and plenty of room for rocking chairs, I pulled over at a little neighborhood bank that had a drive-through cash machine. I suppose one ought not be surprised by anything in the age of the microchip, and yet there was something eerie about the receipt the machine spit out at me along with ten crisp twenties. I was a drifter passing through, utterly unknown to the human population. And yet this runty, unprepossessing little machine, tied in to some unfathomable network of cables and wires and databanks, knew my name, my checking account number, and how much money I had left to spend. Convenience in exchange for privacy in the modern world. Next, I stopped at a grocery store for some bananas and an iced tea. I was eating a lot of bananas these days. They were nature's own fast food, the perfect ready-to-go road lunch, especially when you reached the point where one more grease-stained paper bag shoved through a drive-through window by a pimply teenager might make you give up and go home. Every couple of hundred miles, when I pulled up next to some dumpster to unload accumulated road ballast, I'd find blackened banana peels draped over back-seats, cowering under the brake pedal, moldering in the driver's-side map holder.

I rolled on through a wide spot in the road called Monetta, "Home of the Monetta Trojans," past endless peach orchards with roadside stands selling baskets of hard, firm peaches for a couple of bucks, bleak trailer homes, immense hay fields with the hay bundled in great, tight wheels. Near Ridge Spring, about twenty miles north of Aiken, I climbed a long hill, crested, came down into a dip, and spotted a small sign: "Public Golf Course."

I took a right onto Bogeyville Road, really just a semi-paved drive with ruts every few inches and trailer homes every few hundred yards. The road would not allow me to go more than thirty miles an hour before the car rattled with enough force to reduce kidney stones to dust. Bogeyville Road led to an even rougher dirt road leading to the parking lot and clubhouse for Bogeyville Golf Course.

The clubhouse was a converted trailer, with a large mural out front over the door. The mural, painted by a local artist named Tsabel Vandervelde, showed, on the left, two golfers standing on the first tee under a blue sky, with angel wings on their backs and cupids hovering about. The right side of the mural showed the same two golfers, this time standing on the eighteenth green. Storm clouds had moved in, the golfers were transformed from angels to fork-tailed, cloven-hoofed devils, and the cupids had disappeared, replaced by a dragon. One doesn't usually see the metamorphosis of a golf round quite so artistically or honestly displayed. Golf courses, which want you to play frequently, usually sell the angel side of the equation. But I suppose such cheerful realism is consistent with a course that has the temerity to call itself Bogeyville in the first place. This could only be a mom-and-pop course. The mural and the name would never have survived the marketing department of a corporation or the bureaucracy of a municipal committee.

The mural and the name are the least of Bogeyville's idiosyncrasies. The course, for example, is home to perhaps the world's only single-player best-ball tournament. In conventional best ball, foursomes play together as a team. Everybody hits each shot, but only the best of the four counts. If one player splits the fairway while everyone else slices into the trees, everybody hits the second shot from the spot of the good drive. Best ball is a popular format because it notches down the pressure on individual golfers to perform. Scores tend to be absurdly low. And even hackers can experience the thrill of a below-par round. That's conventional best ball. At Bogeyville, someone came up with a tournament based on the mulligan.

"You know how, when you hit a terrible shot, then tee up again and hit a second, you're more relaxed and you always hit a better shot? Well, why not have a tournament where everybody gets a second chance?" an assistant in the clubhouse explained. So in best ball, Bogeyville style, each player gets two shots per attempt and plays the best one. It has become a popular tournament.

The course itself is one of the most unusual I have played and, I suppose, it's one of those courses you either love or hate. "Don't waste your time with Bogeyville," one man told me. "There are plenty of better courses down in Aiken." But a woman said, "You've *got* to play Bogeyville. It's so fun. It's like golfing in *Deliverance*." After a few holes I found myself squarely in the camp of Bogeyville fans, even though I wanted to snap my clubs in two out of frustration at some of the surprises it had in store. The course has a sense of humor. And you'd better, too, if you play there.

The second hole, for example, is a par-five that turns left across a pond, then turns sharply left again. A complete U-turn! A stand of tall trees discourages ambitious golfers from attempting a shortcut straight to the green. In case the trees don't do the trick, signs posted at the tee box warn that such shots are illegal, since they involve hitting directly over the heads of people teeing off on the third hole. Another hole, the eighth, practically drove me to distraction. Playing alone again, I hit a beautiful three-wood off the tee, straight down the middle. It was one of those sweet shots that puts a goofy grin on your face and adds a quickness to your step as you tromp on up the fairway. My only thought was whether I'd be plunking an eight-iron or nine-iron to the green. The farther I walked, though, the more concerned I became. I couldn't see the ball anywhere. The woods on the far side of the dogleg loomed a lot closer than I imagined. I looked for that ball for at least ten minutes, first on the fairway, then in the rough, and finally in those greedy laughing trees. I never found it. It was a patented Bogeyville "gotcha." Very nearly the same thing happened to me with a pond on the eleventh hole. Then there is the par-five twelfth hole, which takes a wicked turn to the right. Unfortunately the turn is invisible from the tee box, obscured by a mountainous peak in the middle of the fairway. If you hit the ball too straight, you miss the turn and your ball skids to the left of the green into some funky rough.

Despite, or perhaps because of all this, Bogeyville has its charms, starting with the $8 greens fee I had paid to walk eighteen holes. And there is the blissful feeling of being all alone in the middle of nowhere. The sense of isolation is no accident. That's the way the man who built the course intended it to be. The man is Dr. H. D. Wyman, a physician who was wait-listed at a local country club and decided not to wait.

Dr. Wyman and a couple of partners bought a large parcel of undeveloped land and set about designing and building a course from scratch. There was no Donald Ross input here, just eyeballs and a feel for the land, and rough sketches by Dr. Wyman and another local golfer named Rhett Boyd. Nor were there teams of professional contractors and bulldozers to clear the timber and lay the sod. That's what sons were for.

"He wanted to show my brother and me how to work," Neill Wyman said. "We learned everything from agronomy to heavy equipment operation. We learned self-reliance at a very early age. A lot of the work was done by hand. We spent weeks chopping tree roots out of the fairways with axes."

The hilly terrain was left pretty much alone, partly due to necessity (you can't move hills without bulldozers), but also out of respect for the natural lay of the land.

"That's why, no matter how many times you play the course, you very seldom have the same shot twice," Wyman said. "Our biggest attribute is solitude. We offer a lot more than golf. When you were out golfing, did you hear a soul? No. There's been no development around the course, and that's intentional. You can get away from everything out here."

Neill is superintendent of Bogeyville. He is also the manager, teaching pro, marketing representative, chief executive, tee box repairer, ditch digger and holder of a thousand other odd jobs. We sat in his small office at the back of the clubhouse. He was sweaty and grimy from digging an irrigation ditch at the rebuilt fifteenth tee box in the midday heat.

"There is not a job that is above anybody or beneath anybody here," Wyman said. He knows every twist and turn on the course. Every stretch of open fairway recalls a memory of roots and boulders extracted by sweat and toil nearly a quarter of a century ago.

"My brother, Marion, and I were in high school then. We'd get all our friends involved. At one point there were probably a couple of hundred people working with us. For us, though, it was every weekend, every holiday, every Sunday. There was no taking weekends off. On Thanksgiving we'd have Thanksgiving dinner, then spend the rest of the day out on the course. Finally, we had our grand opening on July 4, 1975. There was a big bash."

"You must have felt a lot of pride that day," I said as we sat in his small office at the back of the clubhouse.

He thought for a moment, then said, "You've got resentment as well as pride. It's taken so much of your time, so much of your life, you sort of want to get away from it."

That's exactly what Neill Wyman did for about a decade. After college, he went to work for a defense contractor near Aiken. Wyman worked his way up to supervisor. But when the plant began massive cutbacks around 1986, Wyman could see the handwriting on the wall. It was time to find another job. Bogeyville had never made money. Neill Wyman came home to Bogeyville to try to make that happen. It is still a family-run business. Wyman's wife, Lynn, is the bookkeeper.

"It's strictly a daily fee operation," Wyman said. "We're very low-key, informal. We have a hard enough time keeping shirts on the golfers, let alone collars. It's a no-frills atmosphere. We cater to the workingman's environment. I'm raising kids myself. Incidental entertainment money is not that plentiful. But you'll spend what you've got in your pocket to play golf."

At the time of my visit, a construction crew was busy building a new clubhouse to replace the old converted trailer. A log house, it was going to retain the rustic charms of Bogeyville. And, I hoped, the artwork of Tsabel Vandervelde.

16

Cabbages and Kings

Twenty miles north of the Georgia border, Route 1 intersects with State Route 19 at the busy little city of Aiken, South Carolina, whose whitewashed downtown sparkles with almost tropical cheerfulness. Once a manufacturing and farming town, Aiken has repackaged itself as a warm-weather, low-cost retirement haven, the sort of place that pops up on "Ten Best" lists in *Modern Maturity*.

I arrived at Midland Valley Country Club, a block or two off Route 1, on a Sunday morning. The starter initially hooked me up with a pair of older women, which would have been fun. But when I hit my tee shot, a three-wood that sailed about 250 yards down the fairway, the group just behind, two women and a man, suggested I join them.

"You'll have more fun with a man along," one of the ladies said to me. "So will John."

We let the twosome play ahead and I shook hands with John and Holly Lasienski, and their friend and neighbor, Linda King. John, a New Jersey native gone southern, had spent much of his career as a personnel manager for a nearby nuclear defense plant, the same one where Neill Wyman had worked before leaving to manage Bogeyville. Built at the height of the Cold War, in 1950, the plant occupied 200,000 acres on Route 78 just east of Aiken. Construction required destroying seven rural communities, places with All-American names such as Ellenton, Meyers Mill, and Sleepy Hollow. About the time the towns were leveled, one anonymous resident posted a hand-printed roadside sign: "It's hard to understand why our town must be destroyed to make a bomb that will destroy someone else's town that they love as much as we love ours." Then it added, in a poignant twist, "But we feel that they picked not only just the best spot in the U.S., but in the whole world."

John, now about seventy, had retired just before the plant stopped production, before he had to do the painful firing. Holly, who was from South Dakota originally, and Linda, who was from Augusta, still worked at the plant, as part of the remnant workforce in charge of cleaning up after decades of nuclear weapons production.

I assumed I would be the big hitter in the group, but after I'd hit my great three-wood off the tee and was quietly basking in what I was certain must be universal awe and wonder from my new playing partners, John walked up to his ball, wound an effortless backswing, and outdrove me by twenty yards. John was not a large fellow, either. He was fit but slender and not too tall. Somehow he got every ounce of weight behind that ball.

"Nice shot," I said, abashed.

John, Holly and Linda were members at this course and lived a couple of blocks from the clubhouse. They golfed together frequently.

"You've got to watch out for these ladies," John said confidentially. "You make one mistake and they'll take advantage of it."

Midland Valley was a challenging course with narrow, tree-lined fairways.

"You really came at the wrong time of year," Linda said. "In the springtime, when the weather is cooler and the flowers are out all over the course, it's absolutely beautiful here."

She was right. I had plunged into the Deep South like a moth into a candle flame, at the worst time of the year, the dead of summer. Under the relentless heat, even rounds that I started in the refreshing mildness of the early morning turned into sweaty endurance tests by the fourth or fifth hole. The most carefully watered fairways looked tired and thirsty. The flora, showy as a prom queen during the spring, had retreated into a dull, uniform green.

John wore a peach-colored shirt and a white cap, both bearing the insignia of the Augusta National course a few miles down the road. John told me that he had been able to get into the Masters several times in recent years, thanks to a friend who runs a concession there.

"I was able to do something nice for him," John said. "He was able to do something nice for me. It just goes to show you that if you treat people well, it pays off in the end."

John spoke of the National course with a sort of hushed reverence.

"It's like no other place in the world. Just being there makes your hair stand up on end," he said, tugging at the white hairs on his forearm. "If you're ever passing through here in April, let me know. I'll see what I can do to get you in."

When I asked John how he managed to get such distance from his drives, he just smiled. Then he told me that he had won several long ball contests. We were even going into the last hole, a long par-four. I got into a fairway bunker and double-bogeyed the hole for an 88 on the day. John parred the hole and wound up with an 86. It wasn't the first time I'd been beaten by a man nearly twice my age, but it was the first time I'd been beaten and outdriven by one.

It was late afternoon when I crossed the Route 1 bridge over the Savannah River, pulled off the highway and found myself in downtown Augusta, Georgia. Augusta is the second place along Route 1, after Pinehurst, that claims to be the Golf Capital of the

World. About a hundred miles east of Route 1, along the coast, lies another World Golf Capital: Myrtle Beach. Of the three, Augusta's claim seems the most tenuous. True, Augusta has the National, which, along with Scotland's St. Andrews, is one of the world's two most famous golf courses. The Masters is among the most hallowed sporting contests anywhere. But "golf capital" to me implies something more democratic, more generally accessible than anything brought to mind by Augusta National.

Weary from golf and travel, I zeroed in on the biggest and nearest hotel I could find, the Radisson Hotel, where, despite my sweat-stained golf clothes, they offered me a businessman's rate. In the center of a bricked plaza outside the hotel, a statue of Arnold Palmer gazed intently up a phantom fairway, on his way to Masters victory.

The plaque read:

ARNOLD PALMER WON THE MASTERS GOLF TOURNA-
MENT IN 1958, 1960, 1962 AND 1964. THE MAN WHO
MANY CONSIDER TO BE THE MOST DYNAMIC GOLFER
OF ALL TIME WILL GRACE AUGUSTA PERPETUALLY.

After a shower and a rest I walked along the promenade overlooking the river. I ate dinner in a British pub and microbrewery, then strolled around the faded, charming old downtown, gone halfway to seed in that way peculiar to southern cities—as if one major restoration project would return it to some lost greatness. When downtown areas in northern cities decline, they do it all the way. The blight is uncompromising and stark. In the South, where memory is stronger than neglect, such areas hold on more stubbornly, as if kept alive by ghosts. A couple of blocks from downtown, neighborhoods of grand old wooden homes, once inhabited by the local gentry, no doubt, in the age before the automobile, languished in graceful deterioration. I walked up Greene Street and down Telfair Street, past solid old buildings where, long ago, mothers and daughters, dressed in Sunday hats and gloves, must have come to shop and have lunch, having ridden into town on the streetcar. But now I spotted hardly a soul, save a solitary driver here and there. In Augusta, all the action has moved out to the suburbs, along a series of six-lane, exhaust-scented thoroughfares of fast food and strip malls, indistinguishable from their counterparts in Detroit or Akron or Norfolk—*Welcome to America, may I take your order?*

I drove west out of downtown the next morning on the most prominent of these suburban strips, Washington Road, to find Augusta National. It seems more than a little incongruous to find such an exclusive club in such a banal setting. One expects the course to lie along a winding country road, perhaps, or in an old-money neighborhood of huge homes. Yet Augusta National's neighbors are these: A Steak and Ale, a Dollar General Store, International House of Pancakes, The Chinese Buffet, The Hair Addition, The Scottish Rite Temple, and Pro Cleaners. Over there are the Double Eagle Club "Welcome members and guests," a Domino's Pizza, Whole Life Ministries and Christian Book Store, Economy Rent-a-Car, Flashback Nightclub, Jay's Music and Sound Super Center; Hooters, Books a Million and The Comedy House, featuring (tonight only) Tommy Chong from Cheech and Chong—"He's still smoking!"

And then, at the corner of Washington and Berckman Road, you happen upon the Hedge, and you know you have found Augusta National. Amid all the club's fabled foliage—those fragrant magnolias, white-blooming tea olives, Carolina cherries, and technicolor azaleas, pink dogwoods and fairways softer than a chamois cloth—you don't hear much about the Hedge. Yet it may be the most indispensable piece of greenery on the property. This is no mere courtesy hedge—*here's the property line, friend!* This is a hedge with attitude. Its interlocking arms, stretching for hundreds of yards around the perimeter of the course, form a verdant barrier to prevent passersby from catching so much as a glimpse of the grounds. As if looking were akin to trespassing, as if some curious hacker might take a divot with his eyes. Every so often the hedge parts for a gate, but the gates, colored a somber, dark, get-out-of-here green, seem even more impenetrable than the hedge. They sport signs warning, in case you haven't gotten the message: POSITIVELY NO ADMITTANCE. Like a showy entourage of bodyguards surrounding a movie star, the hedge seems to cry, "Notice me. Now, go away." Augusta National wants your admiration; it just doesn't want you hanging around.

Bobby Jones came across this spot almost by accident, while searching for a place to locate a little golf course he had in mind that would be playable through the winter. Jones had thought first of Atlanta but visited Augusta at the suggestion of his friend Clifford Roberts, a banker from New York who had vacationed in the area. It is said that from the first moment Jones came across a 365-acre parcel at the corner of Washington Road and Berckman Road, with its gently rolling hills and serpentine Rae's Creek running throughout, he knew he'd found his spot. He wrote modest letters to some friends and acquaintances asking if they'd like to join him in developing a golf course. Today, the tournament that developed after the course opened in 1933, the Masters, may be the toughest ticket in all of sports. The club used to hold a lottery for Augustans, with the winners allowed to watch practice rounds. But demand grew so heavy that the lottery was dropped. Residents of Augusta cherish the National, which pours hundreds of thousands of dollars into the local economy around tournament time and puts their city on the world map for a few days each year. Most locals can tell you about the time they got in to see some of the Masters. But when it comes to people who actually get to play here, members tend to be corporate chieftains who fly in from out of town on private jets.

About six blocks away from Augusta National sits another golf course, this one as open and accessible as Augusta National is forbidding. Officially called Augusta Municipal Golf Course, the course is better known locally as the "Cabbage Patch." Even the scorecard says "The Patch." The Patch snuggles up against Daniel Field, a small downtown airport (the larger commercial airport is south of the city). Fairways and runways run parallel to one another. The course is dotted with stern warnings not to hit practice shots onto the runways. To nongolfers this rule would seem obvious. Why would anyone do such a thing? They would not understand, as the course managers obviously did, the preternatural urge to whack a ball out onto that long, flat strip of pavement, just to see it travel. They would not understand why golfers in Memphis stand on majestic bluffs overlooking the Mississippi and drive balls at passing barges and the setting sun.

Augusta National had long since closed for the summer, even to members, in order to protect its fairways and greens from the heat and sun. But the Patch struggled gamely on, its fairways baked hard and wanting a cut. It was open to all takers, those daft enough to go golfing in temperatures that would wilt a steel magnolia. I plunked down $10 and marched off to the first tee box. The contrast was irresistible; this was public golf in its purest form. No Augusta National, perhaps, but a fine venue for the Greater Heartbreak Open. After a couple of solo holes I hooked up with a man named Doug Hopkins, who was fifty-four but appeared at least ten years younger. Doug had grown up in Massachusetts but joined the Navy out of high school, moved south and never returned north for more than a visit. Offered a chance to retire early from his civilian job designing communications systems for the Navy, he didn't have to be asked twice. When I hooked up with him, he had just moved to Augusta from North Carolina to join his fiancée. They were building a log home in a county just north of the city. Doug had reestablished contact with a father who had left home one day when Doug was a boy. Doug had moved his father down to a retirement home near Augusta and begun the process of healing. A soft-spoken man with an accent that was a curious amalgam of New England Yankee and Carolina twang, Doug was embarking on a new life. As a young man in the Navy, he'd golfed several times a week on the base course and worked his way down to a single-digit handicap. In his civilian days he'd let his game lapse. Now, armed with a brand-new set of clubs, thanks to an insurance settlement from a stolen truck, he was teaching himself to play all over again.

The Patch is one of those straightforward courses where you feel it would be a crime to do anything but score the best round of your life. But somehow the very openness kills you. On the first hole, a 478-yard par-five, I hit my first two shots well. My second shot seemed to roll forever on the dried fairway, finally stopping about twenty yards over the green. Looking at my scorecard now, I'm still trying to figure out how that promising start translated into a 6. On the seventh, a minuscule 312-yard par-four, disaster struck. I hit my tee shot off the heel of the club, sending it off into some trees to the left of the fairway. From there I screwed around and wound up with an 8 on the hole. Eight strokes to travel 312 yards. Damn this game.

About the time I hit the skids Doug started to come alive, hitting nice, easy, consistent shots. On the thirteenth, another par-four of 312 yards, he pulled out his new driver and nearly drove the green. He looked so quietly satisfied that I felt I was witnessing a rebirth. On the back nine I settled down with a 42 to go with a depressing 51 on the front. I would have been pleased with a 93 in Maine or Connecticut; by now, I was expecting better of myself. My goal of breaking 80 seemed to be receding before me.

Wrens, Georgia, is a quiet crossroads town about forty miles south of Augusta. It was here that Erskine Caldwell held his first newspaper job, before pushing on up the road to Augusta, where he would scandalize the locals with *Tobacco Road*.

I arrived in town a little after 8 A.M. and found the Four Seasons Golf Club, a nine-hole course, on a state highway a couple of miles off Route 1. The air was still as only country air can be, the silence so full it felt like something stuck in my ears. The only sounds were the chirping of birds and the sleepy, far-off drone of long-distance truckers on their way to Augusta or Waycross.

"How much to walk nine?" I asked.

"Five," said the young man.

"Five dollars?"

He nodded.

I handed over the money.

This pleasant, well-kept little course, with a nice variation of woods, water and open spaces, is just the sort of unexpected gem you stumble on when you travel down lonely roads with a set of clubs in your trunk and no particular plans besides finding another round of golf. A couple of holes were quite challenging, especially the eighth and ninth, with carries over a pond. I parred six of the nine holes but because the other three were a triple bogey and two doubles, I wound up with a 43 for the nine. I finished the nine in a little over an hour. It was still early and I was raring for another go-around. In the quiet clubhouse an older man had just checked in. When I handed over my second five for another nine holes, the man looked my way.

"Are you playing by yourself?"

"So far," I said. "Mind if I join you?"

"Would you?" he said.

Clarence Knighton was in his mid-seventies. He wore a handlebar mustache, a straw hat and a T-shirt celebrating another famous old highway, Route 66. Clarence lived in Gibson, a community not far from Wrens.

"How long have you been a golfer?" I asked as we stretched out.

"Oh, a long time," he said. "Probably forty years."

There was a pause and he added, "I love golf. Golf is a great game. It's a tough game. It's the second-toughest game there is. The toughest game is life itself."

Clarence had been a college football player, a soldier, a teacher. He'd coached football in Zebulon, Georgia, and worked as a youth director for the YMCA in Montgomery, Alabama, and Newport News, Virginia. He'd left Georgia as a young man and lived in Alabama, Tennessee and Virginia. He returned in retirement to this corner of rural Georgia, to be near his wife's family. Fresh out of high school he shipped off to war, where he piloted one of those vulnerable little landing boats that deposited Marines on the beaches at Salerno, Sicily and Normandy. It was at Sicily, when a burst of enemy machine-gun fire pasted the boat but miraculously missed its pilot, that Clarence Knighton found religion.

"In Sicily, I gave my heart to Jesus," he said. "You're scared all the time. Your knees are shaking. You put your trust in the Man upstairs."

A couple of years later, while studying at a small college in Georgia, he found golf.

These days he swung a driver that had a bubble shaft and an expensive-looking graphite head but was actually a cheap knock-off he'd found in the Wal-mart for forty or fifty dollars. He had decent power but, more important, he'd perfected that art that enables old guys to beat players far younger and longer off the tee—he kept the ball on the fairway.

"When I was seventy-three I shot a seventy-three," he told me.

Clarence spoke of his family, and of his travels, and of his experiences in the war. We spoke of golf.

"Boy, that Tiger Woods, he can smack that apple," Clarence said. Clarence did some apple smacking himself. On this fine morning he shot a 41 for nine, a shot better than I.

"I was going to say I hope I can play as well as you do when I'm your age," I told him. "But, since you beat me, I'd better say I wish I could play as well as you right now."

He smiled a satisfied smile. "You're a nice young man," he said.

On the eighth hole I went into some rough next to the pond to help him find an errant ball. He stopped me short, sent me back to my bag for a club. "Always take your fighting stick when you go in there. You'll find rattlesnakes, moccasins, cottonmouth."

When we holed out our last shots of the round, Clarence seemed sorry to say good-bye and I know that I was. We sat in the cart for several minutes, exchanging pictures of our families.

Clarence said, "I've been blessed. Wonderful wife, two wonderful kids, four wonderful grandkids. I've been blessed."

On my way out of town I stopped for gas on a side street in a black neighborhood. Just beyond the gas station was a shack from which poured wisps of sweet-smelling wood smoke. The smell was unmistakable. Barbecue. I paid for the gas and walked over to the shack. The only sign was a hand-painted one over a small window: "Order here." My sandwich came on thick slabs of bland white bread. You can find great barbecue in shacks or fancy dining rooms across the South, but if they serve it on a fancy roll, leave it alone. Bread is merely an edible utensil for true barbecue, a way to keep the sauce from running down your fingers and onto your pants. I headed back out onto Route 1 eating my sandwich and singing to an Everly Brothers song on the radio.

17

Gator Bait

Before finishing my trip through Georgia and Florida, I came off the road for the birth of our second daughter, Caroline. A time of wonder, of happiness. Also a time full of reminders that life, larks or no, moves inexorably on. I spent my weeks home writing, painting the nursery, preparing for the baby, trying to make up for my excursion by being a good husband. My six months' leave from work, which once yawned before me like the end of time itself, was now winding down to a few precious weeks. I'd started this trip in the sweetness of spring. Now, the breeze carried a sharpness warning me the world was turning serious again. Leaving home, leaving my growing family behind, did not fill me with nervous excitement as it had in springtime. That feeling was replaced with a sense of determination, of purpose and also with a sort of premature nostalgia for a time that I could already feel slipping away from me.

I began the final leg, mid-Georgia through Florida, the night before Halloween. The last time I'd seen Georgia, in the swelter of summer, the hills were burned brown by relentless heat and lack of rain. When I returned, the heat and humidity had retreated, and autumn was just beginning to show red and gold in the leaves.

"It's a great day for golf," I said to the pro shop manager at the Swainsboro Country Club in the central Georgia town of the same name.

"I know it," he said, directing me out to an empty first fairway. "I don't know where all the golfers are. Come a rainy day, they all want to play, seems like."

I would play my first round back solo. It was nice to stretch my road muscles and golf muscles. I'd only managed a couple of rounds while at home. In this feast-or-famine season, I'd been famished for two months and now it was time for the last supper. The Swainsboro Country Club, adjacent to a municipal airport, was a nine-hole course when I visited but was in the process of being converted to eighteen. Bulldozers and backhoes busied themselves clearing trees and marking lots for homes fronting the planned holes. The Bermuda fairways on the open nine were spongy and lush, having made it through the broiling summer thanks to frequent watering. The greens were another story. In order to allow golfers to continue playing, a greens keeper on a southern course has to do exactly what a lawn-care expert would tell a homeowner not to do to his own lawn—cut it to within a few millimeters of its life. By late October, with the weather just beginning to turn cooler in these parts, the greens were still scorched. This course would not reach its peak until mid-May. That's when Swainsboro holds its annual Pine Tree tournament. Today the greens were salved in a protective layer of sand, through which a tender beard of fresh grass shoots were struggling to emerge. This made for interesting putting; another obstacle for my Greater Heartbreak Open.

I hit the ball hard but into the left rough on the first hole, a long par-four of 397 yards. A tree stood between me and the green, I couldn't find any distance markers, and was at a loss as to what club to use. After knocking my second shot twenty yards beyond the green, I discovered that the 200-yard and 150-yard distance markers were plates buried in the fairways. Unfortunately, you could not make them out unless you were right over them. This problem was by no means confined to Swainsboro. In fact, it had by now developed into something of a pet peeve. I'm talking about the inexplicable tendency of course designers to make personality statements with their distance markers. I have seen distances marked by small trees, distinctive shrubs, plates, poles, posts, hand-carved wooden signs—too often I had seen no markers at all. What golfers want here is information, not aesthetics, information crucial to averting a disaster. After all, highway departments don't get cute with traffic signs, do they? Imagine one town indicating its speed limits with banners hung from trees, another using colored balls suspended on a chain. Here's to the establishment of a new national standard for fairway distance markers: A blue pole for 200 yards, white for 150, red for 100.

This said, Swainsboro was a fine place to begin again, a pleasant rural course. My score for two times around the nine was a middling but not disastrous 93. I drove south with no particular destination other than a few miles down the road. I passed a series of tiny towns, none with promising-looking lodgings. A radio ad came on for a motel in Statesboro. I pulled onto Interstate 16 and followed it east. Statesboro is a college town, home to Georgia Southern University. I stayed at a hotel not far from Statesboro's historic district, most of which dated post Civil War. Sherman was not as kind here as he was in Cheraw, S.C. He practically burned the town to the ground.

I drove through silent fields early the next morning to Vidalia, about four miles west of Route 1 in central Georgia. My *Golf Digest 4,200 Best Places to Play* had included a Vidalia course called Foxfire on its list of "Great Values." "Best secret in Georgia," one subscriber said of the course, built in the early 1990s. "It has everything," said another.

Foxfire sits in a development of large, expensive-looking homes, but the greens fee was only $16. When the clubhouse attendant directed me to the carts, I said I was planning to walk.

"Oh," she said, surprised. "Then I owe you some money."

The weekday walking fee was just $10. So the great value part was correct. It was a cool, clear morning, just a tinge of crispness in the air for clarity. But there was hardly a soul about. So it would be a second straight round of solitary golf.

The course starts promisingly enough, with a pretty par-four curving around a small pond. A nice par-three, just a few steps from the first green, follows. After the second hole, though, Fox-fire and I started rubbing each other the wrong way. The staff was friendly enough, from the pleasant woman in the clubhouse to the maintenance worker who—and this was the only time this has ever happened to me on a golf course—stopped his tractor, hopped off, and tromped through the underbrush with me until we found my ball. No, the problem owed itself to the layout of the course. Set amid a development of big new homes on rolling hills, the holes stretch so far apart from one another that I lost all sense of being on a golf course. Foxfire seemed like a series of dis-connected holes, as if the architect had been given a mandate to use every bit of the development's too-generous acreage. Built in the age of the golf cart, the course reminded me of those strip developments on the outskirts of every city where barriers to pedestrians make it more convenient to drive to the store next door than to walk. It seemed indifferent, if not openly hostile to walkers. Most courses provide handy shortcuts for a walker, straight trails or footbridges to avoid the long sweep of the cart path. Here, there are so many ponds and other obstacles that the only practical way to walk is to stay on the cart paths.

The course itself, even from the white tees, is too challenging by half for an average golfer, with all sorts of devilish fairway traps, narrow corridors and long carries over ponds or marsh. The eighteenth is a par-five with a pond sitting about 250 yards away from the tee. The pond itself is wide, so that you have to hit a near-perfect drive to have any hope of clearing it with your sec-ond shot. I hit an excellent drive followed by my best fairway wood, and I still wasn't certain until I wandered forever along a path and across a bridge to the other side, that my ball had even made it over the water. For a golfer without much power, the hole would have been more than simply challenging; it would have been impossible. It took me four hours to play the course all by myself, without a single delay for another golfer or a break between nines. An uninterrupted solo round would normally have taken about two and a half. This meant I had spent more than an hour and a half just getting from one hole to the next. As I made my way up the eighteenth fairway toward the green, I shanked a nine-iron. Instead of landing on the green, my ball skipped off to the right, up an embankment and onto the gravel parking lot, a few yards from my car. Perhaps the iron, and the ball, shared my sentiments; it was time to move on.

Vidalia, a town of tidy streets and about ten thousand residents, is famous for the Vidalia onion, a bulb so big and sweet that it has made this small central Georgia town famous with chefs and diners around the world. The whole history of the Vidalia onion started in 1931, when a local farmer named Mose Coleman, searching for some way to make it through the Great Depression, ordered by mail some Yellow Granex Type F Hybrid onion seeds. These were standard seeds, planted in farming communities around the nation. In most areas, they produced standard yellow onions. But what popped out of Mose Coleman's field that spring were not those sharp-tasting little yellow onions but extraordinarily sweet, full, light-brown bulbs. Some combination of sandy, low-sulfur soil and mild temperatures around Vidalia produces an onion with more sugar than is contained in a can of Coca-Cola. Word of Mose Coleman's success spread quickly, and soon everybody was sending off for seeds. The Vidalia onion was born. Now the term *Vidalia onion* is as jealously protected in these parts as *Champagne* is in the Champagne region of France. Only thirteen counties and parts of seven others surrounding Vidalia may call their produce Vidalia onions. Nearly three hundred local growers ship onions around the world. The town boasts a Vidalia Onion Commission and a

Vidalia Onion Hall of Fame (honoring growers, not onions). The spring harvest is marked by the crowning of the Vidalia Onion Beauty Queen. Some people prefer Vidalias raw, peeled and eaten like an apple. But the best way is sliced into thick slabs, brushed with melted butter, and grilled outdoors until just soft enough to cut with a fork.

I stopped for lunch at a place called the Vidalia Onion Company on my way out of town. It was a warehouse with a restaurant and gift shop attached to it. You could have gift jars of Vidalia relish and Vidalia vinaigrette salad dressing and Vidalia barbecue sauce shipped anywhere in the country. Order the onion rings, a woman in town told me.

I'm not a big fan of onion rings. Don't get me wrong. I like fried, artery-clogging snack foods as much as the next American. But onion rings go over the top. Usually they remind me of sneaker laces that have been soaked in motor oil, rolled in sawdust and burnt crisp. Of course, most onion rings aren't made with Vidalia onions. I ordered a burger and the recommended rings. These were lightly coated, crisp but not too crisp, and the onions inside were so plump, moist and sweet that you could have ordered them for dessert. I still hate onion rings, but I'd drive miles out of my way for these.

As I rolled south on Route 1, autumn cotton, not spring onions, dominated the landscape. Plump white popcorn balls, swollen and nearly ready for harvest, speckled the earth as far as I could see. At crossroads farming towns such as Alma and Baxley I saw signs of the Old South and the New intermingling. A booster sign cheered on a local high school football team, the Appling County Pirates. A simple wooden sign by the side of the road in Baxley said: "A day hemmed in prayer seldom unravels." There were Baptist churches and tanning salons. And, off to the left, the stark, ominous towers of the Hatch Nuclear Electric Generating Plant. Each of the towns had, in addition to its Baptist churches, at least one Catholic church, usually housed in a simple white frame building, with the name of the priest out front, unmistakably Hispanic, with a sign indicating that services were held *en español*. This was a legacy of the thousands of Mexican laborers who migrate each year up the eastern United States, following the crops: oranges in Florida, cotton in Georgia, tobacco in Virginia. Along the way they are planting the seeds of a new culture in the Old South.

About sixty miles north of Waycross the land grows more swamplike and shows the first hints of becoming semi-tropical. Short, stubby palm trees begin to appear. A long, raised roadway took me over a swamp. By early evening I was nearing Waycross and the great primeval bowl of the Okefenokee Swamp. From an Indian word meaning "land of the trembling earth," the Okefenokee is a 680-square-mile wilderness of black water, alligators, snakes, cypress trees, red maple and swamp black gum. The trembling earth refers to the vast layer of floating peat covering the water. It was after dark and threatening rain when I pulled into a roadside motel in Waycross, which lies near the northern entrance to the swamp.

As its name suggests, Waycross was born as a place where roads converged. First came the stage lines, then the railroads, then the highways. Back in the days when Route 1 was the primary gateway to Florida, Waycross bustled with roadside kitsch and tourist attractions. But Interstate 95 cut a path down the coast, relegating Waycross to a tourist backwater. It's still an important rail center, though, and the night air was alive with the clack of rails and the forlorn moan of locomotive whistles. The motel parking lot was filled with CSX rail crews awaiting departures. I was in luck, the motel manager told me. It was barbecue night in the buffet restaurant. I lay on the bed in my room, listening to thunder rumble its warning in the distance. On the television, the nation was in an uproar over a British au pair who killed an infant in Massachusetts. A pub full of Brits in some English town cheered because a judge had just decided to let the nanny go. America was stunned; me, I was just lonely. I passed up the barbecue—I'd eaten enough meat on this trip to start my own gastrointestinal cattle drive—and headed over to a supermarket, comforted by generic food smells, produce piled in bright pyramids, Muzak on the sound system and families loading up carts for the week's meals. I bought some fruit, bread, crackers, a hunk of cheese and two bottles of beer and returned to my room. I ate quickly, then lay in bed sipping beer and absently watching some show until I was lulled to sleep by the sound of trains and raindrops on the roof.

When I awoke, the rain from the previous night had only intensified. I ate bacon and eggs in the motel restaurant and considered my options. It was too wet to golf at the nearby state park or to explore the swamp. I was indignant, spoiled. This was the first spate of golf-wrecking rain I'd faced in my entire trip.

I was about ninety minutes from Jacksonville, where, I'd heard, they'd relocated the golf hall of fame from Pinehurst. I decided to use this dreary day to check out the hall of fame. And if the sun came out tomorrow I could backtrack the seventy miles to play at Waycross. I crept through the edge of the swamplands between Waycross and north Florida and then through the gradual buildup of downtown Jacksonville. The St. John's River bisects the city's modest-sized skyscrapers. Jacksonville has the same feel as Charlotte, North Carolina: cities that have suddenly exploded with development and growth and latent civic pride. Both had recently secured pro football franchises. And now you could turn on your radio in either city and hear people talking in voices unchecked by irony about becoming a "world-class city." I checked into a hotel just south of the river, and didn't learn until later how fortunate I was. This was Georgia football weekend, when the Florida Gators, who normally play in their home town of Gainesville, and the Georgia Bulldogs were squaring off in Jacksonville. The game was not until the following day, but already the entire city had football fever. The television stations devoted hourlong segments to pregame predictions and man-on-the-street interviews with the tailgate crowds already gathering in parking lots. On the highways, cars zipped by with flags fluttering from the front side windows. I struck out on the golf hall of fame. The PGA, which has its base here, was building a huge golf complex in the Jacksonville area—courses, teaching centers, hall of fame—but it wouldn't be finished for a year or two.

I drove around the streets at noon in a soggy creep of stop-and-go traffic. I ate lunch, drove some more, restless, antsy, feeling the whole day slip away. The rain tapered off for a few minutes. I rushed over to a course about a half mile off Route 1, called Bay Meadows Golf Club. I hit a few balls at the driving range, waiting to see which way the sky would go. Some loud jokers, in town for the big game, were just starting off on the first hole, adjacent to the range. One of them shanked his drive at ninety degrees into the driving range. He already had his shirt off. Rolls of pale flab spilled over his belt. He swaggered onto the range, retrieved his ball, then started stuffing his pockets with range balls.

"Did you see that?" a woman hitting next to me asked her boyfriend.

Then the sky opened up in a furious downpour and I packed up my clubs and drove back to the hotel.

The next morning broke clear and fresh. The PGA complex hadn't yet been built, but the PGA did operate a course here, called simply the Golf Club of Jacksonville. It was located a few miles down a dull, featureless strip highway on the western side of town. But the course itself was a cool, glistening gem in the early morning. The entire city was apparently nursing a tailgate hang-over because on this lovely autumn morning the course was all but deserted. The starter hooked me up with the only other golfer in sight, Paul Hammarlund.

Paul ran his own lawn-care business. He'd grown up in Connecticut and settled in Jacksonville after a stint in the Marines. He was about my age, maybe a year or two younger, in his early to mid-thirties, with a wife, two small children, a barrel chest and strong arms. He played to about a twelve handicap and asked if I'd mind playing off the back tees. I said sure. Bad move.

The first hole, a par-five that curves gently around to the right, went smoothly enough. I hit my tee shot off into some mounds to the right of the fairway, recovered with my second shot, a five-iron, back onto the fairway, then plunked my third, a nine-iron from about 120 yards out, onto the green. I putted in for my par. But it was on the second hole that I sensed, or should have, anyway, that the Golf Club of Jacksonville was going to be no cakewalk. Not from the back tees, anyway. The second is a par-three that, from the regular tees, is a fairly straightforward 147-yarder, a soft eight-iron. From the back tees it is a tight 190-yarder, demanding precision with a long iron. I hit a three-iron that landed short and off to the right, put the next shot on and putted twice for a bogey.

On many courses, the "championship" tees are merely tees that the management has moved back a few lazy yards in order to give weekend hacks the thrill of "playing from the tips." At the Golf Club of Jacksonville, which, after all, is a training ground for golf pros, the championship tees earn every bit of that title. They are for real golfers, guys who can hit the ball long and straight time after time. I could not blame my poor score here on having a bad day. I didn't play all that badly; I simply was not enough of a golfer for the back tees. Yes, I was improving; slowly but surely I was becoming a decent golfer. But here, I was a club boxer stepping into the ring with Joe Frazier. At the Golf Club of Jacksonville one can't get by with the usual eight or ten decent drives in a round, interspersed with slices, hooks and sky balls. You have to hit the ball long and straight, time after time, just to put yourself in play. From the regular tees, the ninth hole is a nice, challenging 393-yard par-four. From the pros, it's a 463-yard killer. I found myself staring from the tee box at wide ponds or big, funky bogs that I'd have to cross just to have a second shot. Then seemingly a mile or two down the road we'd pass the regular tees. Paul had the power and consistency the course demanded. Rare among muscular guys, he had a fluid swing, which he told me he picked up as a kid on the courses around Hartford. He'd overshoot the pin with his eight-iron from 165 yards out. In the end, Paul shot a 90—not his best, but still respectable. If there is such a thing as a good 102, that's what I shot.

It was not quite noon when I said good-bye to Paul in the parking lot and rolled out into the bright sunshine and six-lane traffic of Jacksonville. I grabbed a couple of cheeseburgers at Burger King and considered my options as I ate and drove. I was tired and disconcerted by the reality sandwich I'd just been fed, courtesy of the PGA. But I had six hours of sunlight left. I hadn't lost all my balls that morning, just most of them. I retraced my steps to Waycross. The sun was shining and my spirits lifted.

The entrance to Laura S. Walker State Park sits just across Route 1 from the entrance to the Okefenokee Swamp. The park, named for a Georgia writer and naturalist, sits on 306 acres of pine-studded lowlands. The golf course was added in 1996. I followed a winding road through the pines for about a mile, until I came to a white clubhouse with a metal roof. The afternoon was beautiful and mild. I walked out to the first tee by myself, hoping to catch up with somebody along the way. Signs around the course advised me to look out for snakes and alligators, but not in the way you might imagine. As one sign stated:

RATTLESNAKES MAY BE FOUND IN THIS AREA. THEY
ARE IMPORTANT MEMBERS OF THE NATURAL COMMU-
NITY. THEY WILL NOT ATTACK, BUT, IF DISTURBED OR
CORNERED, THEY WILL DEFEND THEMSELVES.

In other words, if you get bitten, it's your own damn fault. Political correctness for swamp varmints. I wasn't sure what constituted the difference between a rattler attacking and one merely "defending itself," and I was fairly certain my ankle wouldn't know the difference, either. I made a mental note to leave balls I hit into the tall grass alone.

The first hole is wide and inviting, with a slight dogleg to the right and a green that opened like a promise. Still smarting from my pro tee debacle at Jacksonville, I reverted to the regular tees. I hit a three-wood long and straight and put my second shot, a wedge, onto the green, then two-putted for a redemptive par. I bogeyed the next two holes, and birdied the fourth, a par-five. I felt good. Laura Walker presented its share of challenges, but it was a balm to my damaged psyche. After the first few holes I caught up with a couple, a man and a woman. I tailed them for a couple of holes, playing up as close as I could without actually hitting in to them, hoping they'd invite me to join in. They seemed a little irritated at first. Finally, on the sixth hole, a long par-three, bounded on each side by pine trees, they stopped to let me through.

"You go ahead," the man said.

"Mind if I join you?" I said.

"No, that's all right," he said. "We don't want to hold you up. You go ahead."

I was lonely and far from home. I pressed the point.

"Actually, I was hoping to hook up with someone."

They looked at each other and shrugged, as if I were a head cold they suddenly realized they were bound to catch, then said, sure, if I wanted to join them, I was welcome.

They were Richard and Wanda Miller. They had driven over from Tifton, Georgia, a small city about eighty miles west of Waycross, to play golf and have dinner. They were in their late fifties. Richard taught English at a college in Tifton. Wanda worked in the personnel department of a manufacturing company. Wanda was from Kansas City; Richard, from Pennsylvania. Southerners love to grumble about Yankees who relocate to Dixie (favorite joke: what's the difference between a Yankee and a damn Yankee? A damn Yankee is one who comes down and stays), but transplants such as Richard and Wanda often become the most active boosters of the New South. They liked the pace of life in Tifton. They liked the friendly people, the ease of getting around, the country, the open spaces, the great, uncrowded golf courses. Wanda's only complaint was the vast monotony of pine trees that refuse to turn red and gold in the fall.

Our first hole together was the sixth, a par-three. All three of us hit decent but not spectacular shots. That's the best way to break the ice. Sending your first shot screaming into the woods is like belching at a cocktail party. But acing one to the center of the green can be equally poisonous.

I uttered something inane, like "Those'll play," and we proceeded up the fairway as a happy, collegial group. Richard had a swing so full that from a distance he almost appeared to be throwing a discus. It probably didn't help his golf game. A pro would have told him to shorten up considerably. But the flexibility impressed me. Richard and Wanda had been married about twenty years, golfing together for five. They traveled all over southern Georgia playing courses, sometimes venturing another hour or so down to the seaside courses at Brunswick. They played seriously but cheerfully. They had mastered the art of married golf. She politely asked for advice from Richard, Richard gave it politely but not overbearingly.

"Watch out, here comes wild Wanda," she announced when she lost control of her drives for a couple of holes. I shot a reassuring 41 on the front nine. The sun was already pushing the horizon when we teed up at number ten; we would have to move quickly in order to beat the darkness. We had the course largely to ourselves.

Laura Walker quickly became one of my favorite courses. It sits in a flat, open plate of land surrounded on all sides by pine forests. Fresh winds washed constantly over us, as if we were playing an oceanside course. The flatness is compensated for by ponds and doglegs, and by soft moguls and contoured greens and bunkers that give the course the appearance of a gently swelling sea. Laura Walker is neither tricky nor obvious, but somewhere in between. Perhaps owing to its newness (the course had only been open a year) the tee boxes and greens were pristine. I'd played flashier courses, and ones that cost a whole lot more than Laura Walker's $20 weekend walking rate, but none I liked more. It was the sort of course you could marry. I was jealous of Waycross residents who got to play there week after week. I'll bet you'd find new things to like about this modest, unpretentious gem long after the tricks of some overpriced resort course had grown stale.

The only sore point came on the par-four fifteenth, a 362-yarder with a waste bunker running up the right side. I hadn't run into one of these vile things since Northwoods in Columbia, South Carolina. You never lose a ball in a waste bunker—it sits up as plain as a zit on your nose on prom night. Unfortunately, it is also about as difficult to remove. So there I was, maybe 150 yards from the green for my second shot, with no obstructed view. I was damned if I was going to lose a stroke hitting sideways out of this stuff. What could be so difficult about plucking a ball off the hard tack? I selected a six-iron, figuring on a nice, easy swing. I kept my head down, swung easy, and struck the ball so softly that I swear I could hear it sigh as it fluffed a few miserable yards forward. No problem, I thought, I still lie just two. I'll plunk it up to the green and one or two putt for a par or bogey. Fluff! Damn! Fluff! Damn! Fluff! *Damn!* Richard and Wanda had been such pleasant playing partners, and so cheerfully tolerant of their own mistakes, that I had to keep my anger under wraps. I kept a sort of bemused, lighthearted smile fixed on my face, but inside I was swearing like a sailor. Was I going to throw a fine round away? Finally, I struck the ball solidly enough that it hopped out of the trap and onto its grassy lip. I pitched onto the green, and two-putted for my 8. Richard and Wanda remained politely silent.

The next hole curved around another waste bunker, this time to the left. Fortunately, it was a short hole. I took out a three-iron and played the ball as far to the right as I dared, regaining some of my equilibrium with a par. On the eighteenth hole I hit my ball into a long pond running up the left side of the fairway. At first I was mad; later I was grateful. As I walked the length of the pond searching the shallow fringe for my ball, Wanda called out, "Watch out for the alligators." It was one of those warnings like "falling rock zone." Do you ever really see a falling rock? I was looking so intently for my ball that it was only by chance that I looked up in time to see a four-foot-long gator taking in the last rays of sunshine, directly in my path. He didn't seem to think much of me, one way or another.

"Look at that! Look at that!" I screamed excitedly. Richard and Wanda watched nervously.

"Don't get excited," Wanda said. "Keep your distance." The alligator did not budge. That ended my search for the ball in the pond. I was jumping up and down, pointing and exclaiming, probably violating every rule of gator-human interaction. The gator was perhaps ten or fifteen yards in front of me, although I must admit the distance has shrunk steadily through my retellings. Talk to me in a year or two and I'll tell you how I jumped the beast, pried its jaws open with my bare hands, and retrieved my ball from its slimy gut.

"Careful," Wanda said. "They're pretty fast." But the gator seemed no more inclined to attack me than he was to run away. He was an "important member of the natural community" and seemed to know it. Something about his sly grin told me he was waiting to see whether I'd screw up my approach shot, just as I had my drive. Come to think of it, I'd seen expressions like that on the faces of guys I golfed with back home. I took a lateral drop and, under the gaze of the big reptile, placed a nice shot to the edge of the green. I got down with a 6, a decent final hole considering the pond, and finished up with an 87 for the afternoon.

I chatted with Richard and Wanda for several minutes in the darkened parking lot. They were glad we'd hooked up, they said. They wished me good luck as we parted. Waste bunker or no, Laura Walker State Park had been just what I needed. I rolled south again on Route 1 with the sun disappearing in my rearview mirror. I returned to Jacksonville to find the entire city plunged into gloom. While I was gone, Georgia, a poor team that year, had defeated the mighty Gators. Just a few hours before, smug radio commentators were questioning whether the Gators should even continue to keep Georgia on its schedule; the rivalry had become a mismatch. Now all over town those same commentators were having crow for dinner. Still covered with a layer of old sunscreen and sweat from two rounds of golf, but too tired and hungry to return to my hotel, I stopped in at a restaurant not far from the hotel, where I sipped cold beer and ate some chicken wings and listened to subdued families around me discuss how Coach Steve Spurrier and his Gators could possibly have lost the big game. The hotel was a different scene entirely, packed with ecstatic Bulldog fans. Several of them raised collegial fists to me, yelling "Go Dogs!", and then I realized that I was wearing a red shirt of approximately the same shade as a Bulldogs jersey, and was being taken for another fan. "Go Dogs!" I shouted at a man I passed in the hallway.

Part Four

Florida's Gold Coast

18

For the Snowbirds

I rolled out at sunrise, after breakfast in a Cracker Barrel restaurant next to my hotel. The Sunday-morning streets were empty, as the city slept off its party weekend. Route 1 south of Jacksonville, called Phillips Highway, is like Route 1 on the edges of most large cities—seedy and industrial. But in the pearly mist it attained the faded majesty of a Woody Guthrie song, all boxcars and rail yards, diners, industrial parks and tough-looking bars caught in a moment of repose. A few miles south of the city, the road cuts east, passes under Interstate 95 and heads down the Atlantic Coast, which it follows the rest of the way to Key West.

My next stop was St. Augustine, America's oldest city and, appropriately, home to one of its oldest golf resorts, the Ponce De Leon Golf & Conference Resort. The seaside course, located right on Route 1, is yet another design by Donald Ross, whose stamp on older American golf courses seems as ubiquitous as Edith Head's on costumes for movies from the golden age of Hollywood. The course was built in 1916 to snag the first generation of well-heeled tourists who made their way down from the Northeast for sun and palm trees.

The sun was just beginning to shine when I pulled into the resort, its low-rise guest buildings nearly hidden behind live oaks dripping with Spanish moss. The pro shop manager sent me out to see the cart man (carts were mandatory), who in turn directed me to the starter. You can judge the fanciness of a course by the number of employees you must get past in order to play. On the tee box I hooked up with a threesome, a dad and his two sons.

I loaded my bag onto the cart of the elder son, Pat, a freshman at Flagler College in St. Augustine. His dad, John McDermott, a big friendly man with a red mustache, was assistant fire marshal for the city of Newport, Rhode Island. The family had traveled down to St. Augustine for parents' weekend. Pat was a friendly, smooth-talking kid, one of those nineteen-year-olds who already seems to know what he wants and how to get it. He was majoring in sports management, he told me, and then after graduation was going to become agent extraordinaire to the Michael Jordans and Troy Aikmans of his generation. He'd chosen Flagler College because it was one of the few schools in the country with a sports management major. The kid had plans. He'd been managing his high-school basketball team and now, two months into college, he seemed to have wangled himself a position helping manage the college team. I knew this kid had the makings of a first-class sports agent because by the time we were halfway down the first fairway, he had me convinced that he was practically a scratch golfer.

"I was five over on this course yesterday," he announced, shortly before I sliced my drive irretrievably into some tall grass standing between the fairway and the Atlantic Ocean. I'm in for some humiliation, I figured. But fortunately for me, Pat had transformed back into a mortal overnight.

The front and back nines at Ponce De Leon play like two entirely different, equally intriguing courses. The front runs wide open next to a wide marshy expanse of the Intracoastal Waterway.

The only trees are a few lovely clumps of palms. The constant sea breeze provides the major challenge. The front nine has the feel of a British links course gone tropical; from anywhere on the nine you can gaze out across the undulating berms and see every other golfer on the course.

The back nine plunges into the jungle with the suddenness of a Disney ride, into a lush, dark, secretive world of mangrove swamps and ponds curving tantalizingly like lost lagoons. Moving from the ninth to the tenth holes is like putting down a volume of P. G. Wodehouse and picking up *Heart of Darkness,* all in one morning. Even the sun played along. On the front nine, once the fog burned off, sunshine danced gaily off the shimmering greens and the ocean. On the back nine it hid behind clouds, casting shadows into shadows, threatening rain.

I had one of those outings when you feel as though you are constantly on the verge of breaking out and playing some great holes, but don't. The wide-open front nine made you feel like you should shoot a record round. But I kept getting into trouble or missing putts. I was playing bogey golf and couldn't seem to break out of it. Pars slipped from my grasp for stupid reasons. I finished the nine with a 47 and logged a 92 for the round.

John McDermott, the dad, was a good golfer and a good father, gentle with his sons. He had a big swing but surprisingly delicate control for a large man. Coming up to the last hole, a par-four of nearly 400 yards, he hit a booming drive that put him maybe 150 yards out. He lined up a seven-iron and swung. The ball sailed toward the green, rolled a few feet toward the pin and disappeared.

"It's in the hole!" Pat cried.

John maintained a noncommittal expression, not wanting to play the sap in a practical joke.

"It's in the hole," I cried.

It was a great moment for John. Coming up the eighteenth fairway, playing with his sons, he'd eagled the hole from 150 yards out. John maintained his composure, no whoops or hollers, the coolness born of fighting three-alarm fires, no doubt. But you could see in his expression he'd savor the moment for years to come.

I followed the highway south straight into St. Augustine and parked at Ripley's Believe It or Not Museum. St. Augustine is an odd but agreeable mixture of historic Spanish buildings, gracious inns and shady downtown squares, overlaid by good old American kitsch provided by Ripley's and assorted other attractions, such as 3-D World—"A Voyage Beyond Reality." Everywhere I looked, little, slow-moving, gas-powered trains, bulging with tourists, crept through the streets. I walked around the town, past an archway on Magnolia Street marking the Fountain of Youth ("Snacks available at the Forever Young Depot") and pretty, shaded squares and down narrow alleys with restaurants, gift shops and bars.

On a grassy promontory next door to the Ripley's museum sits the Castillo de San Marcos, a three-hundred-year-old fort that took the Spaniards twenty-three years to build. Despite repeated attacks by the British, including one in 1702 in which they occupied and then burned the town, the fort never fell, although it changed hands diplomatically several times. The Brits took over the fort in 1763 as part of a treaty that gave Spain Havana in exchange for Florida. Spain got Florida and the fort back after the Revolutionary War. Finally, the United States took over the fort when Spain ceded Florida in 1821. As I walked around the massive fort, now run by the National Parks Service, I could see why no military forces ever conquered it. I walked down into the old storage rooms and soldiers' quarters, where centuries-old graffiti carved by bored soldiers marks the walls. Although impregnable to opposing forces, the fort is finally facing a dangerous enemy threatening to wear away the sedimentary rock of which it was built—the footsteps of hundreds of thousands of tourists a year.

In St. Augustine I had noticed signs at some of the restaurants, saying "Bikers Welcome." I wondered whether this was some sort of general policy of the St. Augustine Chamber of Commerce, until I got back on the road and noticed a thickening clot of motorcycle traffic leading to Daytona. It was the last vestiges of "Biketoberfest," an annual gathering that just now, two days into November, was winding down. By the time I reached the northern sections of Daytona, an enormous flatulent roar of an escort swept me into town. Every couple of miles traffic slowed to a creep, and on either side of the road would be tents with rows and rows of motorcycles parked outside. Bikers and bikers' babes were everywhere. Alongside the bikers were representatives of the other state vehicle of Florida, the enormous, late-model sedan, always in some pastel color; you didn't even realize they made these cars anymore until you came to Florida. Ensconced in noise-proof, air-conditioned splendor, retired couples rolled on to some early-bird special. Everybody comes to Florida seeking something. It isn't so much one society as a dozen separate ones existing side by side. The bikers vroomed on by and the oldsters coasted along and nobody paid the slightest bit of attention to one another, or to me.

The next morning, a Monday, I woke early and headed from my motel over to the Daytona Beach public golf course. Lining up to tee off on the first tee were at least twenty-five golf carts filled with women. The backup extended onto the fairways. Normally on a par-four hole, one group hits, then proceeds to the fairway, hits its second shots, and clears out toward the green, whereupon the group behind hits. But these women were hitting the ball not much farther than sixty yards up the fairway at a pop. So on the first hole there were three foursomes working the fairways and a fourth putting away on the green.

A man saw me standing, holding my bag and looking at the scene.

"They call themselves the 'Forty-niners,'" he said. "Don't know why. Every Monday morning. You'd better come back around noon if you want to golf." I looked over at the Forty-niners, laughing and having fun. I thought about trying to break in and join them, but I didn't see a twosome or threesome among them. Besides, with the space separating the groups, I'd have to use my sand wedge the whole way around. I took the man's advice and headed down the road, figuring I'd come to another course sooner or later.

I drove due south from Daytona, expecting the road from there to Miami, a distance of more than five hundred miles, to be little more than an ever-increasing buildup of condominiums and beachfront life. To my surprise, the road from Daytona plunged into a sort of old rural South, small villages and tin-roofed shacks and encroaching vegetation. Interstate 95 ran twenty miles west and had taken the development with it. I came upon a village, little more than a wide spot in the road, called Oak Hill and, off to the right, the Oak Hill Golf Course, situated next door to a gift shop called Manny's Alligator Center.

Oak Hill is a par-three course carved out of a choking swamp and tangles of subtropical vegetation. Streams and ponds run throughout, and ants have built hills the size of pitcher's mounds. A reluctant and jealous landscape of sable palms and southern pines encroaches everywhere, still debating whether to allow a golf course to exist here at all. The course ends after eleven holes, as if the owner wearied of the fight and declared a stalemate. I paid the woman in the pro shop a few dollars and walked over to the first tee. At Oak Hill, the shortness of the course is compensated for by the postage-stamp greens and thick ball-eating growth on all sides. A groundskeeper kept busy sweeping sand traps and cutting grass. The fourth and seventh holes border on a trailer park. After a while I caught up with a couple of Johns. That's the way they put it, anyway.

John Goetze and John Pomfret had grown up within a few miles of each other outside of New York City. Together with a third fellow named John, they had attended Westchester Community College, then all three transferred together to State University at Oswego, New York. After graduation, they had fallen out of touch for nearly forty years. It was the Internet that brought these old buddies back together in retirement. John Pomfret, who had taught shop in suburban New York, found his friends through an Internet white pages search. John Goetze, a former teacher and administrator at SUNY at Canton, was now living in retirement in Edgewater, Florida, a few miles up the road from Oak Hill.

John Goetze said he came out to the little par-three course frequently, because the price was right, and so were the crowds.

"Guy who built this course did it all himself," he said. "Bull-dozed, cleared, designed the holes himself."

"Why'd he stop at eleven?" I asked.

"Some kind of zoning dispute with the town. He sold out to a Japanese guy. He still comes down here, though."

"Now you're playing with the pros," John Pomfret said cheer-fully, after swinging and topping the ball a few feet forward. I found their goodwill infectious. Within a few minutes, we were laughing like old buddies. They had fallen back into their old ways and old laughs, as if they were twenty-two again, as if they shared a lifetime of stories and memories instead of a few years at the very outset of life.

I asked them as we stood on the eleventh and final hole if they planned to stay in touch now.

"Oh, yeah," said John Pomfret.

"Absolutely," said John Goetze. "We're inseparable."

A few miles south of Oak Hill, Route 1 reaches an elbow, the land and the ocean taking a concerted inland turn in order to make way for the large, irregular burr of Cape Canaveral. I passed an orange grove off to the left, the trees standing at attention in smart, military rows for what seemed like miles, bearing their fruit like gaudy medals. In a way, agriculture provided the most stirring reminder of how far I'd come, and of the immensity of this country. Navigation by fruits and vegetables. I'd sliced off just one narrow corridor of the United States and managed to run from the raw, chilled potato fields and blackened blueberry barrens of northern Maine, down through the cornfields of Pennsylvania, the tobacco fields of Virginia, to the cotton fields of Georgia. And now the land of oranges burst upon me like a tropical dream. The sight both thrilled and saddened me. I realized for the first time how close I was to the end of the line, the point where I would turn my old car around and point it north for home. The road home would be easier. I'd leave behind this old Route 1, with its thousand interruptions and distractions, this stop-and-go hell, for a bland, blessed strip of interstate blacktop. Once you were on the interstate you were almost home, it seemed, wrapped in that familiar cocoon of rest stops and service stations. I'd stop in a Barnes and Noble or Books a Million and buy myself some unabridged, multi-cassette book-on-tape, drive through the night, be home in a couple of days. I longed to be back with Barbara and my girls, to hold my infant daughter, Caroline, in my arms, to wave Natalie off to kindergarten. I missed my job, or at least the regular rhythms of a morning cup of coffee, a day of work, returning home at night. It all seemed achingly wholesome to me now. The appearance of oranges on the landscape also signaled to me how near I was to wrapping up this journey. It was getting close to the time for summing things up, pondering just what I had accomplished. As long as the road stretched far out in front of me, I could put that one off. But now the road was coming to an end.

The area around Oak Hill is the last of the rural South along the Gold Coast of Florida, or, at least the last that I saw. The road took me through towns named Mims and LaGrange, and then Titusville, and the turnoff for Cape Canaveral space center. Titusville has a tidy, friendly, old-fashioned-looking downtown, like something transposed from the early 1960s. Every business seems to bear the name Spacecoast This or Spacecoast That. A few miles on, at Cocoa, I stopped at a sun-baked, eighteen-hole "executive" course with a driving range. I briefly debated playing the course, which started at the top of a treeless hill. But I'd already played a par-three course at Oak Hill that morning. I bought a small bucket of balls and went out to the range to unwind from the road. The "grass" tees were more like packed mud and crabgrass. I set a few balls down and struck a few crisp irons off the hard tack without teeing up. It was not an optimal golf surface, but it was the composition of choice at the Greater Heartbreak Open, of which I was now a qualified touring pro. I found a hard-packed surface good for my concentration. Hit too far behind the ball, and your club would bounce off the surface like a plane flown by a student pilot on his first solo landing. You had to hit the ball dead on. I found the narrow demands liberating. I'd hit under these conditions so many times now it seemed like second nature. I plunked eight or ten five-irons far out into the range. The only other people around were a scraggly-haired young man of about twenty-five, a beginner in T-shirt and jeans, and an older gentleman giving him pointers. Out of the corner of my eye I noticed them watching me. I switched to a five-wood and struck a few line drives that rose slowly as they screamed into the distance.

I pretended not to hear this exchange:

"Hey, you see that? He's not even using a tee."

"That's what practice will do for you. Keep playing and you'll be able to hit like that."

I placed my last ball down on a slab, brought my five-wood back and creased the ball. I observed it for a moment or two, as if deftly judging its placement and distance, making critical notes in my mind. Then I turned casually away, picked up the empty basket and headed back to the clubhouse past the young man and the old man.

"Nice hitting," the older man said.

"Thanks," I said, feeling flattered and trying not to show it.

At mid-afternoon I arrived in Melbourne, where I figured I'd stumble upon a course. At random I turned right on Route 192, mainly because it was a busy intersection, and within a mile came to the Melbourne Golf Course.

I did not complete a foursome here but rather helped construct one from scratch, picking up members along the way like the Pied Piper. My first partner, walking from the clubhouse, was a young guy, in his early thirties, with dark curly hair and a heavy New York accent. His name was Don.

"You alone?" he said.

He lived in Manhattan but was in Melbourne visiting his mother. He'd spent years as a doorman at a Manhattan apartment building but had just finished training as a court cop in the Bronx. He played with some old bladed clubs and said he only got out a few times a year.

"I've been a doorman for five years," he said. "Always wanted to be a cop. I took the exam a year ago and passed. Did my training. I just started."

On the first tee we hooked up with Ray, a retired Navy man who'd spent the last couple of decades before retirement working in maintenance at the Library of Congress.

Melbourne is a wide-open, straightforward municipal course. The holes are packed together so that each hole borders others on either side. The greens sported a five-o'clock shadow of unshaved grass.

"This is for the snowbirds," Ray muttered, invoking the dismissive term year-rounders in Florida use for winter-only residents. "They'll cut it in a day or two. They want the course in good shape for when the snowbirds start arriving next week. Prices go up, you can't get a tee time." He shook his head. "Snowbirds."

On the third hole G. W. Sutter joined our group. Sutter had lived in Florida for about thirty years, had come down from Michigan for his job, raised his family and retired here.

The course isn't very long, just 5,300 yards from the regular tees. If you hit a decent drive you can approach most greens with a short wedge. I had no doubts about why it was popular with snowbirds and other weekend golfers, and I liked it for the same reasons.

I bogeyed the first two holes, then parred the next two, a par-three and a par-five. The par-five, the fourth hole, is an odd hole that crooks back and forth like a backward Z, just 445 yards long. Rated the most difficult on the course, it is protected in front by a stream and on the right by a pond. I hit a fine drive to the right rough and found myself on the second shot just about 200 yards from the pin, if I cut off the final zag of the Z and hit over the pond and some trees. Should I try to be a hero? I decided to lay up. Call it playing smart, call it playing chicken. By this point in my trip, I'd seen too many rounds take that crucial bad turn and go down in flames from getting greedy.

Here's something else about laying up: It only pays off if you are a decent golfer. Novice golfers always go for the green, no matter how difficult the shot, and it has nothing to do with reckless stupidity. It makes perfect, logical sense. When you don't golf well, there is absolutely nothing safe and secure about a safe and secure shot. A nice little seven-iron to the middle of the fairway has every bit as much of a chance of being topped lamely a few feet forward, or sliced into oblivion, as a fairway wood from the rough, over trees and a pond. A layup only becomes a layup when you have the confidence to hit one. Laying up in this case was not simply a matter of caution. I now had the skill to lay up with confidence. My seven-iron landed just short of the stream. Then I hit a soft wedge to the green and made my par.

Don, who had dug his bladed clubs out of a closet of his Manhattan apartment, also parred the hole, and it was a great thing to see the look on his face. You could see his faith in himself bolstered as he parred the toughest hole on the course.

"I need to get out here more often," he said. "Hey, maybe I need to get some new clubs. What do you think?"

"You might want to think about some cavity-backed irons," I said. "You get a lot more control from your shots. With the blades, your sweet spot is much smaller. With the cavity backs, the weight is all around the perimeter of the club face, so the distribution is more . . ." This from a guy who had bought his irons out of the trunk of a stranger's Buick.

But I did feel Don would benefit from a new set of clubs, if not because of my expertise on blades versus cavities, then certainly because of the New Stuff Buzz. The New Stuff Buzz is that surge of confidence you get with any purchase of new golf equipment. It's stronger in golf than in any other sport. It doesn't matter what the new technology is spouting—better control, better distance, thick shafts, thin shafts, eternal arguments on weight distribution. The most significant impact of any new golf development is the surge of confidence you feel when you hold it in your hands. The New Stuff Buzz allows you to transfer responsibility for your next shot from yourself to the stuff. It's a roundabout way of not overthinking your swing. Well, this titanium bubble zinc-tipped death stick is going to hit the ball great, so I might as well relax and enjoy. And you do hit the ball well, not because of the titanium bubble zinc-tipped death stick, but because you're relaxed. Of course, the drawback to the New Stuff Buzz is that it has a life span ranging from a few holes to two or three rounds. Then you begin to forget that your stuff is new. You forget the scientific principles that sounded so convincing a short while ago. The old imperfections creep back into your game. The laws of physics reapply themselves, and you must deal with the mundane realities of your own body and swing. Or else, of course, you can go out and buy some even newer stuff.

The New Stuff principle is why the market for used golf equipment is so much larger than that of any other sport; why it is possible to find pristine castoffs in almost any golf shop. It is why, also, if you are just learning the game and know somebody, a father-in-law, for example, who is serious about the game, you will not have to buy any equipment for the first several years. Their garages or cellars are mines of good golf equipment that has lost its magic for them.

Ray begged off after five holes. With his membership, he didn't have to pay daily greens fees and usually came out for a few holes a day. Especially before the maligned snowbirds arrived. Don, too, drifted away after the front nine. He had to get home to take his mother out to dinner. It was just G. W. Sutter and me. The sun already showed large and orange in the western sky. I had finished the front nine with a 42 and was determined to complete this round. The course was clearing out. We zipped through the next four holes, which brought us more or less within shouting distance of the clubhouse. On the thirteenth green, G. W. paused for a moment. He was practically at the parking lot; the sun was going down, he was tired, the pull cart feeling heavy. Playing the fourteenth would commit him to finishing the course with me, since it headed straight away from the parking lot and didn't return until the eighteenth.

All afternoon, G. W. had been the quietest of the foursome, content just to be out golfing.

"Hmmmm," he said. "I'm just thinking if I should . . . We'll, no, I think I'll keep going." We trooped on. It was a fresh, cool early evening. The balls flew straight. I racked up pars. We came upon a foursome in front of us. Two men and two women. Playing as if they had all the daylight in the world.

"They just come out at twilight for a few holes," Sutter said. "They're not planning to finish." But we were on a mission. Finally, they turned around and spotted us, then waved us through. One of the men winked conspiratorially at us.

"We got a couple who are just learning," he said, nodding to the women up ahead on the ladies' tee. Slow play always gets blamed on the women. I parred the sixteenth hole, a 152-yarder with a pond on the left, by placing a lovely eight-iron a few feet from the hole, then two-putting through the unshaved grass. It was my last par of the day. I finished with three bogeys, but no disasters, and an 85 for the round. The seventeenth, a par-five, turns sharply to the right at the end of the fairway, to a green protected by two ponds. I hit a nice three-wood to the right rough, dangerously close to the long pond on the right. I got back to the fairway with a seven-iron, then pitched over the green but safely between the ponds.

We played the last hole almost by feel through the darkness, groping with safe irons. We walked up the eighteenth fairway, past a stand of cabbage palms. Unlike the coconut palms with their lazy, romantic curves and gracefully asymmetrical fronds, cabbage palms are short, squat trees with rigid, upright stalks topped by a large ball of fronds. They are not the sort of palms to conjure up romantic idylls from Rupert Brooke or Robert Louis Stevenson, but cabbage palms are perfect for a golf course, because they resemble nothing so much as a large golf ball sitting on a tee, like Nature's own Titleist, ready to be whacked away by God's three-wood.

"Supposed to be good eating," Sutter mused as we trooped toward the last green. "I have a friend who's lived here all his life. He said cabbage palms got him through the Depression. Cabbage palms and gopher turtles. Gopher turtles and cabbage palms. That's all he had to eat."

The sunset or the thought of his friend or the end of the round put him in a reflective mood. He looked out at Hibiscus Avenue, the busy thoroughfare of chain motels and fast-food restaurants, now swollen with commuters on their way home. Melbourne, the sleepy orange-grove-cum-retirement-community, now bustled like any other American city.

"When I came here this was just a dirt road," he said. "Interstate 95 wasn't even here. Route 1 was the big highway. That's how you got anywhere."

I said good-bye to my new friend, Mr. Sutter. As always, it seemed, we made vague plans to hook up for another round sometime, the next time he drove north or I drove south. I checked into a motel a couple of blocks from the golf course and showered. Then I called home and hung up, feeling particularly lonely. For the past few days I had been bothered by an infected big toe, which I worried might disrupt my journey as it neared the end. Once, several years earlier, I had been laid up for several days after a blister on my foot led to a spreading infection up my leg. Without antibiotics, I might have died. Ever since, I've been acutely—read: unreasonably—aware of infections. This throbbing right big toe had begun to make walking painful, especially with the endless miles of fairways I'd trudged. It also put me in a low mood, in the way that only loneliness and distance from home can accentuate an ailment. Sitting on the bed, still wet from the shower, I imagined the infection racing up my leg. I saw myself lying delirious in some hospital room, surrounded by doctors deciding impassively whether to amputate. As my mild case of worry swelled into full-fledged hypochondria, intensified by hunger and fatigue, I began to calculate my distance to the nearest airport, the flying time home. I paced the room like a zoo animal, checking the pressure of each step, trying to convince myself the infection was all in my mind. I checked my right big toe next to the left, looking for signs of extra swelling or redness. It was red and tender, but there were no signs of streaking. I felt higher up on my leg for the telltale pains I'd felt that other time, signaling the spread of the infection. Come off it, I told myself finally. Relax. Get some dinner. I dragged myself across the street to a Friday's for a chicken breast smothered in something and a cold beer. I'd thought the lights and activity of the restaurant would divert my attention, calm me down. But somehow the odd familiarity of the chain restaurant here on another exhaust-scented commercial strip just intensified my jitters. After dinner I drove to a nearby mall and walked for what seemed like miles, feeling every step, until I found a drugstore. I bought a plastic tub and some salt. Back at my hotel room I filled the tub with warm water and lay on my bed with my foot dangling down in the water, until I slept.

19

Papa Could Beat Anybody

I woke the next morning with the first shafts of sunlight stealing into my room. Everything seemed different in the morning. I examined my toe and found that the virulent infection had, against all my fears, failed to materialize. The toe was still sore, but it was noticeably less sore than it had been the night before. I walked around the room and felt only the grateful harmless muscle soreness that greeted me every morning after a day of golf. I walked to the sliding glass windows and opened them, welcoming the milky dawn into my room. The room, which had seemed like some kind of cage the night before, had reverted back into a harmless motel room. I felt pleasantly hungry, after having only picked at my food the night before, and looked forward to breakfast. I spread some ointment from the drugstore on my toe, applied a Band-Aid and a sock and laced my shoe up snugly. As I dressed, I shook my head and laughed at last night's fool.

I proceeded south on Route 1 with no particular course in mind. I figured in this land of sunshine and plenty the golf courses would practically grab me off of the highway and beg me to play. The portion of the coast from just south of Melbourne to Jupiter is known as the Treasure Coast. The name derives from a fleet of Spanish galleons, carrying New World gold, that sank along the coast during a storm in 1715. The Spanish recovered some of the treasure, but much of it lay hidden until the mid–twentieth century, when developers building fortresses along the shore for a new wave of conquistadors, these wearing straw hats and flip-flops, started discovering gold coins buried in the sand.

Around Ft. Pierce the highway slowed to an agonizing pace, short-circuited every half mile or so by another six-lane intersection. The road was flanked by bleak strip malls, RV dealerships, leisure-furniture outlets, used-car lots and the like. After a while I spotted a large, friendly sign for a golf course beckoning me off the highway. "Public Welcome! 1,500 feet." I followed the directions through a subdivision of single-story homes.

I hardly had time to change into my golf shoes when a course attendant pounced upon me, grabbing my bag out of the trunk, loading it onto a cart and driving me to the clubhouse. I fished a couple of bucks out of my shorts for a tip and mumbled thanks, even though his aggressive courtesy put me on edge. I expected it at Pinehurst; not here. I like to scope out a course at my own pace, carry my own clubs to the clubhouse, mill around for a few minutes, get the feel of the place. I don't like guys showing up from nowhere and handling my stuff, especially if I haven't made an advance tee time.

There were only a couple of golfers in the pro shop, and from the sign on Route 1 you would have thought they loved walk-ons. But when asked if I could get on as a single, the man behind the counter looked at me as if I'd strolled into Spago on Oscar night and asked to be seated next to some movie stars.

He looked at his ledger, tapping it impatiently with his pen, and said, "*Hmmm*. I can get you on at eleven forty-five. Why don't you come back then."

I looked at a clock on the wall. It was twenty past eight.

"You don't have any threesomes going out before then? No cancellations?"

He shook his head. "I've got four groups coming on in about five minutes. Maybe someone won't show up. Why don't you go out to the putting green and I'll let you know."

I remembered I was hungry.

"Where's the snack shop?"

"Upstairs. It's not open, though."

"Do you have anything to eat?"

He nodded at a basket filled with crumbly muck-filled cheese crackers. I made my way out to the green with my mouth full of gravel snacks. Several golfers had arrived in the past few minutes, and the putting green was a busy jumble of pastel pants and cheerful profanity. The primary subjects of conversation appeared to be, in no particular order, sex, bad knees, bad kidneys, bad livers, bad hips, boats, golf, investments and guys who weren't around to hear what was being said about them.

"Hey, what's up!" one man called out when a friend arrived.

"Me, this morning."

"*Ahhh,* bullshit."

"How would you know? You weren't home. Just your wife!"

A man named Joe, wearing a peach golf shirt, missed a long putt just short of the cup.

"Goddammit," he growled. "Story of my life. Two inches short. Just like my dick."

There were embarrassed chuckles all around as everyone thought, "Hey, aren't you supposed to say that about somebody else, not yourself?"

The men paired neatly into fours on the first tee, with no sign of a threesome. After a few minutes I wandered back to the clubhouse.

"Sorry," the man said without apology in his voice. "Like I said, come back at eleven forty-five. I think I can get you on then."

I wanted to say: "Eleven forty-five? *Eleven forty-five?* Listen, jackass. I am a wanderer, a nomad. I do not have time for *eleven forty-five.* I have seen Cape Arundel at dusk, swung my eight-iron in the Bronx, and in Newark. I have been cooled by the potato fields of northern Maine and dodged an alligator in the Great Okefenokee Swamp. Yea, and I have walked in solitary splendor at Mid Pines, parred the fifteenth hole at Pinehurst No. 6, and been humbled by the twelfth hole at Franklin Park in Boston, where the great Bobby Jones tested himself in his youth. I have been high and I have been low, but I would not wait five . . . more . . . minutes to soil my irons on this mangy patch of crab-grass you call a golf course!"

I said: "I'll pass. I have to be moving on."

I didn't have much better luck at the next two places I tried. The first was a swank club set among million-dollar homes; it looked like the sort of place where golfers might pull out sand wedges worth more than my car. The course was open to the public, the starter told me, but not until 2 P.M., because of a tournament. Probably just as well. The second course was less swank but more crowded. Amid a sea of retirees, I was learning fast, there's no advantage in showing up on a weekday. As I lugged my bag with faltering confidence toward the starter, a friendly young attendant approached.

"Golfing today, sir?"

"I don't know," I said. "I don't have a tee time."

He winced. "That's going to be tough. It's pretty crowded." He pointed me toward a gazebo where the starter stood. I felt like Oliver Twist. Please, sir, may I play some golf? There were about fifteen people waiting to tee off. There was a line to speak with the starter. I moved on, beginning to grow concerned. The Single Golfer Rule, which had carried me through a charmed summer's worth of courses in the most congested cities in the United States, suddenly seemed in danger of collapsing here in the Land of Golf.

A few miles later I was down around Hobe Sound when I saw another sign for a public course. I've been down this road before, I thought. But I was getting desperate. It was already after eleven. Another morning had ebbed away, and I had yet to take my first swing. I wound through another development of single-story houses, this one called Heritage Ridge. The course was as crowded as the others, but this time I lucked out. There was a threesome getting ready to tee off, the woman told me.

"Do I have time to use the men's room?"

"Real quick. Your threesome is getting ready to tee off."

I ducked into the men's room. I didn't think too much about the fact that there was no urinal. I just flipped a lid and began my business as quickly as I could. I had just reached the point of no return, when it occurred to me that this was an exceptionally well-maintained men's room. One didn't often see flowers and sachets and . . . oh, God. I had to get out of there as quickly and quietly as possible. At my moment of realization a woman poked her head in, glanced at me with a mixture of amusement and suspicion, gasped and ducked out. I finished and stepped back into the pro shop, my face burning. I looked back at the bathroom door. From the angle I had originally seen it, a doorjamb had blocked the "wo" from "women."

Two women in the pro shop laughed nervously as I fumbled for an explanation and the door.

I loaded my bags onto the cart of an attendant, who drove me through a tunnel to the first tee. My playing partners were Howard, Vannie and Lewis. Vannie and Lewis Weber were married and riding together. I loaded my bags onto Howard's cart.

Howard Tidy had met Vannie recently on a nearby course where Vannie had been golfing with her son. Howard had held a variety of jobs in Florida and Pennsylvania, and wound up in Hobe Sound running a snack bar on the beach for fifteen years. He was retired now.

Howard had once played minor-league baseball in Pennsylvania, in the Yankees' farm system, as a shortstop.

"Ever heard of Phil Rizzuto?" Howard said, as if the name of the Yankee Hall of Fame shortstop would by itself explain why Howard never made it to the majors.

"In those days you had guys who could really play ball," Howard said. "The basics. That's what we knew. Hitting, fielding, throwing. None of this hot-dogging crap you see today. And you felt lucky to get the chance. You didn't get a million dollars for putting on a uniform."

There was a long line going off the first tee. We waited about fifteen minutes. It looked like a long round. I hit my first shot, a three-wood, off to the rough near some houses fringing the fairway, then screwed around for a double bogey, hardly the best way to start off on a fairly easy hole.

We sat at the next hole, a par-three, forever, waiting for slow foursomes ahead to clear the green. Slaves to "proper" golf etiquette, they politely waited for whoever was farthest from the green to hit, oblivious to the pileup of carts on the tee box behind them.

Howard muttered, "Jesus Christ, they're slow."

With the green at last cleared, I hit a fair eight-iron that landed just to the right of the green, but safe from the water. Then I parred the hole with a long, arcing, lucky but beautiful putt. Howard had a nice, easy swing. He'd only taken up the game in recent years, since retiring from his snack shop, but the old athleticism that had carried him through minor-league baseball held him in good stead out on the golf course.

The next hole at Heritage Ridge, number three, is a par-five. The front nine has an odd layout, with three par-fives and three threes. All told, the course has six threes and five fives. When the course is crowded, the layout makes for stop-and go traffic; every time you build up a head of steam on a par-five, you queue back up for a three.

But the oddest thing about Heritage Ridge was the frogmen. Our first encounter came on the third hole, when Howard hit into a pond along the left side of the fairway. The ball hadn't seemed to go in too far, so we poked around the edges looking for his ball. We spotted a couple of other balls and were in the process of fishing those out, too, when we realized we were being watched. A head had emerged from the pond, then a body, in full scuba diving gear, dark and threatening. He was not pleased with our lingering at the edge of the pond. Many courses retrieve and resell balls from their ponds. But this was the first time I had ever seen it done so aggressively. These frogmen—there seemed to be a half dozen scattered around the course—used vacuum hoses that combed the bottoms of the ponds, sucking balls into large bags. They did not smile, they seemed vaguely menacing, and this fellow in particular did not seem to acknowledge the unwritten right of all golfers to keep balls they find on a course. You'll never find as many as you lose, but stumbling across a near-perfect Titleist under an oak leaf or a pristine balata at the edge of a pond is one of those pleasant, serendipitous pleasures of life, a sort of grown-up's Easter egg hunt.

"I think we made that guy mad," Howard said. He decided to go over and smooth things out. "Hey, how about selling me a few of those balls," he said cheerfully, pointing at Frogman's bag.

"No."

The answer was so cool and impassive that Howard hurried back to the cart. We were glad the frogman didn't have a speargun.

Heritage Ridge is not an especially difficult course, but there is enough water and tight out of bounds near houses that you can run into some trouble if you don't hit straight. Fortunately, that was not my problem today. I swung easily and cracked my woods and irons. It helped that Howard and Lewis and Vannie were kind and appreciative with soft whistles and head shakes every time I hit the ball more than 180 yards. I began to feel like the Incredible Hulk. But beyond that, I was placing the ball well, chipping and putting consistently. I had come across stretches like this in the past, but they were more frequent now. I finished the front nine at 45 but improved as the day wore on and came home with a 40 for an 85.

The slow play meant it was already late afternoon when I bade good-bye to Howard, Lewis and Vannie. I continued south on Route 1 under a tropical sky that seemed heavy and full of meaning, like one of those Dutch oil seascapes you see in museums. A streak of brilliant sunlight ran down the center of the sky, as if guiding my way down the road. On either side boiled huge, black clouds. Near dark I passed through the rundown center of West Palm Beach. Somewhere off to my left, across a section of Intracoastal known as Lake Worth, lay the *other* Palm Beach, that gilded sliver of private beaches and fabulous estates where generations of millionaires have found refuge from the cold. Over there is where the awnings of shops on Worth Avenue and Royal Palm Way go *snap snap snap* in a cheerful chorus of privilege and money.

The intertwined history of the two Palm Beaches dates to the 1890s, when railroad tycoon and Palm Beach visionary Henry M. Flagler built one of Florida's earliest and most magnificent pleasure domes, the Royal Poinciana Hotel. Flagler needed a labor camp to house droves of imported construction workers. He selected a spot just across the water, and that was the start of West Palm Beach. By now, of course, the relentless push of development means there is plenty of money on both sides of the Intracoastal. But West Palm Beach remains the poor relation, and Route 1, weaving in a series of hard-to-follow turns through the center of town, shows off perhaps the bleakest side of West Palm Beach. South of West Palm Beach, in Lantana, I passed the headquarters of the *National Enquirer*, the supermarket tabloid. I stopped for the night in Boca Raton, where Ed, an old, close friend of mine, had recently been transferred. Ed's family hadn't yet moved down from Connecticut; he was staying in a hotel and offered me the spare bed. Two lonely married guys, we went to dinner, drank beer and talked about our families.

I pulled into the Pompano Beach Golf Course, on Route 1, next to the Pompano Beach airport, just after daybreak. Here was another thread of Route 1 running through my life. Pompano is where my grandparents had spent their retirement and where my grandmother, now nearly a century old, still lives. My early trips to Florida had left happy memories that could not be erased by the current reality of southern Florida, the strip malls sprouting like toadstools, the restless masses seeking salvation under the palms. Whatever South Florida had become, it retained for me the magic of my early youth, when my family, bundled against the cold, would take off from a snowbound winter airport and land in the sunshine, shedding our coats like repentant sinners. In those days, the Fort Lauderdale airport was so small that I have vivid memories of walking down the steps of the plane onto a shimmering tarmac and seeing my grandfather waiting and waving from behind a chain-link fence.

My grandfather, Charles Morse Slack, was a physicist, who, as a director of research for Westinghouse, invented a high-speed X-ray tube and oversaw development of the engine for the U.S. Navy's first atomic submarine, the Nautilus. Though not a celebrity of the Oppenheimer order, he held a certain place in the scientific firmament of the twentieth century. My father remembers as a child Hyman Rickover, the legendary (and legendarily abrasive) Navy commander, coming to the house in Pittsburgh for dinner. There were pitched battles, with Rickover pushing and cajoling for this or that alteration or concession, and my grandfather, more quietly but just as stubbornly, refusing. I remember my grandfather principally for taking us fishing off the Pompano Beach lighthouse in his boat, the *Beacon*. The *Beacon* was a heap, painted a sort of workmanlike gray-green. In a marina filled with sleek, gleaming pleasure craft, my grandfather's boat was notable for not having a single luxury item on board. It was the sort of boat a professional waterman might use to haul in his shrimp nets. In hindsight, I can admire Papa's austerity. But as an eight-year-old kid I longed just once to shove off in one of those *other* boats, with their gleaming rails and stocked galleys. Broken fixtures on the *Beacon* were never discarded; they held fast under copious splotches of my grandfather's beloved Epoxy glue. According to Papa, no broken object was beyond salvation, as long as you had enough Epoxy. Back on Beacon Street my grandmother stoically endured a world held together by glue. Seams of hardened Epoxy bubbled like prehistoric amber from china teacups, dinner plates, shoe heels, toy airplane wings. When the gear shift stick on his ancient Oldsmobile sedan snapped off, Papa glued a screwdriver in its place. His brother, an auto-parts dealer from Georgia, spotted the contraption one day and groused, "Charles, with more people like you around, we'd all go broke."

My grandfather felt that tough feet were directly related to a strong character—he'd lead my cousins Gordy and Walter and me (the girls were spared this particular drill) up to the flat, pebble-covered roof to walk around barefoot. Each morning it was my duty to retrieve the morning paper from the mailbox over a moist gauntlet of spiked tropical grass and gravel.

As a physicist, my grandfather developed a technique for isolating uranium in beryllium crucibles. The innovation provided a crucial source of uranium to scientists working on the Manhattan Project during World War II. But it ultimately killed my grandfather. Traces of beryllium, dormant for decades in Papa's lungs, attacked with a vengeance during the 1960s. He died, essentially by suffocation, in 1970. After Papa's death, his reputation within our family, prodded by my grandmother, only grew. One of the stories concerned his prowess as an athlete. It became the stuff of family legend. He was a tennis champion at the University of Georgia and, in retirement, the shuffleboard champion of Beacon Street. His finest sport was said to be golf. Just as he stubbornly refused to buy a new boat, he would never join a private course. He preferred the Pompano public course and carried old, mismatched clubs. He walked the fairways in paint-stained trousers, had the worst form of anyone on the course and never lost. Or so went the family legend.

I can still hear my Aunt Winnie's musical intonation: "Nobody beat Papa."

It was so early when I pulled into the parking lot at the Pompano Beach course, I figured I could walk right on and, in the solitude of the early morning, gain a sort of mystical connection with my grandfather. But it was not to be. The lot was already filled. The Pompano Beach Golf Course is actually two eighteen-hole courses, the Pines and the Palms. The Pines wraps all the way around the Palms, encircling it.

"They start lining up here at sunrise," the starter told me.

Of the two, the Pines is the longer and more difficult and is generally considered the better course. It's the one Papa played. A man approached me, a French Canadian in his late seventies named Claude. He was from a small town a few miles from Clair, New Brunswick, that town just across the river from Fort Kent, where I'd begun my trip. I had traveled a straight line, it seemed, and come full circle.

"You are playing the Pines, yes?" he said.

"Yes."

He nodded. "You play with me, all right?"

Claude had already hooked up with another twosome of retirees, Frank and Joe. I paid the starter inside the clubhouse.

Claude offered me a seat on his cart, but I declined. Something about my grandfather and tough feet. My sore toe had improved. It still ached, but the infection had subsided. If you worry about something enough, it's bound not to happen.

I hit my first tee shot, a three-wood, sky-high and to the left, in the rough and short, but safe. It wasn't a great shot but it got me safely past the gallery of crotchety old regulars who stood just behind the tee box, hoping to see someone other than themselves screw up. To the left as we headed out was the tarmac of the Pompano Beach municipal airport. I could see the Goodyear blimp, tethered on its mooring, resting just off the ground. I bogeyed the first hole. On the second, a par-three, I hit an eight-iron to within twenty feet of the pin. I left my first putt two feet short.

"Nice putt, Sally," said Frank. Frank was in his late seventies, from Ohio. He'd lived in Pompano for a decade. I sank my next putt for a par. Frank said he'd rather be fishing, but just golfed for the exercise.

When, later, I hit a nice, long drive and Joe whistled and said something wistful about lost youth, Frank barked at me, "How old are you?"

"Thirty-six."

"That's not young. That's old."

The sixth hole, a long par-five, carries straight for a little over two hundred yards, then doglegs ninety degrees to the left. I pulled out my three-iron.

Frank saw my iron and snorted. "Uh oh, Joe, looks like Sally's afraid to hit his woods off the tee."

"It's not that," I said calmly. "I'm just worried about over-shooting the fairway."

"Hah!"

I needed a good, strong iron shot. I came back slowly and uncorked a beautiful shot. Of all the good shots you can hit in golf, there's none more pleasing than a long iron off the tee. For pure sensory satisfaction, I'll take it over a booming drive with the Big Bertha any day of the week. It's that delicious sense of control combined with the surprising distance you can get from an iron when you hit it just right. And, under these circumstances, it couldn't have been better. The ball bounced, rolled and came to rest just kissing the light rough at the far side of the fairway. Any more club and I would have been underneath the rest rooms positioned a few yards beyond the elbow.

"Damn," I said, feigning concern. "Hope I didn't put it over."

"Beautiful, beautiful!" cried Claude. Frank said nothing.

On my second shot, I had a clear view of the green. I hit a five-wood that arced straight toward the pin. Now, from fifty or sixty yards out, with serene confidence, I plucked out my sand wedge and with about a half swing popped the ball up into the air. It landed about two feet from the hole.

It is these situations for which the "furthest away" courtesy rule was made. You calmly stand by while everybody else works his way to the green. It's a license to gloat, albeit in a gen-teel fashion. You stand patiently by the side of the green until everybody gets reasonably close. Then you casually mark your ball, just as a courtesy, because you are absolutely certain that everybody else is going to knock their ball within two feet of the cup as well. When nobody does, you wait patiently while they take their putts, adding gratuitous comments of encouragement: "Go ball! Go ball! Break!" As though their putt for a triple bogey is the number-one thing on your mind, not your own imminent putt for a bird. Then, with all the pretenders cleared away, you line up your own putt at last. Well, it ain't marching up the eighteenth at Sawgrass with a three-stroke lead and 20,000 spectators cheering madly, but it'll do.

I placed my ball down.

"Don't miss this one, Sally. Don't leave it short."

"Thanks, Martha, I won't," I said, and sank the putt. Frank laughed. The ice melted.

"Nice birdie," he said.

I finished the front nine with a 43, not bad considering that I hit sand on the majority of the holes. Just a few weeks earlier, sand spelled automatic disaster. I had never felt comfortable hitting a couple of inches behind the ball and swinging fully, as we are all taught to do in sand. Use that kind of force and accidentally hit the ball instead of the sand and your Maxfli may wind up in a different area code. So even while my brain said Hit! Hit! Hit! some rogue impulse sent treasonous warnings to my arms: Not too hard! At the last instant my arms would go limp and the ball would hiccup eight inches forward. I can't say exactly how I surmounted this impasse, except that pure repetition seemed to have eradicated my fear. Fear is all about the unknown. After this many rounds of golf, I knew sand.

On the thirteenth green thieves struck the carts. Frank, Joe and Claude had parked next to a stand of pines. We were putting out when I glanced over and saw them, four or five of them, crawling over the carts. Raccoons. They moved with the stealth, coordination and bravado of Navy SEALs. One checked out the bench seats and dashboards. The others rummaged through the golf bags strapped to the rear of the carts. We were standing just a few feet away and hadn't heard a thing. And when we spotted them and waved our arms, they didn't scatter as expected. They glanced lazily at each other as if to say, "Relax, Mac, they think we might be rabid." After a few moments of fruitless searching, the raccoons sauntered back into the woods to await the next foursome.

I'd hit a rough patch coming around the turn, bogeying the tenth, eleventh, and twelfth holes, two of them par-fives, leaving ugly 6s on the scorecard. I had no idea what Papa used to shoot here, but I hated the thought of not shooting in the eighties. I answered with three straight pars. The sixteenth is the tester, the sort of hole that for some reason never gets rated as the toughest but inevitably is. The tight fairway is bordered by out of bounds on the left and a slicer's nightmare of a pond on the right. A stiff cross breeze tries to blow everything into the pond.

I went with a three-iron. My play had been inconsistent through the day, and this hole would make or break me. I hit a long, straight shot that split the fairway, maybe the best three-iron I had ever hit. I hit another good long iron on approach that came to rest on the fringe of the green and got down in two for my par. I double-bogeyed the seventeenth, a longish but easy par-three, and bogeyed the last hole—a poor finish but still salvaging an 88. I had yet to shoot that magical round in the seventies and began to suspect dishearteningly that it wouldn't come. In my defense, I can only say that playing a different course every day contributed to my inconsistency. If I'd stayed in Richmond and played one course over and over, I might have broken 80 several times. Now that goal seemed to be slipping away from me as the trip wound down. Still, I had proceeded from being happy to break 100 in my early rounds to being disappointed if I didn't break 90. I had shaved ten strokes off my game, under ever-changing conditions, and that was saying something.

Claude offered to buy me a beer in the clubhouse, and we sat and drank slowly. Through his thick accent he told me of the hazards of potato farming in New Brunswick and why the car business was what had allowed him to retire in Florida. I couldn't help looking for the face of my grandfather in this old French Canadian. Pompano Beach had always been to me a land for the very young and the very old: the very old being my grandparents and their contemporaries; the very young being myself and my sisters and cousins. My grandmother was still living in a retirement home a couple of miles from the golf course, and as long as she was there this impression, however fragile, remained intact. But it occurred to me suddenly that this old man sitting next to me in the bar was closer to my father's age now than to my grandfather's.

I thanked Claude for the beer and drove through the streets of Pompano. I crossed over the Intracoastal Waterway, with its white boats bobbing next to tidy docks, and kept driving east toward the ocean. At A-1A, the oceanside spur of Route 1, I turned left and wound past residential streets until I came to a small side street called Beacon Street. I drove slowly past the house my grandparents had designed when they first moved to Florida in 1956, five years before I was born.

The circular driveway of rough stones, my route for retrieving the morning newspaper, had been paved over smooth. No tough feet in this house. There had been a time, shortly after my grandmother moved to a beachfront condominium in the mid-1970s, when the house and all of Beacon Street seemed destined for shabbiness. Trips to Pompano had always included a ritual drive past the old house, but these had become sadder and sadder exercises. The houses and lawns were neglected. But now the houses seemed revitalized and loved. Two children, about the age I would have been when I visited nearly three decades earlier, played on bikes on the driveway. They obviously weren't visiting. The minivans in the driveways and play equipment in the yards testified to Beacon Street's transformation from a neighborhood of retirees to one of young families just starting out. It was my grandparents and their peers who had built these homes, carving their retirement dreams out of the thick Florida vegetation. I remembered all the names: the Ruckleses, the Edwards, that man we knew only as Harvey, with a perpetual uncleared gob in the back of his throat. I remembered endless shuffleboard games on the court in the backyard, the shoe-shiny smell of shuffleboard wax, the clinking of ice in plastic cocktail glasses with a fishhook imbedded between the layers, the mysterious, reassuring music of grown-up conversations on the screened-in porch and the feel of cool, fresh-washed sheets against a sunburn. Returning here to Beacon Street I longed to have all that back. But the images were closer when I closed my eyes than when I opened them.

All those original settlers were long gone now. They had left behind these shells to be inhabited by a new generation that would pursue its own Florida dreams. It was just like all those great old golf courses I'd been playing down the length of the coast— Cobb's Creek, Franklin Park—built, loved, neglected, then redis- covered all over again. Here was the continuity of life, and golf.

I made my way back to A-1A and crossed over the Intra- coastal, past the old Oceanside Market, now closed, where my grandmother used to take us to watch ladies in smocks squeeze fresh orange juice into cone-shaped containers. It seems almost foolishly old-fashioned to recall the delight we took in that orange juice. But that was when the juice you drank up North dropped like a gelatinous slug from a tube of frozen concentrate and tasted like chilled dishwater. At breakfast one morning I tried to explain to my daughter, as she turned up her nose at a glass of fresh-squeezed Tropicana, about the magic of orange juice from the Oceanside Market. She looked at me the way I must have looked at my own parents when they described for me the won- ders of watching the first grainy images flicker across a black-and- white television screen. I wound my way to the retirement home to see my grandmother.

20

Land's End

It was bound to happen, I suppose, given the number of rounds I had been playing, that I would come across a day when my game would completely blow apart. If Claude at Pompano, with his connection to New Brunswick, had brought my trip full circle in one sense, then my round at Bayshore Golf Course in Miami Beach brought it back depressingly in another. I played as badly here as I had at the beginning of my trip. Maybe worse. In this sense golf, in my experience, differs materially from every other sport. You can have a bad day in tennis, when your serve is off or your backhands down the line all seem to fall a foot long. But once you have reached a level of proficiency at tennis, you can only play so badly. Not so with golf. It's the only sport I know that can humble you to the extent that you may as well never have played the game before.

Bayshore is a faded but grand old municipal course in a residential section of Miami Beach, well inland from the ocean. I crossed over the Intracoastal from Route 1 to its seaside adjunct, A-1A, after passing through Fort Lauderdale and Hollywood. The clubhouse at Bayshore is a cavernous old building with high ceilings, almost like a train station. It's one of those old municipal courses, like Cobb's Creek in Philadelphia or Franklin Park in Boston, that can still take a bite out of you. Bayshore starts right off with a par-five 538-yarder. My playing partner was a young guy named Don. Don was in his mid-twenties, crew cut, handsome, stocky, friendly, a little cocky, a uniform salesman for a company in the Midwest. He'd won a regional sales prize, a Bahamas cruise, and was staying at a beach-side hotel awaiting the ship. His girlfriend had obligingly agreed to sun herself by the pool while Don headed out in a rental car to find a round of golf.

I christened my round with a ball in the water to the right of the fairway. My 8 set the tone for the day. I double-bogeyed the next two, before finally chalking up a par on the fourth hole. I had lost all feel for the clubs. I shanked and duffed and sculled the ball. Soon Don, this well-meaning twenty-four-year-old, was taking it upon himself to offer me all sorts of unasked-for advice, attempting to salve my shaky ego with shreds of golf wisdom he'd picked up on the courses back home.

"Everybody hits bad shots," he said after I bladed an easy chip shot over the far side of the green. "It's *how bad* your bad shots are that determine whether you're a good golfer."

Then I took a mighty swing at a fairway three-iron, only to watch the ball skip fifty feet forward. "This game will make you pull your hair out, if you let it," Don said.

"You really need to turn your shoulders more on the backswing," he added later. "Your follow-through is stopping way short. Try swinging through the ball."

Don was too young still to know what a bad idea it is to give unsolicited advice to strangers on the course. For one thing, they might have a gun in their bag. For another, they might take your advice seriously, and screw up their swing for months to come. Golf advice that comes free from strangers is almost always useless, and frequently harmful. During my entire journey I had not offered a word of unsought advice, and even on those odd days when I was playing well and someone asked for my opinion on his swing, I gave it only reluctantly and with disclaimers about my own lack of expertise. Don was young; he would learn this one day when some golfer chased him across the eighth fairway with a six-iron.

For myself, I was too dismayed to be angry. Dismayed because I was now nearly at the end of my grand adventure and could still be taken for a poor sap who needed the advice from strangers to get him through a round of golf. I had imagined that by this point in my trip the standard response to my swing would be a long, low whistle, accompanied by an admiring shake of the head, as the ball screamed down the center of the fairway and hopped lightly onto the green. I had imagined that my trip would be the golfing equivalent of *Flowers for Algernon,* the story about a mentally retarded man who by the grace of an operation is transformed by degrees into a genius. Instead, I was reverting to idiot status without having graduated from junior high school.

The only consolation was that Don soon began to play badly as well, worse than I was, as a matter of fact. He had started off hitting long, straight, powerful drives and arcing wedge shots. But a nasty hook had crept into his swing, and once that happened he lost confidence in the short game and began making horrible chips that careened over the green in search of tall grass, trees and sand. I almost told him to try taking a half step away from the ball, but kept my mouth shut.

I leveled off a bit toward the end of the front nine and finished the nine with a 48, the same score as Don. We were both hot, tired and pissed off at our mutual misfortune. As we turned the corner on ten, I could see him weighing his options. On the one hand, there was playing nine more holes of bad golf with a sweaty stranger. On the other was sipping a rum-laced fruit drink by the pool with his bikini-clad girlfriend. Somehow, I didn't make the cut. After plunking his drive on the tenth hole into a pond, he said cheerfully, "That's it for me."

I trudged on alone. This would be a fresh start, I told myself, and continued to tell myself that even as I followed Don's shot into the pond, then screwed around in a sand trap or two and pulled down a quadruple-bogey 9.

On the eleventh tee I encountered a pair of golfers who had started on the back nine. The older man was slender and dressed all in white, with a white mustache and a straw hat. The younger man was in his early forties, stocky.

"Would you care to join us?" the older man said.

"Sure. I didn't see you before. Did you just start?"

He gave a little bow and smiled coyly. "You're quite right. Maybe we should ask to join *you*."

Their names were Sherman and Paul. Sherman, the older man, had retired to Miami Beach from New York, where he had followed a number of careers but spent most of his time driving a cab. Paul was an electrician and part-time karate instructor, who had moved to Miami from out west someplace.

Paul and Sherman had met on the golf course one day and become fast friends.

"Soul mates," Sherman said.

"Brothers," Paul added. "Brothers who just happened to meet each other a few years ago."

It was on the par-four thirteenth hole, when I hit a lousy drive and must have grimaced, that I got some more unsought counseling.

"You know, Charlie, you really shouldn't get upset. You've got a good swing. You're a good player. You need to relax and have fun." This was Sherman.

Which, of course, guaranteed that I would neither relax nor have fun for the rest of the afternoon.

Somehow the subject turned to marriage and child rearing, and Paul announced, "I married the first time for sex, the second time for money. The third time . . . I married for love." And, later, "Want to know the secret to raising your kids right? The belt."

Bayshore, meanwhile, was having me for lunch. It was a long course, unforgiving of error. I slipped into those hot-sun, golf-fatigue blues, no hope, get me out of here. Sherman and Paul, lost in the magnificence of their own friendship, soon decided that I was too taciturn, and more or less pretended after a few holes that I wasn't there.

I shoved my bags in my trunk, my scorecard (103) in my pocket and my pride in a hole in the ground. I wound back along Alton Avenue until I came to a bridge back over the Intracoastal to Miami and Route 1. I had never driven through downtown Miami before, though I had been to the airport and other outlying spots many times. I don't know what I expected—chaos? Carjackers? I found the downtown to be far more neat and orderly than I had anticipated. Route 1 slices right through the center of town before cutting down to the southern suburbs.

I was near the entrance to the Keys, well after dark, when I checked into a motel. I stopped at a convenience store for crackers and cheese and a quart of beer. I showered, changed, and lay down on my bed, eating the crackers, sipping my beer, and watching the colors of some cable news weather report flicker across the screen. My body was tired and sore; my mind was tired and sore. Could it be that I had golfed too much?

No, I decided the next morning.

It was a beautiful morning, lonely birds calling in sea air. I headed out toward the Keys. Right near the entrance I saw a sign for Keys Gate Golf & Tennis Club. The name brought back a memory from the beginning of my trip. My old friend Joe O'Neill, one of my first golf partners, in Northport, Maine. This was the place he'd told me about on that June morning two thousand miles ago. Nice course, he'd said. Free glass of beer when you finish your round.

It was early enough that I'd beat the crowd. Keys Gate has a rather ornate clubhouse, with a long entranceway supported by columns, like a Cadillac dealership. Its most notable gimmick is a sunken driving range. All your shots go straight out into a pond. Keys Gate has an odd rule that only members may walk the course. I shrugged and loaded my bags onto a cart. I was all by myself. I felt I was playing with Joe O'Neill. I struck my first drive of the morning well. It was cool and fresh, and my ball lay some-where in the distance. There were only a few tracks ahead of me on a fairway as inviting as a newly vacuumed carpet. On the fifth hole I played through a couple of guys who had started early, and from then on I was the original explorer, the first golfer of the day, carving my own tracks across virgin fairways. The holes flew by, I felt the cool wind brush my face as I whipped along. The principal hazards of the course were the numerous ponds, but I managed to avoid most of them. I finished in about two hours, shooting an 87. It was a little after 9 A.M. when I walked into the empty bar/restaurant next to the pro shop.

"I understand there's a free beer here at the end of a round."

The man looked at his watch, smiled and shrugged. He drew me a plastic cup of beer from the tap.

"This is for you, Joe," I said, and drank a long, cool draught of breakfast.

I expected the bridges to be longer and the Keys farther apart than they were, perhaps because photos often feature the dramatic ocean spans from farther down the Keys. It was early enough in the day and the season that traffic was relatively light as I crossed a bridge into Key Largo, a congenially seedy outpost of dive shops and inexpensive resorts. The lore seemed half native grown, half imported from some Hollywood back lot image, a peculiar amal-gam of Ernest Hemingway (who lived farther out, on Key West) and Humphrey Bogart. Until the Bogart movie *Key Largo,* there was no Key Largo. This largest Key was called Rock Harbor but changed its name as a tourist draw in the wake of the movie. Today, the Bogart legacy has been cheerfully muddled still further with infusions of *Casablanca* and *The African Queen*—"Ride Bogey and Hepburn's *African Queen* Glass Bottom Boat"—as if Morocco and Zaire were just over the next bridge.

It was fitting for the end of my trip that Route 1, freed from its long waltz with I-95 (that highway petered out ignominiously somewhere around Miami) would once again be the sole and primary highway, and also the main street for each Key, just as it had been at the start of my trip, in Fort Kent, Maine. Here Route 1 is a two-lane, pass-when-you-can thrill ride called the Overseas Highway. The only way to get from Key to Key, it does not end until the land itself runs out, a hundred miles shy of Cuba. At Indian Channel Key the land narrows and stretches out, and the bridges become longer, as though the land has been sucked through a straw. Fiesta Key is barely wide enough for the road. On both sides of the road, tropical waters run from light green in the shallows to deep blue farther out. I crawled across the Seven Mile Bridge, separating Marathon Key from Pigeon Key, behind a recreational vehicle. At Big Pine Key, twenty-five miles from Key West, a radio message warned me to watch out for "America's tiniest deer," the key deer, only three hundred of which were said to be still roaming Big Pine Key.

Just at the entrance to Key West came a sign for the Key West Golf Club, a key lime's throw from the highway, off to the right. As I wound slowly toward the clubhouse of this, the final course, I thought of the June morning when I'd pulled up outside the Fort Kent Golf Club in northern Maine, at the headwaters of that long asphalt river. Back then Key West had seemed unreal to me, beckoning like a mirage of swaying palm trees. Had I really come this far? Though I had done nothing to announce my arrival today, I felt suddenly as though the occasion called for a ceremony—a brass band, speeches and a plaque. But the golfers dotting the fairways under a cheerful tropical sun took no notice of me or my faded Pontiac as we rolled past them and into the parking lot.

Once a military course, the Key West Golf Club had been purchased by a private developer and spiffed up. A neat row of carts flanked a shiny white clubhouse. I figured the combination of upscale pretensions and this being the only course on Key West was going to cost me, and I was not surprised when the clubhouse attendant calmly asked for $85.

My partners on the first tee were Larry and Aaron. Larry was a piano player at a Key West nightclub, Aaron a concierge at one of the fancy hotels. We also picked up a retired military man named Dick. Larry and Aaron were both married and had moved down from New York, but hadn't known each other until they got to Key West.

I cracked my first drive long and straight down the left side of the fairway. The course winds through tropical marshes, with fairways fringed by tidy homes built in the Key West style—row houses gone tropical, with arched metal roofs glinting in the sunlight. There were pockets of "wildlife areas" in keeping with the trend of environmentally friendly golf courses.

Wild roosters wandered the course, descendants, Dick told me, of the roosters owned by the first Spanish settlers on the Keys. Adding to the atmosphere on the day of my visit were Christian monks in long flowing robes, gathered for a convention on the grounds. They wandered the cart paths on their way to and from a large meeting tent.

Larry, the piano player, was a boisterous fellow who seemed to take umbrage at my emotional control.

"How come you don't get pissed off?" he demanded. "Me, I yell and scream." I was amused that anyone could accuse me of being too good a sport. The sixth hole was the toughest on the course, a narrow fairway with a dogleg to the right, a pond to the left and another to the right. I put my drive in the water, reteed, hit again and hit a poor shot off to the left that barely missed going out of bounds. My second shot, actually my fourth, was a great five-wood that got me out of trouble and put me on the edge of the green, bisecting all the trouble spots, and I wound up with a double bogey. On the next hole, a short but tricky par-four, I hit my drive into some trees off to the left, and hoped I wasn't coming unglued. My drive engendered a spirited debate between Larry and Dick. They were debating where I would have to drop my ball, whether I would get a lateral drop or stroke and distance.

They kept at it for a few minutes until the conversation broke apart and they went off for their balls. I dropped mine and hit and wound up with another double bogey.

The eighth hole, a par-three, was one of the funkiest of my trip. It's just 141 yards, but you hit over a swamp and tall grass to an obscured green. An elongated flag stick provides the only target. I hit my ball to the right of the flag stick. Not a great shot, but I figured I'd be okay. It turned out that I was in a sand trap just below the hole and to the right. I dug my feet into the sand, swung back and hit a pretty sand shot up onto the green, spraying sand all over my arms. I was pleased with my shot and with myself until I got up onto the green and felt a sharp sting on my right forearm. I brushed my arm quickly, then felt another sting on my left hand, then one on my right calf. By now I was hopping around the green like a madman, swiping and batting at my own limbs. I tore my shirt off and swung it wildly. Fire ants.

Dick, Larry and Aaron were sympathetic but unmoved by my anguish.

"Happens all the time," Dick said. "You'll be standing in your garden, minding your own business, and suddenly your legs are covered."

Apparently, I had surprised a nest of them with my sand wedge. After a time-out to clean the sand off my body and shake out my shirt and socks, we moved on. It was the hardest-earned bogey of my trip.

Throughout the afternoon the monks wandered the fairways like our conscience. Some particularly ambitious member of the order had found a novel way of spreading the Word. As we were coming up the seventeenth hole, there was a broad sand trap to the right of the fairway. In it, one of the monks had scratched the words, with a large stick, GOD LOVES YOU. A nice thought, but if he really wanted to draw converts from a golf course he would have communicated some divine guidance on the perfect swing.

The eighteenth hole, a difficult par-five, was the last hole of the journey. I had 84 so far, so if I wanted to break 90 on my final round I would have to par the hole. But I was tired and hungry and my arms wouldn't follow my heart. I hit what I thought was a nice drive, to the left of the fairway but straight. But when I headed up the fairway I saw to my dismay a low-lying pond I hadn't noticed. It was a cruel twist, but not the first time something like this had happened. That was the penalty for playing a different course every day. Disillusioned, I hit a poor recovery shot from my lateral drop, and limped home with an 8, for a 92.

"Now, I want to see you pissed off," Larry said. "Throw your clubs. Swear. Say 'Shit!' Before you leave you have to say 'Shit.'"

"Shit."

"Now throw your putter."

I tossed it at my bag.

"Very good. All right."

I turned out onto Route 1 to follow it to the end. As I drove past the string of chain motels that in Key West pass for suburbs, I tried to put the trip in some perspective, to grapple with What It Means. But it was wonderful moments rather than big lessons that crowded my mind:

Best course: Mid Pines, in Southern Pines, North Carolina. **Best day:** Riverside in Portland, Maine, in the morning; Cape Arundel in Kennebunkport in the afternoon. **Funniest partners:** Sam Ellis and Robert Kendall at Van Cortlandt Park, the Bronx. **Best close call:** the alligator on the eighteenth hole, Laura Walker Golf Course, Waycross, Georgia. **Best road breakfast:** blueberry pancakes at the Bluebird Ranch Cafe, Machias, Maine. **Best doughnuts:** Krispy Kreme (around the South). **Best shot:** uphill, five-iron approach shot from 175 yards out, on my way to a birdie on the par-five tenth hole, Pinehurst No. 6, Pinehurst, North Carolina. **Best shot (someone else's):** John McDermott's eagle at St. Augustine, Florida, in front of his sons. **Best golf course name:** Bogeyville, Ridge Spring, South Carolina. **Best**

golf quote: "It's the second-toughest game there is. The toughest game is life itself."—Clarence Knighton, Wrens, Georgia.

After 2,200 miles of Route 1, I was road weary, to be sure, my appetite for fast food cured forever (or at least a month), my wanderlust muted. It was time to go home. Home. But I was not weary of golf. Standing on the first tee at Key West, I had felt as new and fresh with possibility as I had on those spring mornings in Maine. In that sense, the journey had never grown old.

Nor had the irritations specific to public courses ruined them for me, though some came close. Among these irritations, slow play was the worst. It plagues public golf courses North and South, in big cities and rural burgs. I'll never understand how a nation that prizes speed and efficiency in all else tolerates such a glacial pace on the golf course. Here's to importing a legion of crotchety, whip-cracking British marshals and setting them loose on America's public links. They'll have us all playing three-hour rounds in no time. In all, though, my affection for public golf courses only increased. What appealed most was the unexpectedness, the discovery, the chance that just around the next bend I'd stumble upon a little gem like Loch Nairn in Pennsylvania or Laura Walker in Georgia. And, as one of my earliest partners, Stacey Kelly, that logger in Maine, said, the best thing is the people you meet. I had ventured into huge, rough cities and forgotten rural communities, and found friends, at random, in both.

As for my own accomplishments, I had set out to shave ten strokes off my game.

Done.

As to whether that made me a happier golfer, or a happier person, as I'd hoped, that's a tougher question. Still, I'd reached a point where I could reasonably expect to shoot in the 80s and feel justifiable disappointment when I failed. I was in all respects a better player than when I started; longer off the tee, more precise with the short chips, steadier with the putter. I walked confidently instead of fearfully into a sand trap. I had expected improvement to come in more or less linear progression. Instead it came slowly and unpredictably. A couple of early successes filled me with false expectations, and some notable meltdowns late in the trip filled me with despair. I never did break 80. In defense I can only point to the stiff penalty I paid for playing an unfamiliar course every day. I suspect there are more than a few golfers in America whose low handicaps wouldn't survive an extended journey beyond the snug, worn paths of their home course. But no matter. What I lost in strokes I gained in experience, in adaptability. And 79 is still out there waiting for me. Somewhere.

Before, during and after my trip, people asked me, in tones ranging from eager to faintly accusatory, how did it *feel* to take off, to leave being daddy and husband and working stiff behind and hit the road? Overall, fantastic. Of course, the trip and my time schedule imposed their own limitations and demands, but I may never again savor the sense of freedom I had when the only obligation, from the moment I rose, was to find another place to play golf. On leaving the daddy and husband duties, well, the odd thing is that within a few days of leaving you begin to remember all the reasons you got married and had kids. No, I didn't long to change diapers. But I forgot about diapers completely. All I could think of were the sights and sounds and smells of home. Would I take a trip like this again? In the interest of marital preservation, I'll plead the Fifth Amendment. But I have noticed on my U.S. maps that a certain U.S. Route 50 carves a tantalizing East-West path across America, all the way from Eastern Maryland to the very shadows of Pebble Beach . . .

· As for anything I learned about life, only this: All my life I have operated under the belief that happiness or contentment were things you strove for and once you found them, you had them for keeps. I hadn't gotten to that mythical place yet, but I believed it surely existed. More money, a better job, a bigger house. Then, life would slip into cruise control. But the ups and downs of my golf adventure, the wonderful peaks and agonizing slides, finally disabused me of this notion. And, too, the ups and downs of the American landscape itself, the procession of cities and golf courses rising, fading, rising again, struggling to reinvent themselves. It doesn't mean you stop trying to get there, but perhaps you find a way to enjoy the ride a little more. It took sixty golf courses to convince me of a truth about golf and life so obvious and facile sounding, I probably could have gotten it from a fortune cookie or a Salada tea bag: Getting there is nothing; the journey is all.

As I drove on into downtown Key West, the chain motels gave way to charming older buildings and homes, pedestrians filled the streets. It was difficult to tell exactly where Route 1 ended. There is an official sign beside a beautiful old kapok tree in front of the town hall, designating the spot as the end of Route 1. However, another sign, and my map, indicated that Route 1 actually becomes Duval Street and heads straight through the little downtown. I followed that path, to mile marker zero, then found a place to park my car. It was almost dusk. The streets were filling up. The changing of the guard between afternoon tourist traffic and the rowdier drinking traffic of the night was just beginning. I pulled up a stool in a bar on Greene Street called Captain Tony's. You can buy a beer and a Hemingway T-shirt in a crowded tourist spot called Sloppy Joe's on Duval Street, but the original site of Sloppy Joe's, the bar where Hemingway got sloppy and picked fights, is the place now called Captain Tony's. Nailed to the ceiling was a stool with Hemingway's name on it, alongside a stool bearing the name of John F. Kennedy. I drank a cold can of Budweiser. Then I wandered down to the end of Duval Street and sat on a bench on a pier staring out at the final sunset of my trip. The red ball of the sun, resting half in the water, half out, seemed to smile knowingly at me as though it, too, had rolled all the way down from Maine on Route 1, then splashed into the sea when the land and road finally gave out.